Winning

Winning

Reflections on an American Obsession

Francesco Duina

PRINCETON UNIVERSITY PRESS

PRINCETON AND OXFORD

Library of Congress Cataloging-in-Publication Data
Duina, Francesco G., 1969–
Winning : reflections on an American obsession / Francesco Duina.
p.   cm.
Includes bibliographical references and index.
ISBN 978-0-691-14706-2 (hbk. : alk. paper)   1. Social values—United
States.   2. Losers—United States.   3. Success—United States.   4. Failure
(Psychology)   5. Competition (Psychology)   6. National characteristics,
American.   I. Title.
HN90.M6D85 2011
303.3'720973—dc22   2010000808
British Library Cataloging-in-Publication Data is available

To My Children Sofia and Gianluca

New Lights in My Life

Contents

Acknowledgments

SOCIOLOGISTS BELIEVE THAT individuals produce very little on their own. They think that much of what we do benefits from our engagements with other people, places, and institutions. This book proves the point.

I spent most of the 2007–8 academic year in Denmark as a visiting faculty at the International Center for Business and Politics (Copenhagen Business School). There, I enjoyed what most academics would probably call heaven: ample time to research, the opportunity to present my ideas to excellent colleagues, and exposure to a very different system and set of values. For that, I will be forever grateful. Thanks, then, to Professors Ove K. Pedersen and Lars Bo Kaspersen for making it possible.

I first tested my ideas in 2004 at Bates College by designing a course called the Sociology of Competition. Students in that course helped me think through many of the issues and problems that this book addresses. In the subsequent years, a host of colleagues provided me with powerful insights and challenging questions. John A. Hall (McGill University) and John L. Campbell (Dartmouth College) urged me to think about the intellectual roots of the project and its practical implications for readers. Liah Greenfeld (Boston University), through conversations and her own wonderful writing, helped me see how the United States is indeed a rather unique place in the world—a place of great freedom but also considerable risks. Bruce Sacerdote (Dartmouth College), an economist, provided me with alternative and valuable explanations for why people compete. Paulette Kurzer (University of Arizona) and Gordon Fellman (Brandeis University) pushed me to reflect more about my own motivations for engaging in this project. Valuable comments came, as well, from Joshua Margolis (Harvard Business School),

Shelley McDonough (Northeastern University), Grahame Thompson (Open University), Michael Sargent (Bates College), Emily Kane (Bates College), Tore Vincents Olsen (Copenhagen Business School), Jette Steen Knudsen (Copenhagen Business School), and the anonymous referees who read this book for Princeton University Press.

Outside of academia, Emil Dabora (Harvard Management Company) and Alan Kantrow (The Monitor Group) shared with me insights into competition from the worlds of finance and management consulting. John K. Glenn (United States Global Leadership Coalition) did the same from the perspective of countries and their foreign policy. Patrick Lohier, a freelance editor, and Gianfranco Duina, my father, read and commented on the entire manuscript. Conversations with family members and friends such as Andrew Blom, Lisa Ceglia, Phil Cunningham, Paul Gastonguay, Ariel Kaminer, Emilie Nakayama, and David Schab proved enlightening and fruitful. In both the United States and Denmark, I conducted several formal and informal interviews with business people, athletic coaches, teachers, and state officials. Most asked that I refer to them anonymously. I thank them here for dedicating some of their precious time to me.

This book would not have been possible without the steady and wise guidance of Eric Schwartz at Princeton University Press. He exhibited the qualities any author would want an editor to have. He was supportive above all. But he was also enormously constructive and motivating in his criticisms. I am grateful to Eric for all his help. At the press, Kathleen Cioffi oversaw the production phases of the book, which included the meticulous copyediting work of Jack Rummel. I could not have asked for better support. Finally, I wish to thank my wife and companion Angela. Once again, she supported me with great wisdom and patience through years of hard work and reflection.

PART 1

Introduction

Chapter One

THE PROBLEM

Now of all good things, truth holds first
place among gods and men alike.
—Plato, *Laws,* book V

ALEXIS DE TOCQUEVILLE MARVELED at the American spirit. His travels through the country in the early 1800s revealed a people with great ambitions, in constant motion, with remarkable ingenuity, and an appreciation for getting things done. In Europe, people seldom dared to dream. In the United States, where the established social and cultural orders of the old continent had been set aside and everyone had been given a fresh start, people could aspire to great things. A new society founded on equality unleashed fantastic energy, freedom, and movement. When Tocqueville asked an American sailor why the ships of his country were built to last such a short time, he was told that technological advances made any given ship obsolete in a few years. The "great nation" of the United States, Tocqueville reflected, "directs its every action" ultimately towards one goal: "indefinite perfectibility" (Tocqueville 2003: 523).

This may have been too simplistic an interpretation of the new country. But my recent yearlong stay in Denmark helped me see that Tocqueville captured something of life in the United States.

Anyone spending some time in Denmark will eventually run into Jante's Law. The law was formulated by Aksel Sandemose in his 1933 novel *A Refugee Crosses His Tracks*, where he portrays the culture and beliefs of the residents of the small Danish town of Nykøbing Mors. Virtually all Danes are familiar with the ten principles of the law. Many embrace them to a good extent. They permeate public and private life, the education system from kindergarten on, politics, business, sports, family life, and more. Here is what they say:

1. Don't think that you are special
2. Don't think that you are of the same standing as us
3. Don't think that you are smarter than us
4. Don't fancy yourself as being better than us
5. Don't think that you know more than us
6. Don't think that you are more important than us
7. Don't think that you are good at anything
8. Don't laugh at us
9. Don't think that anyone cares about you
10. Don't think that you can teach us anything.

Without a doubt, most of us in the United States are raised to believe exactly the opposite of Jante's Law. We are told to feel special and strive for new heights. Being smarter, better, and more knowledgeable than others are virtues, not faults. And most of us certainly believe, if not pray, that we matter and are good at something. While we do not necessarily want to laugh at others, we work extremely hard to make sure that others care about us and that we, in turn, have something that they can learn from us. Indeed, as recent comparative studies of American and Danish cultures show, Americans "hold unrealistically positive views of themselves and believe that they are much better than average on many attributes." Quite the opposite applies to the Danes (Thomsen et al. 2007: 446). Danes, in turn, "show aversion to conspicuously successful persons," while "Americans aspire to such distinction" (Nelson and Shavitt 2002: 440).

We live in an intensely driven and dynamic society—a life, in the words of Tocqueville, of fervor. But while this is clear, it is also true that we seldom stop to think and analyze what exactly we are after and why. Instead, we subject ourselves with little awareness to the profound demands that our society imposes on us. As Liah Greenfeld recently put it, we are overwhelmed by "busyness" but lack understanding: convinced that the "sky is the limit" and conscious that it is our duty to "find" if not "make" ourselves, we are breathlessly running from task to task, place to place, and mission to mission (Greenfeld 2005a: 331). Max Weber wrote that our Puritan ancestors taught us that idleness is a sin (Weber 2002). One could say that we learned that lesson all too well. We have been running ever since even if—as Weber himself predicted—so much has changed around us.

Nothing represents our restless and confused mentality better, perhaps, than our great love of "winning" and deep fear of "losing." Americans embrace competition. According to the World Values Survey,[1] as table 1.1 shows, our approval of competition is unmatched by any other major industrialized country on earth. Nearly half of our population firmly believes in the goodness of competition. This is much more than the numbers in Germany, Great Britain, and Italy. It is twice the number in France. In Japan, less than one fifth of the population values competition decisively. The figure for Denmark is 27 percent. Indeed, when we consider the whole world, the United States is more positively inclined toward competition than most countries—a fact that is well established among comparative psychologists and sociologists (Nelson and Shavitt 2002). As we shall see throughout this book, Americans also believe more strongly than others in the fairness of unequal outcomes, rewarding those who try and succeed, and leaving those who fall behind to their own devices.

At the same time, despite all this and the pressures it generates, *we have remarkably little understanding of what competition— and winning and losing in particular—are all about.* We use the terms with different and sometimes contradictory, but never explicit, connotations and meanings. We often think of winning as

TABLE 1.1
EMBRACING COMPETITION

	United States	Germany	Great Britain	Italy	France	Japan	Canada
No reservations	29%	16%	12%	18%	16%	11%	24%
Minimal reservations	17%	17%	17%	10%	7%	7%	15%
Total	46%	33%	28%	28%	23%	18%	39%

Source: World Values Survey, Question E039.

the opposite of losing, but we are unsure about how the two concepts relate to each other. We push ourselves, congratulate winners, and console losers—all without knowing why. Indeed, we are not even clear about what, exactly, we are after on any given occasion. Winning and losing have become "taken for granted" aspects of our "everyday reality" about which we know much too little (Berger and Luckmann 1967: 19–21).

We should pause and analyze. According to the World Values Survey, the Danes, with their apparently odd approach to life, rank among the most satisfied and happiest people on earth—well ahead of the United States on both counts.[2] According to a recent comparative study of forty-two nations across the world, happiness decreases as the level of competition increases in a given society (Van de Vliert and Janssen 2002). The United States cannot and should not turn into a Denmark, of course. We are too diverse a society and our approach generates valuable benefits. But those reports suggest that something may be amiss in our mind-set.

The purpose of this book is to explore in detail our ideas of winning and losing. The task is certainly challenging. Tangible things in life, like bicycles or telephones, are relatively easy to take apart and study. With some effort, we come to understand their makeup: their components, how they are put together, and so on. But the values, ideas, and concepts that frame or underpin our societies are more difficult to deconstruct. They are invisible and cannot be held. They are nowhere in a sense, yet also everywhere. We can say that they exist in the minds of people. We can also say, however, that they have an independence of their own and exist separately from each individual consciousness (Durkheim 1965: 269). How, then, should we carry out our investigation of winning and losing?

For guidance, we can turn to the foundational works in sociology of Georg Simmel and Max Weber. They offered two different but complementary methodologies for examining life in society. According to Simmel, social life takes on particular forms (Levine 1971). We come to know any given social phenomenon when we understand how it is ordered or set up: What elements are at play? How do they relate to each other? Who gives what to whom? Parents, for instance, are authoritative figures who provide love and protection to their children. Those children reciprocate by giving their parents joy and affection. Prostitution, in turn, entails an exchange of money and sex between two individuals with asymmetrical power. Simmel urged us to look at the structure of things.

Weber, by contrast, thought that we should pay far more attention to what goes on inside people's minds. People interpret themselves and the world around them. They endow things with significance. Understanding something in society is best done by grasping the meaning it holds for its members (Runciman 1978). If, for instance, we see a mother buying an ice cream for her daughter on the first day of summer, we can understand what is happening when we discover that the mother is motivated in part by memories of her own mother doing the same thing for her years ago. For Weber, our attention should go to what people make of things—to the attributions and thought processes they bring to the world around them.

Both approaches inspired my investigation of winning and losing in America. In line with Simmel, I examine two fundamental aspects of winning and losing. Both have to do with what is at stake or what we *pursue* when we seek victory and try to avoid loss: What prizes do we get or give up? Second, what powers does victory give us over those prizes? How does loss limit us? These are structural questions—they are about the way winning and losing are set up in our society. The answers will reveal a great deal about the hidden qualities of victory and losing as well as what moves us to pursue victory and dread loss so passionately. Chapters 2, 3, and 4 explore the prizes. Chapter 5 focuses on power.

In line with Weber, I explore how we conceive of winners and losers—how we think of them and therefore make them into what they are. Who, in our minds, is a winner? Who is a loser? What do we believe a person must do to earn those titles? Moreover, how do we think about competitive events and the world in general that allows for the existence of winners and losers as well as for their central position in our culture? We are interested in our *beliefs* about the constitutions of winners, losers, and the world around us. This will be the topic of chapters 6 through 9. We will cover much ground. Figure 1.1 summarizes the road ahead. Above all, the analysis will make clear one fundamental fact about winning and losing: they are not endpoints or final destinations but gateways to something of immense importance to us. This is *the affirmation of our place in the world*. We desperately wish to know that we belong to this earth and society—that our presence is legitimate. This doubt is characteristic of modern societies but especially the United States (Greenfeld 2005a, 2005b). Americans, according to the World Values Survey, are among the most preoccupied people in the world about the meaning and purpose of their lives.[3] We are an unsettled people. Behind the drive toward "perfectibility" that Tocqueville saw in America one finds *profound doubt*. In victory we hope to find a positive answer to our questions. In loss, we fear rejection and, with that, the abyss.

Our investigation will also make clear that, unfortunately, we are bound to be disappointed over and over again—regardless of whether we win or lose. This is because, as we compete, we are not aware of what we are really after. It is also because we rely on arbitrary and faulty or inconsistent logic to assess the world around us, to draw conclusions about others and ourselves, to motivate us and interpret events and outcomes. All this creates problems. The intensity of our drives, coupled with our ignorance about what we are doing, ensures that we have a very *obsessive* or compulsive (Fellman 1998) relationship to competition: one that is marked by

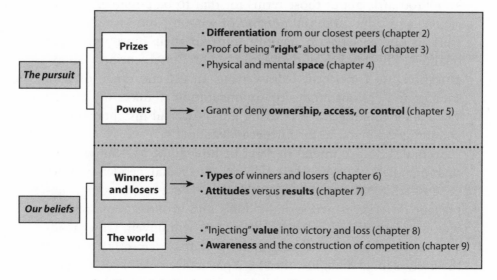

Figure 1.1. Exploring winning and losing in America.

strong urges, repetitive but never satisfied behaviors, and a continuous need to produce evidence about ourselves.

The bulk of this book is descriptive. But in the last chapter I pursue a very normative question: Should we continue to embrace the language of winning and losing in our everyday life? If winning and losing have become "inflationary" and are, at the same time, very messy concepts, is this not an indication that the time has come to reassess our use of those concepts? Are we depriving ourselves of more appropriate language, of sounder and therefore healthier attitudes toward so many different situations and events in life? Is our approach ultimately *inefficient?* I will propose that there are advantages but also serious problems associated with our current approach to winning and losing. Thus I will close by proposing an alternative mind-set for how we pursue our aspirations and dreams.

I shall end this chapter with three caveats. First, our investigation will not be exhaustive. While the task before us is of the most serious nature, I do not intend to offer a conclusive description of winning and losing backed by a comprehensive set of data. We know too little about those terms for that to be possible. My objective is to offer an initial *portrait* of winning and losing as they exist in our society—to identify some of their most important qualities. This book is not a treatise but an "intervention," an exploration. As I proceed, I draw from an eclectic range of data sources and various modes of argumentation to make my point.[4] The reader looking for provoking and powerful insights will encounter good material for further reflection.

Second, I do not intend to describe how all of us—individually or as members of particular socioeconomic, racial, gender, or other groups—think about winning and losing. There are, of course, important differences across individuals and groups. Some readers will not identify with what the discussion will unveil. Other readers, such as myself, will recognize (perhaps hesitantly) parts of themselves in it. What lies ahead is a particular type of sociological effort. My mission is to shed light on a set of powerful concepts *that occupy a dominant place* in our society and which, by virtue of their privileged position, are incessantly before us as we go about our everyday life. To use the language of Berger and Luckmann, this is a book about two socially constructed ideas that have firmly taken roots in our society and which many, though not all of us, accept without question (Berger and Luckmann 1967: 19–21). We are after what Emil Durkheim called "social facts" that mold in a multitude of ways our reality (Durkheim 1982: 70).

Third, we shall focus on the characteristics of winning and losing, not how those concepts originate from, are maintained by, or stand in relation to broader societal factors. What roles do our political system, professional and nonprofessional sports leagues, education system, and economy—to name a few of those factors— play in the making of our competitive mind-sets? Do they benefit from our preoccupation with winning and fear of losing? Are there significant differences across contexts? I do not systematically answer these important questions. Still, given that I speak to them at various points in the book and that some readers may be looking for answers, I outline here my position.

When it comes to broader factors, we should pay special attention to institutions. Institutions are the formal and informal programs, rules, and practices found in our political, economic, athletic, educational, and other systems. We find them at our workplaces, leagues, the state, associations of various kinds, our schools, and beyond (Campbell 2004: i; Fligstein 1996: 658). Institutions are especially responsible for fostering, supporting, and making possible our approach to winning and losing. Research should turn to institutions when investigating the broader context of our competitive mind-sets. By and large, the organizations, associations, and systems that house those institutions benefit from what they produce: individuals are encouraged to give far more of themselves to any given cause than is reasonable or healthy. More of everything is therefore generated—goods, services, professional and athletic achievements, money, entertainment, to name a few. Matters are unlikely to change fast: institutions are sticky (Mahoney 2000) and cannot be easily dismissed, although each context is likely to have unique dynamics at work. In all of this, individuals clearly find themselves in difficult circumstances. The most promising path for them to follow is a change in their own personal perspectives, as I argue in the closing chapter of the book.

PART 2

The Pursuit

Chapter Two

DIFFERENTIATION

What a way to win, as well, with my
brother so close behind me.
—John Grossman, on winning the 2003
World Surf Kayaking Championship

Victory in and of itself is not necessarily what brings us satisfaction. If that were the case, most of us would put ourselves in situations where we would be assured of beating our competitors. Chess masters would play with five-year-olds and professional golfers with people who do not know the difference between a golf club and a walking stick. Instead, quite the opposite happens: we take steps to ensure that we participate in competitive events where we face off against competitors of near equal skill or ability and where the outcome is, therefore, uncertain. In this and the next two chapters, I explore what is behind our love of winning and distaste for loss. What prizes are motivating us?

In this chapter, I identify a set of subtle and somewhat darker things: uncertainty, the thrill of seeing but then avoiding danger, the pleasures that come from seeing others struggle, and above all, the possibility of differentiating ourselves from our closest peers. Close competition provides all of these. We as a society have, therefore, devoted enormous resources, and crafted rules and practices—whether in business, sports, education, or other areas—to ensure that competitive events remain close.

The Competitors

Victory itself is not very interesting. What gives it special flavor is close competition. Without close competition, very few of us would be eager to compete. So, how does close competition make victory thrilling? Figure 2.1 specifies the dynamics at work. Consider each step in turn. Close competition increases the risk of loss. The resulting uncertainty gives victory part of its flavor. We can recall here the words of French sociologist Roger Caillois who, in his classic study of competition and games, stated that "the game is no longer pleasing to one who, because he is too well trained or skillful, wins effortlessly and infallibly" (Caillois 2001: 7). We must be running a risk. If things go wrong, we will find ourselves in an undesirable position; if things go well, on the other hand, we will be quite happy. Because we do not know the outcome yet, we feel excitement. Social psychologists have known this for quite some time: "unpredictability," note two researchers, "is important in creating the tension and excitement for the participants and spectators" (Frazier and Snyder 1991: 380). And "doubt," if at all possible, "must remain until the end," so as to create the maximum excitement (Caillois 2001: 7). But what causes uncertainty? One factor is our opponent. We are facing a partly unknown challenge, one that is potentially bigger than we can handle. Only engagement with that challenge will reveal the truth. A second, perhaps more important cause, is ourselves. To return to Caillois' insight, we know that we are not infallible: "Every game of skill, by definition, involves the risk for the player of missing his stroke, and the threat of defeat, without which the game would no longer be pleasing" (Caillois 2001: 7). We are capable of making mistakes and hurting ourselves. The challenge becomes to see how we perform. We choose situations, then, that test our abilities. We can certainly run faster than a five-year-old. But can we run as fast as our peers?

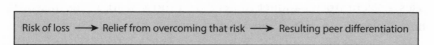

Figure 2.1. Close competition and the thrill of victory.

The risk of loss generates other dynamics as well. We must struggle and exert ourselves in order to overcome the odds. We have to labor for the desired outcome. We must, in other words, make an effort. Such effort implies that we have invested a part of ourselves, that we have taken time to gather our energy, to concentrate, to turn our attention to the task before us. We have not only spent part of ourselves but also dedicated our minds to it. Loss becomes painful because of all that we have invested. Winning vindicates us. Rewards, then, are available only for those who have struggled. And, in fact, psychology experiments confirm this much. In one study, for instance, researchers found that progress in attaining certain objectives at the workplace caused feelings of self-esteem only when those objectives were deemed *difficult* to attain. "Goal difficulty," wrote the researchers, "emerged as the clearest moderator between goal progress and well-being over a period of 3 years" (Wiese and Freund 2005: 298). The attainment of easy goals generates no real pleasure. Other researchers reported more generally that for most people the attainment of hard goals generates more pride and self-respect than is the case for easier goals (Mento et al. 1992).

The effort-reward mentality is quite central to American culture and its roots. According to the General Social Survey—the most authoritative and comprehensive source of attitudes in our country—75 percent of Americans believe effort to be an essential driver of one's social standing.[1] Success, they believe, requires and reflects hard work. Our mythologies, in turn, are heavily preoccupied with the close relationship between effort and rewards. Think of Ulysses' adventures in *The Odyssey*: they are a sequence of challenges and obstacles that are overcome through courage and skill. Ulysses' reunion with his wife Penelope and Penelope's own faithfulness in the face of doubt and pressure from numerous suitors are deeply meaningful because of their travails. Tellingly, once back, Ulysses uses a celebratory banquet to get rid of those who, in his absence, had aspired to marry Penelope and replace him in his own home: close competitors indeed! When it comes to Christianity, only those who heed the word of God and avoid doing evil are granted salvation. Eve in the Garden of Eden could not resist temptation: God deemed her unworthy and sent her and Adam away. Since then, all humans have come into this world burdened with original sin. They must toil to survive on this earth: "Cursed is the ground for thy sake," said God to Adam; "in sorrow shalt thou eat of it all the days of thy life" (Genesis 3). And, of course, they must cleanse themselves to reach the heavens.

The second element in figure 2.1 follows closely from the first. Victory confirms for us that, *even though we could have lost,* we have in fact won. We delight in not having lost, with all the terrible consequences that that can bring. Insofar as this is the case, victory is then a sensation of pleasure based, in part, on something that has not taken place: we stand by the abyss that we previously saw and delight in the idea that we have not fallen into it. Without the abyss, the delight would not be there. In terms of uncertainty, victory is then the *elimination* of that doubt. Note, therefore, that the pleasure comes not from the mere absence of that doubt but, rather, from its acknowledged presence and, in a later moment, its deletion. It is the sequence—doubt and then no doubt—that causes pleasure.

There are plenty of studies that show that inordinate pleasure can come from seeing danger and then avoiding it. In a recent experiment measuring the pleasure associated with winning and losing, students at Ohio State University were put before a computer and allowed to gamble money. Outcomes were fixed, so that all participants neither lost nor made money. Yet the paths to those outcomes were different. One group of students was in positive territory until the end. The other was in negative territory until the end. Which group reported the most overall pleasure from the experiment? The one that was losing throughout and then saw the losses go away (Heyman et al. 2004). But we need not turn to experiments to understand this process. The logic is embedded in many of our daily activities and social rituals.

What happens, after all, when we take a shot at a basket? If we knew beforehand that we would make the shot, we would be less interested in taking it. Michael Jordan said on many occasions that he took each shot with the conviction that he would make it. But this cannot possibly explain the joy he displayed on so many occasions when making the shot. The possibility of failure, confirmed by more than 9,000 missed shots and a career's percentage of shots made from the field of 47 percent, had to be always in his mind (Reilly 2002). The realization that he avoided a negative outcome in turn surely was at least part of the pleasure. Much the same can be said of the ritual that takes place every spring with high school students opening their admission letters from the various colleges to which they have applied. The anxiety that mounts in the days before the letters arrive is by and large fueled by students imagining rejection letters in their hands: "What would a rejection from that college say about me, my intelligence, how I rank in the world of my fellow peers?" The arrival of positive news erases those memories and provides much welcome relief. "I am not that person," the student feels, "but rather this smart, interesting person." Parents as well experience positive feelings out of the confirmation that their child is, indeed, not a "failure." Even the best of parents, with the best of children, harbor their doubts and rejoice when the good news erases their fears.[2]

And the same can be said of what happens at the workplace, in the business world, and elsewhere. When we await a job offer, work hard to launch a new company, or wait for end-of-year bonus decisions, we entertain negative outcomes. We engage in thought experiments, contemplating the consequences of failure. What will I do if I receive no offer to join the company? What will a failed business say about me and what I am capable of? How will I communicate to my spouse that I received the smallest bonus in the firm? We work hard to avoid those outcomes. We train, read helpful books, devote extra hours, and sacrifice precious time with families and friends. When good news comes, part of its significance is that we will not have to hear bad news that would make our efforts and sacrifices seem futile.[3]

The third and final component of this process is perhaps the most important. The great psychologist Erik Erikson explored in detail the importance of *differentiation* between human beings. Identity for groups and individuals alike is created not so much by an independent process of self-definition. Rather, it is attained by somehow asserting that we are different from someone else: that we belong to a class or group of people that stands apart from other classes or groups. The very fact of standing apart from someone else *is* what defines us. Erikson calls this tendency toward separation "pseudospeciation"—the artificial (i.e., human-made) setting of boundaries among people:

> The term denotes the fact that while man is obviously one species, he appears and continues on the scene split up into groups (from tribes to nations, from castes to classes, from religion to ideologies) which provide their members with a firm sense of distinct . . . identity—and immortality. (Erikson 1968: 7)

In primitive tribes, individuals and groups attained differentiation by simply decorating their bodies "with feathers, pelts, and paints" (Erikson 1969: 431). In our society, the process of differentiation continues to rely on basic physical signs—such as clothing, physical appearance, and our material possessions. But our reality is also more complex. There are more symbols, a larger number of groups to which we can belong, finer differences between groups, and so on. We also employ a variety of nonmaterial tools to separate ourselves from others. Our level of education is one example: those with a college degree feel themselves different from high school dropouts. Those with advanced degrees, such as physicians, feel that they stand higher than those with "only" a college degree. There are even differences within a given level of educational achievement. A doctorate in theoretical physics, for instance, sends a different message about a person than a doctorate in social work. Education is but one tool for differentiation. The way we speak—our choice of vocabulary, our choice of subject matters, and so on—communicates something about who we are, and who we are not. So do our professions and the way we decorate our personal spaces. In the words of French sociologist Bourdieu, we are constantly "distinguishing" ourselves by our tastes, knowledge, dispositions, and behaviors (Bourdieu 1984).

Americans deeply value differentiation, of course. When asked in the General Social Survey whether their country should promote equal opportunities or equal outcomes, nearly 90 percent answered opportunities. When asked whether the government should be responsible for reducing income differences between the rich and the poor, the majority said "no." Most believe that social (and not only economic) differences in life are "justified." And when they were asked whether people should be allowed to accumulate as much wealth as they can even if others live in poverty, nearly 60 percent of respondents said that they should be. Only 31 percent disagreed.[4] We believe in and indeed crave all sorts of signs of distinction.

In competitive events with close rivals, then, we have the special opportunity to *separate* ourselves from those who, until then, we and others thought to be like us. We have before us *peers*—persons belonging to the same general category of people or groups: colleagues at work and in our profession, our neighbors in the next town over and their children, our siblings, and so on. The competitive arena allows us to set boundaries between ourselves and others—it gives us grounds and tools for making distinctions. This is ultimately what is so special about these events that one cannot find when facing, and beating, far weaker opponents. We seek our equals in the hope of proving to ourselves and the world that they are not, after all, equal to us. We seek to distance ourselves.

The winners in particular obviously benefit from this process. They become different from the losers by virtue of having become the winner: "I won, therefore I am different from you." The winner is catapulted into a new space—a space that is closed to those who lose. But what does this space look like? It is a rarified and, to some extent, mysterious space. One of its characteristics is that fewer people belong to it: it is a selective space. Thus, on learning in 2005 that he had been awarded the prestigious prize of best economist under forty by the American Economic Association, MIT professor Daron Acemoglu felt it "was a great honor" because "the cast of people who have been awarded this is staggeringly strong" (Gavin 2005). With similar language, genetics researcher Marlene Belfort described her joy at the great honor of becoming a member of the National Academy of Science. "One of my kids," she reported "said it was like making the All-Star team." She then continued by saying: "I was very happily surprised . . . it's something that every self-respecting scientist aspires to" . . . but only very few manage to get (Wood 1999). As I win, then, I join the elite group of those "who know," "who can." It is also a place of blessed people: people who—in line with the first two steps of figure 2.1—have lived through uncertainty to be rewarded with the sensation that comes from having avoided the abyss and overcome the odds. It is, therefore, a place of honor and, with that, of some measure of immortality.

For the losers matters are quite different. They, too, undergo a process of definition. But they are left with significantly less information about themselves than the winners. The separation from the winner—so crucial for the winner—equates primarily to a feeling of having been "left behind." Losers are thrown back into a large pool of competitors who aspire to become distinguished but have yet to find ways of making this happen. Their distinguishing mark is that they are *not* the winners. Physiological events that take place in competitors' bodies confirm this. Before a competitive event, players experience a rise in their testosterone levels. After the event, winners experience a further increase in those levels, while losers remain closer to normal. The rise appears to be especially steep when the competitive event was close and the outcome uncertain (Mazur et al. 1992).

Thus, "to come close and lose," said Leon Panetta, a former White House chief of staff under President Clinton, about losing presidential nominees in the United States, "tends to magnify everything the candidate did wrong." The loser's task becomes then "to go back to the drawing board," "re-find themselves," and search for the motivation to aspire again. In the words of Walter Mondale, who lost the presidential elections to Ronald Reagan in 1984, this is exactly what happens when you have the privilege of running for the top political position in the country and lose: "If you come back and expect to be, quote, the titular head of the party, you're bound to have a bad day." Instead, assuming you are a person of character, you have to look around, ask yourself what is next, and find a new path. As Michael Dukakis, who lost to George H. W. Bush in 1988, recently put it: "I ran a lousy general election campaign. . . . [A] lot of people were upset. I was upset. You can't expect your party to wrap you up in love and affection . . . but there's a role you can play" (Leibovich 2006).

Competition among close rivals, then, provides the victor with the opportunity to assert themselves vis-à-vis others thought to be, until then, of equal skill. It is often a momentous occasion. But we should stress that its intensity is even greater when the competitors share similar backgrounds, histories, physical appearance, and other characteristics. Then, the separation that results from the demonstrated skill superiority acquires even more significance: we feel good when we beat a stranger of similar rankings in chess at a tournament, but we feel even better if that stranger is in fact no stranger at all. This is indeed what was at stake in most struggles for secession. The American Civil War saw a close and long fight between one group of states (the southern states) wishing to assert its difference from another group of states (the northern ones) which were quite similar for the most part. For the South, the difficulty of the struggle would have made a victory all so meaningful. But that meaningfulness could not have been separated from the fact that the warring parties shared so much in common.

The same can be said of siblings who, close in skills at a given game or enterprise, push themselves to extremes in order to win. Recent research shows that competitive events among siblings are uniquely charged with emotions and psychological tension (Nickolas and Meyer 2008). There are many reasons for this but one is surely that a hard-won victory gives one of the siblings the license to distinguish herself or himself from the person who otherwise resembles them more closely than anyone else on the planet. What happens at home will, of course, later happen in college. From September to April, otherwise very similar schools stake their grounds and assert their personalities on the football field, basketball courts, and elsewhere. On this point, I recall vividly a conversation with the coach of a NCAA Division III men's basketball team. Without a sign of doubt in his eyes, he told me that his season was not so much defined by the number of wins over losses but, rather, by whether his team would beat the school's two archrivals—both of which were very close in skill but also had nearly identical student populations, rated very similarly in the national ranking of schools, and were located within sixty miles of each other. "As long as we do that," he said, "I have achieved my mission and done my job . . . the rest of the season no longer matters . . . that is what they told me when they hired me."

The Spectators

Most of us enjoy watching competitive events. More than 56 percent of respondents in the General Social Survey reported attending an amateur or professional sports event in the last year.[5] But we are picky. Few of us would go to see a game between the Los Angeles Lakers and a high school basketball team. Many of us would, however, enjoy seeing the Lakers against another professional team, or two high school teams play against each other. Political races where polls predict landslide victories by a candidate seldom generate excitement. Viewers of popular television reality shows such as *Survivor, Fear Factor,* or *American Idol* would be quite bored if it became clear from the start that a certain team or individual was very likely to dominate over all others and win the grand prize.

All this tells us that we, as members of an audience, enjoy a competitive event for reasons that have little to do with strictly witnessing someone win and somebody else lose. What, then, draws us to a competitive event? What rewards do we gain? There are several factors, all of which require that competitors be quite close in skill or level. Research in psychology and sociology suggests that four are especially important, with "differentiation" once again being perhaps the most critical.

Most obviously, as is the case for the competitors themselves, *uncertainty* itself generates a certain thrill. The more the uncertainty, the greater the thrill, as experiments have shown.[6] Here the question is not whether we or someone else will win. Instead, the question is who, amongst these more or less equal competitors, will prevail. Why does this uncertainty cause excitement? The main reason is, again, our fear of uncertainty. In almost everything that we do, we prefer to know what is about to happen in the near and not-so-near future. This gives as a sense of security: we can prepare for the events ahead, plan our activities, and rejoice at the fact that we will be safe tomorrow. Studies in economics and psychology have shown rather convincingly, for instance, that the majority of people are risk averse and, as such, are willing to settle for less with certainty than take the chance to risk (getting nothing or a possible loss) for more.[7] We surround ourselves with routines and predictable environments. Consider, for instance, the music we listen to: the most enjoyable pieces are those we have heard at least once before. Or consider that order and predictability allow children to develop their cognitive, analytical, and emotional faculties (Dumas et al. 2005).

From this perspective, a close competitive event affords us the chance to experience the sense of freedom and possibility that is otherwise so very much missing from our lives. Most Americans, according to the General Social Survey, do not find everyday life exciting. They define it, instead, as routine driven (49 percent) or outright dull (5 percent).[8] For a limited period of time, then, we play with what is otherwise too risky, dangerous, and therefore normally forbidden and out of reach. We enjoy the diversion, recognizing that the competitive event is organized in a way that maximizes what is normally minimized in everyday life. As an astute observer of American football put it:

The football fan's world of everyday work is generally characterized by limited opportunities for self-expression. In the

role and status of football fan, and in the passion and meaning emanating from the act of rooting, the football fan can
assume a new identity in life. In playing the role of fan, the
individual finds a haven for escape from work and a forum
for excitement and adventure. (Miller 1997: 125)

The experience is exhilarating and, as a result, we lose our normal
composure. We no longer have to restrain ourselves. Some of us
scream and shout, jump up and down—very much as we did when
we were children. If we are in a group, sensing the power of the
collective excitement, we let ourselves go even more. If others are
doing it, so can we. Suspended for a moment from the constraints
of everyday life, we feel exceptional. Along with our accomplices,
we feel that we are stealing time from time itself. These are powerful moments. They remind us of the sense of "collective efferves-
cence" that Durkheim described in what became arguably the most
important text of sociology, *The Elementary Forms of the Religious Life*: moments when members of a society, excited by each
other's presence, gather around a totem or other symbol of their
group and feel transported to an unconventional place where the
rules and boundaries of everyday life are no longer in place (Durkheim 1965). Society is a safe place built on the suppression of our
darker instincts (Freud 1989: 73). Because of that, it has mecha-
nisms that allow us to explore and express what we otherwise seek
to control in normal life.

But to make all of this possible, a second crucial condition has to
be met: we must be at a *safe distance* from the event. This means
that the outcome of the event cannot have serious consequences
for our well-being. If it did have such consequences, we would be
resolute in wanting no uncertainty whatsoever.[9] Instead, though it
may have a major impact on the competitors, the competitive event
is not that important for us, all things considered. The possible
damage that might come from the loss of our favorite competitor
(if indeed we have one) is thus outweighed by the positive feelings
that come from taking a mental vacation from our otherwise con-
strained and controlled lives. We "play," in other words, with un-

certainty. And here we would do well to recall the words of the great Dutch scholar of culture, Johan Huizinga, concerning play and its function for human beings: "Summing up the formal characteristics of play we might call it a free activity standing quite consciously outside 'ordinary' life as being 'not serious,' but at the same time absorbing the player intensely and utterly" (Huizinga 1955: 13). We flirt with uncertainty, watching it while knowing that it cannot have any real consequences for us. Thus, as we watch, we are likely to be doing other things that are pleasant—such as eating food, talking to our friends, and occasionally taking a break.

There is a third, perhaps darker dynamic at work that accounts for our interest, as spectators, in competitive events. We are watching competitors as they struggle to succeed, react to events as they unfold, and suffer in what is a tense and closely fought battle. We are aware of the enormous pressure that they are experiencing. We examine their eyes, sighs, and body language. We observe their reactions, their emotional ups and downs as the competition progresses. The more drama we witness, the more delighted we are. Missed opportunities, belligerent behavior followed by punishment, and dashed hopes are prime material for our excitement, especially when the stakes are high. Psychologists and economists have documented and researched in detail this tendency of ours to feel some level of pleasure at the sight of others' suffering (or at very least doing less well than us). Its intensity can vary depending on the observers' mind-set and the nature of the misfortune (if very serious, we do not feel pleasure), but many of us—whether in the United States or another country—are likely to feel it to one degree or another.[10]

Public excitement thus grew multifold when Alaska's governor Sarah Palin gave her awkward interviews in September 2008 as vice-presidential candidate on CBS and ABC. The media incessantly discussed her strange statements about Russia and her foreign policy credentials. On YouTube, in early October a search for her name retrieved forty-eight thousand videos. A search for her opponent, Senator Joe Biden of Delaware, yielded only fourteen thousand results. Many of us therefore watched their debate in early October 2008 both out of a genuine interest in the issues at hand but also to "see" how the candidates—and Palin especially—would perform under extreme pressure. Like hawks, we waited for the slip, the error, the wrong statement or choice of words. Then, after the debate, we watched television and read newspapers to find out what others "saw." It was no different in the 2004 debates, when journalists paid great attention to the facial expressions and body language of both Senator Kerry and President Bush. "From the outset," wrote Alessandra Stanley of the *New York Times* about Bush after their second debate, "his clenched jaw twitched, and he blinked repeatedly, like a man whose contact lens hurt" (Stanley 2004).

We are engaging, in other words, in a *sadistic* exercise. We feel a sort of pleasure when we see others struggle. We marvel at the spectacle of human efforts and emotions that are on display. We enjoy seeing players suffer as the tension mounts, the outcome is repeatedly put into doubt, and temporary relief is followed by renewed tension. Indeed, the more the competitors give of themselves, the more we enjoy ourselves. Do we suffer or feel pleasure at the sight of a baseball pitcher hitting a batter on the thigh with a ninety-mile-an-hour fastball? If watching it gives us pain, why do we stretch our necks when the slow-motion replay shows us more clearly what happened? Indeed, why do television networks show such replays? The answer is quite simple: within certain limits, we are interested in seeing others in pain.

Appealing to our sadistic side, after all, is how promoters of competitive events try to lure us into watching this or that event. The advertising for upcoming games in the National Football League (NFL) inevitably shows receivers and quarterbacks getting hit hard—with amplified sound effects—by defenders flying helmet-first into their bodies (ideally, without the victim seeing this coming). Those for the National Basketball Association (NBA) show images of exhausted players rejoicing or despairing after their last-minute efforts to overturn or put closure to a wide open game. Stories profiling the lives of Olympic athletes portray their previous failures, victories, and hopes. And advertisements for presidential debates show snapshots of candidates making errors, being caught off guard, or crushing their opponents with clever one-liners. With all of these, the message is clear: there will be pain and joy, and we—the viewers—will have a chance to witness them.

Close competitive events, then, maximize the chances that competitors will suffer and that we, as a result of that, will be entertained. But there is a fourth, final, and perhaps more innocent and important, aspect of the audience–competitive event relationship. This has to do with the *vicarious differentiation* that comes from witnessing others—especially those whom we support—try to assert themselves and their uniqueness. We often become virtual participants in the competitive event, feeling its ups and downs. We suffer and rejoice with "our" players on the field, sensing their fears, hopes, and if victorious, joy and elation at their successes. Their happiness becomes our happiness. Indeed, we see in their superior performance evidence of our superior abilities, and in their failures our weaknesses, as recent experiments have demonstrated (Hirt et al. 1992). Thus, simply put, we "become" them and join them accordingly in their quest for differentiation.

Our Society

The previous two sections suggest that we have a collective interest in close competition, whether as players or spectators. This, coupled with the other benefits that close competition can generate for society,[11] is responsible for making sure that we are constantly devising rules and practices that ensure that many aspects of our lives—even those that do not require a competitive dimension— unfold in spaces where the competitors will be a match for each other. We, in turn, duly flock to participate or watch. We should be cognizant of what those rules, structures, and policies are. After all, often unbeknown to us, they profoundly shape our lives: our ambitions, choices, sense of self-esteem, relationship to others, and much more.

The world of sports is especially organized and run to ensure that competition remains close. We keep teams and players separated by skill level. At the college level, there are divisions. In professional sports, there are different professional leagues (major versus minor leagues in baseball, for instance). Among children, we separate children first by age (a good proxy for ability) and then ability (varsity versus junior varsity, A versus B teams, and so on). Once we make sure that fairly equal competitors meet each other, we devise rules that ensure that no one competitor can, over time, become dominant. In the United States, draft rules in basketball, American football, and hockey give the weakest teams access to the best new players. Salary caps—introduced for basketball in the mid 1980s, for American football in the mid 1990s, and for hockey in 2005—limit how much talent any given team can buy. In baseball, the recent introduction of revenue-sharing structures provides financially disadvantaged teams with much needed resources, much to the delight of its commissioner, Bud Selig, who recently shared his enthusiasm for what these could mean for the sport: "I had dreams of things getting better but, no, in many ways this has exceeded my fondest expectations. This sport has more parity than ever" (Schmidt 2006).

Importantly, the rules of the games themselves are often designed to keep the competition in any given event or through a series of events as open as possible. In some sports, such as tennis or baseball, a comeback is possible until the very last point, regardless of what the deficit might be. Playoffs involve multiple encounters, such as best of five or seven series. A heavy defeat in the first games does not mean definitive loss; the losing team can still win the series by beating the opponent in the next games by a smaller margin of points (and thus with fewer points overall for the series). In some cases, the good players are penalized: in golf, stronger players start with a handicap precisely so that the outcome may be more in doubt. In some sports, different kinds of scoring can be worth different points; as a result, comebacks from large point deficits are more possible than otherwise. This is true for basketball (two versus three point shots) but also gymnastics, skating, diving, and other sports where athletes can attempt more arduous, though also riskier, routines or moves.

Our education system as well has plenty of measures that ensure close competition among students—in this case less for the purpose of keeping large audiences enthralled and more for the purposes of establishing differences and identities among the competitors. Early on in their educational careers, children of similar intellectual levels are put together in the same classes. On paper, this is designed to "stimulate" and "motivate" those children: surrounded by others of similar abilities, the children will strive to demonstrate to themselves that they are indeed equal to, if not better than, the other "advanced" kids. The possibility that others will perform better pushes those kids to study harder. The results—uncertain until grades become available—provide kids with meaning and a sense of self as well as a good dose of excitement. But here, too, we cannot forget that there is an audience: the parents. They have a vicarious interest in these affairs. Their child—their life's work—"has to be tested," over and over again, for his or her worth to become clear. Each success provides relief but also signals the possibility that the child could go further. New challenges, appropriately calibrated to be within possible reach, are brought on. Thus parents wait anxiously to discover if their child, already attending an elite preparatory school, can further distinguish herself (that is, separate herself from her current peers) by being admitted to a more prestigious college.

Later, colleges continue the formal and institutional segregation of students. This guarantees not only four challenging years with equally capable peers but also easier entry into competitive circles and careers that can guarantee not only a lifetime of productivity and comfort but also close competition. Now in question is not only the parents' own self-esteem but also the child's, who is old enough to appreciate the consequences of differentiation. The stakes are consequently very high. Thus, should there be any doubt as to which category a college belongs, a variety of sources provide us with updated and influential rankings of schools. The most popular source, *U.S. News and World Report*, releases on a yearly basis in late summer its eagerly awaited segmentation of schools. Undergraduate programs are mercilessly divided into "top," "tier

3," and "tier 4" (tier 2 is not used). For each school, the report gives the average scores for the SAT and ACT entrance exams, the percentage of students in the top 10 percent of their high school class, and the rate of selectivity: "Am I among the few, select ones?"[12] What happens for colleges happens again for graduate schools. The best students will go to the best programs in the arts and sciences or the best professional schools—of law, business, education, medicine, journalism, and so on. The weaker students will attend more modest schools. Each student will thus meet his or her intellectual "match" and thus move into a space of calibrated uncertainty and stimulation.

What is true for sports and education is also true for a third, major sphere of social life: the workplace. Most professional fields—medicine, law, education, engineering, healthcare, finance, computer programming, and so on—are hierarchically organized in ways that group people of similar skills and experience together. Those people are then evaluated against each other in a process that causes anxiety but, in the case of positive results, also grounds for differentiation and satisfaction, as well as a fair degree of sadistic pleasure in seeing others run into difficulties. The process of evaluation is highly formalized and in theory objective, so that everyone in principle has a shot at success: there are awards, pay raises, prizes, and other types of rewards that await those who can outperform their peers. Of course, the fact that everyone can in principle win is what makes victory for the eventual winner meaningful. Importantly, the struggle is not only with one's immediate peers but with the profession as a whole and with the task itself, which is rather challenging but within reach. Thus becoming a partner at a law firm is meaningful precisely because it is challenging in several respects: one is fighting against other capable candidates, the legal field itself, and the work that one encounters throughout the years. Throughout we are reminded in various ways of both the difficulty of the task ahead but also the real chances of success. Tenure rates in given academic institutions or disciplines are made public, large financial institutions make known who was promoted to director level, and prestigious management consulting firms, like

McKinsey & Company, remind their employees of their "up or out" policies—according to which somewhere between half and two thirds of second-year consultants are sent packing.

We could discuss additional examples. What is important is to recognize that we have built a society replete with environments where competition is fiercely close. Those environments infuse victory and loss with their meaning. They could certainly be designed differently. They could be less competitive, for instance. Or they could make sure that everyone wins in some way or another. This is what happens, after all, in some children's clubs, leagues, and summer camps, where everyone is recognized for something, and even in some adults' organizations—especially those where the members are suffering from addiction, depression, or other problems. They could even do away with competition as a whole, as Alfie Kohn (Kohn 1986) suggested should happen in *No Contest: The Case against Competition*. There could be no language of winning and losing, comparative performance ratings, prizes for the better performers, and so on. We could instead make wide use of alternative terms and concepts, such as personal fulfillment or professional and client satisfaction. Many of us would certainly welcome such an approach. We have chosen not to follow those paths, opting instead to create a host of very competitive environments.

Conclusion

The primary conclusion we draw from all this is straightforward. We do not have a simple love of winning and dislike of losing—despite what one might think when listening to coaches, parents, friends, colleagues, leading authors, commentators, and others talk about what matters. Much more is at stake. We are interested in the thrill and subliminal satisfaction that come from contemplating but then avoiding danger, the subtle pleasures we feel from seeing others suffer, and above all, our desire to be different and define our own identity—especially vis-à-vis our closest peers. That is what many of us are after, and that is why we are interested in winning (and not losing) in competitive events that are very close in nature.

Several implications stem from this realization. First, we should now be clearer about *why* we take competition so seriously. Second, we should begin to wonder whether competition, winning, and losing are the best venue for the satisfaction of our drives. Third, we should inquire further about those drives. Why, for instance, do we so desperately wish to differentiate ourselves from our peers? If, after reflecting on things, we no longer felt this impulse, we would be free from having to compete or we could change drastically how we compete. These are but the first steps toward a better understanding of what is at stake in our competitive events. The next two chapters shed further light.

Chapter Three

I WIN, THEREFORE I AM RIGHT

The only good thing about losing is that
it sounds an alarm bell.
—Harvard Business School professor
Rosabeth Moss Kanter, *Confidence*

As we have just seen, competition is seldom only about the particular event, game, or sport at hand. Why would ambitious and hardworking adults dedicate the best years of their lives—most of their waking hours, their emotions, their bodies—to trying to put a leather ball in a basket a few more times than others in the space of forty-eight minutes? Are CEOs really sacrificing their personal relationships, their interests (actual or potential) in other things, and their peaceful nights of sleep so that their companies can make better shampoos, glass bottles, and nail polish? What really drives people to compete? Victory must endow the winners with something truly sweet and engrossing. In the previous chapter, we learned about differentiation. In this chapter, I explore a second major "prize" that is at stake in our competitive events: *being right*.

Winning often serves as an objective and external validation that we are *right*. But right about what? Certainly, we have a better grasp of the competitive event itself: the required skills, the clever tricks, the needed resources. Yet there is more. We feel, by an odd twist of logic, that we have a better grasp of the *world* in general—its laws and workings. We establish that we are *overall* right, and therefore feel at peace with ourselves and life. Therein lies one of the most important—and most luring—aspects of victory: it tells us that we are clearheaded, correct, sharp. It confirms that our perceptions, until then not fully tested, are faithful to reality. Losers, by contrast, are wrong in a general sense. Their defeat tells them that they must engage in some "soul searching": they have limitations, faults, and misperceptions that require investigation. Competitive events in our society offer a battleground where alternative perspectives on life meet head to head and where, we hope, our doubts about ourselves are finally put to rest.

On Top of the World

In a recent study of ten-year-olds' reactions to the outcome of a soccer match, psychologists from North Carolina State University found that children from the losing team, when asked to reflect on what had happened and their performance, provided more causal and introspective interpretations of the turn of events. Those from the winning teams instead offered more factual and less inquisitive accounts (Baker-Ward et al. 2005). Victory, in other words, is liberating. Unlike the losers, who have some painful homework to do, winners need not spend much time agonizing over the past in search of their errors. If interested in winning again, they will surely revisit their performance to identify what they did, or did not do, correctly. But this will be a relatively pleasant exercise—a matter of refining what already worked well. It will be a question of adjustments and fine-tuning, rather than of searching for serious faults and revamping. The winner may even think about the past with some humility, but this will be without the guilt and sense of failure that plague the loser. In the words of Harvard University Business School guru Rosabeth Moss Kanter, winners must turn their good "habits of responsibility, teamwork, and initiative into routines, processes, and practices that encourage and perpetuate them" (Kanter 2004: 30). "Success," she adds, "stems from a great deal of consistent hard work to perfect each detail. It is even a little mundane. Win, go back to work, and win again" (Kanter 2004: 62). Winning, in other words, does not shake one's foundations but rather confirms their solidity. Winners must keep on working so as to ensure that they build on what they already have. Losers have it much harder, by contrast. "Losers have more problems to solve," Kanter notes. "Their energy is depleted just keeping things from falling apart" (Kanter 2004: 125). "The only good thing about losing," she emphasizes, "is that it sounds an alarm bell." It should trigger, she adds, close "scrutiny of taken-for-granted assumptions" (Kanter 2004: 356). Losers need to stop, look deeply inside of themselves, reassess, and try again.

Hence, it is not uncommon to hear winners proclaim, soon after prevailing, that they feel "on top of the world" or utter other similar statements of joy and triumph. "For the last nine years," Michael Jordan reflected in 1994 when taking a break from basketball, "I lived in a situation where I had the world at my feet" (Berkow 1994). "We are walking on top of the world," said Steve Forbes's campaign manager after an impressive performance in the Alaska's Republican primaries for the 2000 presidential elections (*Union Leader* 2000). Those around winners often concur with such claims: to them, winners seem to be in a fantastic position. They seem to inhabit a different realm—that of the blessed, anointed, beautiful. We watch them with admiration and some envy. This contrasts with the sight of losers often looking deeply distraught. With their heads down and subdued voices, they feel at the "bottom" of the world, dejected, last in line. We detect signs of shame or guilt. Losers feel empty, spent, finished. They question—as countless psychological studies have shown—their worthiness, cognitive abilities, judgment, physical skills, and prowess.[1] And we in the audience agree with that assessment: having seen their limitations, we lose interest in them. We realize that there is something wrong with them, that they carry a burden that requires some "fixing."

But what, exactly, makes winners feel so good about themselves and losers so upset? Through a strange twist of logic, we use victory and loss at something quite specific (elections, basketball, selling home goods, etc.) to *generalize* about our position in, and our understanding of, the world. We see in victory some specific evidence that our understanding of the way things work in general, what causes what in the world, how people think and act, what it takes to succeed in this or that endeavor, what follows from what, is accurate, appropriate, lucid—in a word, *right*. Victory tells us that we are competent not only at the specific task in which we have shown our superiority but in general, as whole people. We now feel that we no longer have to prove ourselves, not only at the specific task in which we succeeded but in other realms as well. The feeling generates a sense of peace and satisfaction: freed from doubts, we have finally found our place in the world. We feel wholesome and complete.

Loss, by contrast, raises profound questions not only about our skills in the particular competitive event at hand but about us as persons and the way we approach the world. Defeat tells us that our vision of the world is flawed. Our perceptions are misleading. We have miscalculated, misjudged, misinterpreted. We failed to see things as they truly are. There is, in brief, something wrong with us—*as persons*, and not only as business persons, athletes, or politicians. On closer scrutiny, this process of generalization is rather odd. Why do we make this leap from the results of a specific activity to a judgment of our entire selves? We will address this question later in the chapter. First, let us examine some telling examples of the process of generalization itself.

During the Cold War, victory in athletic events was seen by both sides—the West led by the United States and the East led by the Soviet Union—as a validation of their views on politics (democracy versus communism) and economics (capitalism versus planned economies), even though there was clearly little, if any, connection between sports and economics and politics. As one scholar of the Cold War recently put it, competitors were "projectors of national values and strengths, as well as weaknesses . . . political-ideological considerations, then, imparted an extra edge to the usual element of sporting competition" (Beck 2005: 170). A gymnastics victory for the West was thus taken as proof of the superiority of the principles of individualism, freedom of thought, and the private pursuit of wealth as articulated by Adam Smith, John Locke, the Founding Fathers of the United States, and many others. A victory for the East was seen as proof of the correctness of the writing of Karl Marx, Vladimir Lenin, and others calling for equality and the importance of a powerful state in society.

The leaders of the Soviet Union were clearly very interested in using sports to demonstrate to themselves and others that the socialist way of life was indeed superior. "The Olympic Games," wrote an expert on Russian history and sports, "made Soviet athletes ambassadors for the state and Party, and victories in soccer, by far the most popular game in the USSR, were particularly valued by Stalin and his successors" (Edelman 1993: 46). Thus a 1948 Communist Party resolution decreed that sport should be used not merely to prove athletic ability but also the superiority of the socialist way of thinking. That line of policy would remain the same for decades to come. In the words of Vladislav Tretiak, the legendary goalkeeper of the Soviet hockey team between 1972 and 1984, "Every time our government wanted us to prove that communism was better than capitalism. We were programmed to prove this to the world. . . . It was up to us to make sure that the public knew that communism is far superior to capitalism" (Davey and Mac-Askill 1997, as quoted in Beck 2005: 273).

Government officials, the public, coaches, and players alike in the United States also saw sports as something that could reveal something far beyond athletics. The U.S. hockey victory in the 1980 Olympics against the overwhelmingly favored players from the Soviet Union was perhaps the single most important athletic event of the Cold War. The victory, known in the United States as the Miracle on Ice, had little to do with hockey. It had everything to do with reassuring Americans that their culture, ideology, and life philosophy was superior to those of their Soviet counterparts. The timing was crucial. The economy was miserable. Two months before, the Soviet Union had invaded Afghanistan. A few months before that, Marxists had launched a successful coup in Nicaragua and Iranians seized control of the U.S. embassy in Teheran, taking sixty-six Americans hostage. President Carter had warned the nation that it was facing a crisis in confidence. The Miracle on Ice became for many a momentous turnaround point, a much-needed confirmation of the worthiness of the "American spirit."

The "generalization" started with the American coach himself, Herb Brooks. Journalist Gerald Eskenazi recently wrote about his meeting with Brooks a few months before the game. Eskenazi "was immediately struck by his [Brooks's] hatred of the Soviets and his evangelical belief in the American system that could topple them. Indeed, we had a fascinating discussion about capitalism and communism, and how the entrepreneurial spirit would translate to the athletic field or the rink . . . that someone would rise above the collective to create an American victory—on and off the ice" (Eskenazi 2004). The coach's spirit was shared by his players, who, after their victory, became convinced that the outcome had not only proven their worldview right but that it had helped the Soviets see the fallacy of their own philosophy. The reflections of Jim Craig, the goalie, are worth capturing at some length:

> We saw the Russian team as a steely-eyed, cold group of assassins, but they were wonderful men with extreme talents who were never allowed to express themselves except on the ice. The game was the start of the end of the Cold War for them [the players]. Vladimir [a Soviet player] would tell me that it started as a revolt against the coach, and with people getting the courage to speak out against what they didn't like. It's probably the best thing that happened to them. It started a fight for independence . . . the men and women who die for our country have done so much more, but in our own way we did everything we possibly could. You do not know what it means to wear that USA until you actually do it and hear the national anthem . . . that moment wasn't for us, it was for everyone. (O'Connor 2005)

Certainly, most Americans who watched or heard about the game (practically everyone in the country) felt "lifted" by the turn of events. The country erupted with joy. People old enough to follow the game remember where they were in the final seconds. Celebrations lasted for weeks. Major newspapers covered the event on their front pages for days. President Carter invited the team to the White House. The players became instant heroes. When the fifty-two remaining American hostages held in Teheran's embassy were released in 1981, they were shown a tape made by the State Department summarizing the world events they had missed during their 444 days of captivity: the tape ended with the stunning hockey victory. "The group," reported a journalist, "applauded the most for the hockey team" (Sandomir 2001). "Besides the cheers on the plane leaving from Iran," reflected one of the hostages years later, "I don't remember cheering for anything else as I did for the hockey team . . . that game may have been the moment when Americans starting feeling pride again" (Sandomir 2001). A number of documentaries and movies followed (one, *Miracle*, as late as 2004). Amazingly, then, the victory on ice had done so much to reassure Americans that their worldview was, despite recent setbacks, just fine.

Sports in general provide a great number of people with repeated confirmation of the "rightness" of their position in the world. Whether as children in school or as professionals, athletes see competitive events (or sequences of events, such as an NBA season) as the place to test themselves in general—and not only as athletes. Winning provides them with enormous boosts to their self-esteem, their abilities, and their worthiness as people. This has indeed been proven to be the case in a variety of psychological studies (Gould et al. 1993). What is most interesting about sports, however, is the reaction of audiences and fans to a victory. As the Miracle on Ice showed, those around athletes are remarkably prone to interpret a victory by their athletes as confirmation of *their own* approach to the world. Hence, teams winning national titles in American football, baseball, and basketball make the residents of the cities and localities where they come from "proud"— not of their athletic abilities but of their way of life. The fact that many of those teams are privately owned by wealthy individuals or organizations who may have little affiliation to those places and that they have players who are not from there seems to have no relevance. By winning several NBA titles in the 1970s and 1980s with their "show-time" style of basketball, the Los Angeles Lakers demonstrated to the nation and the world the worthiness of their city—much of which thrives on entertainment and creativity. Michael Jordan's Chicago Bulls made their city "proud," earned it respect and admiration, and—above all—demonstrated to other cities that Chicago was better, greater, more "right" than other cities. The Boston Red Sox victory in 2004, after a drought of nearly nine decades, proved to the world, and New York especially, that "Red Sox nation" was not, alas, a collection of incompetent, backward, and outdated (about life and not only baseball) people. Bostonians—their approach to life, their way of life, their values and beliefs—were proven to be right. All of this explains, in part, the otherwise puzzling joy and intensity with which victories are celebrated.

Several psychological experiments have demonstrated the curious impact that victory can have on the minds of people witnessing an athletic event. One experiment in particular is worth noting. After exposing a number of college students to a Division I NCAA college basketball game, Hirt and his colleagues measured those students' estimates of their own performance at mental and social skills. The mental skills tests centered on solving five-letter anagrams: participants were asked how many anagrams they could solve in five minutes. For social skills, participants were presented with pictures of individuals rated differently in terms of physical attractiveness and asked to imagine themselves asking those individuals to go to a concert with them. As it turned out, fans of the winning teams exhibited significantly higher estimates of their mental and social skills than those of the losing team (Hirt et al. 1992). Their favorite team's success at basketball boosted their confidence in their analytical and interpersonal skills.

We need not engage in psychological experiments to learn about audiences and how they feel fundamentally vindicated by someone else's victory. The common sight of parents screaming at coaches and referees, jumping up and down, and cheering on their junior high school or high school children suggests to us that those parents view a victory by their children as evidence of the correctness of their own approaches, philosophies, and worldviews. How else to explain the fact that the National Association of Sports Officials (NASO) receives weekly reports of parents assaulting referees during games, that the association now offers assault insurance to officials working in youth leagues, and that in a recent survey 37 percent of children aged five to twelve said they preferred their parents not to watch them during their games (David 1999: 75; Still 2002: 20)? Noting that "attacks by parents continue to rise," NASO reports on a number of recent accidents. Some, such as the following three, are deeply perplexing:

- Georgia (Wrestling)—After announcing to fellow spectators, "if my kid loses, I am going after an official," a forty-six-year-old man made good on his threat and slugged a high school wrestling referee. The assaulted official spent one night in a hospital as a result of the attack. (February 1999)

- Virginia (Soccer)—A "soccer mom" slapped and scratched the face of the game's fifteen-year-old volunteer referee following a soccer game involving nine-year-olds. (October 1998)

- Pennsylvania (Wrestling)—A parent was criminally charged for biting a coach and shoving the official after his seven-year-old son lost a peewee wrestling match. (February 2001) (Still 2002: 19–20)

Losing hurts the parents and their vision of who they are, and how they stand, in the world. "His old man is going to kill him," said one parent at the 2005 Little Caesars Hockeytown Invitational featuring sixteen of the best teams of eleven-year olds in North America, when a child failed to score after a gorgeous move. "And rightfully so," replied another father (Weber 2005). An athletic error is equated to a character flaw, a fatal imperfection in the person as a whole, a profoundly mistaken approach to the sport and to life in general. A victory confirms instead that they, as parents, have succeeded at producing a successful child: their child is physically strong ("we fed her right!"), mentally tough ("we prepared her right"), and courageous and capable of overcoming the odds ("we taught her the right values"). Indeed, the entire family as a group is proven to be "right": a healthy, strong unit that shows to the world the way to be.

As puzzling as some of the previous examples might seem, some of the most powerful generalizations come not from sports but war and military interventions. The leaders and people of the United States have relied extensively on military success for overall confirmation of their beliefs; indeed, they have gradually come to expect that as a natural outcome of their virtues. This was already evident in the notion of Manifest Destiny in the nineteenth century, according to which every success was to be understood as a fulfillment of a divine plan that rewarded the overall greatness of the American people with territorial conquests. As influential journalist John L. O'Sullivan put it when coining the term in 1845 in support of the annexation of Texas and the taking of Oregon, the American armies conquered *because* they were right: the United States "is by right of manifest destiny to overspread and to possess the whole of the Continent which Providence has given us for the development of the great experiment of liberty and federated self-government entrusted to us" (as quoted in Zoysa 2005: 134).

Only a few decades later, the Civil War became for many a test of two competing ideologies, two "incompatible civilizations"—with at stake fundamental views about the foundations of society, slavery, education, whether to run an agricultural or manufacturing economy, the virtues of city versus country life, and the larger place of the country in the world (McPherson 2004: 423). Indeed, each party claimed that it, alone, had the correct interpretation of the U.S. Constitution and all it meant for life: "With complete sincerity," famous historian James McPherson wrote recently, "the South fought to preserve its version of the republic of the Founding Fathers—a government of limited powers that protected the rights of property and whose constituency comprised an independent gentry and yeomanry of the white race undisturbed by large cities, heartless factories, restless free workers, and class conflict" (McPherson 2004: 423). Victory would thus serve the fundamental function of reassuring the victor of the rightness of its position. Defeat, by contrast, would let the loser know that it was holding on to the wrong interpretation of things. Thus, McPherson continued, "Union victory in the war destroyed the Southern vision of America and insured that the Northern vision would become the American vision" (McPherson 2004: 433).

A belief in higher moral causes explains much of our invasion of Iraq. Codenamed Operation Iraqi Freedom, the operation was from the start predicted to succeed by its planners because, in part, of the superiority of the values of the United States, which would ensure two things: a higher, and therefore "destined to succeed," moral ground and the related quick embrace of the proposed values by the Iraqi people who, despite belonging to one of the earth's oldest civilizations, were expected to welcome U.S. soldiers with flowers and open arms. The United States would win because it was fighting on behalf of irresistible and universal values: freedom, the natural desire of human beings for a safe and predictable bourgeois life, secular law and order, individual rights, and democracy.

Various speeches and statements by Secretary of Defense Donald Rumsfeld, Vice President Dick Cheney, and other senior leaders of the Bush administration exhibit elements of this logic. Deputy Defense Secretary Paul Wolfowitz spelled out without ambiguity why the noble warriors of the United States would win during a speech to the Senate Armed Services Committee on September 9, 2003, a few months after the invasion:

America's troops and those of our coalition partners—among whom we would emphasize are the Iraqis themselves—are determined to win. And they will win . . . as the president said recently, our forces are on the offensive. And as Army Vice Chief of Staff Gen. John Keane said in congressional testimony, "They bring the values of the American people to this conflict. They understand firmness, they understand determination. But they also understand compassion. Those values are on display every day as they switch from dealing with an enemy to taking care of a family." . . . In many ways, the people of Iraq are like prisoners who endured years of solitary confinement—without light, without peace, without much knowledge of the outside world. They have just emerged into the bright light of hope and fresh air of freedom. It will take time for them to adjust to this new landscape—but, all things considered, they are doing rather well. (U.S. Department of Defense 2003a)[2]

Rumsfeld's speech to the troops at Baghdad's Airport on April 30 of the same year, six weeks after the invasion, echoed the same worldview:

What you have accomplished is truly remarkable. You've rescued a nation, you've liberated a people, you've deposed a cruel dictator, and you've ended his threat to free nations. You've braved death squads and dust storms, racing across hundreds of miles to reach Baghdad in less than a month. Some people call that a quagmire. It was possibly the fastest march on a capital in modern military history. And unlike many armies in the world, you came not to conquer, not to occupy, but to liberate and the Iraqi people know this. And when you arrived in Baghdad many of the Iraqi people came to the streets to welcome you. Pulling down statues of Saddam Hussein, celebrating their newfound freedom, freedom that you helped restore, and what a sight that was. You've unleashed events that will unquestionably shape the course of this country, the fate of the people, and very likely affect the future of this entire region. Take great pride in your accomplishment. Not only for what you've done but also for how you've done it. You've done it well. (U.S. Department of Defense 2003b)

For Rumsfeld, the fast and stunning race to Baghdad spoke volumes about the ideology propelling it. It seemed natural that those with noble instincts who risked their lives to "liberate" others would prevail, and would do so quickly and with honor. It also seemed natural that these heroes would be welcomed by most Iraqis with open arms. After all, as two astute observers of American society put it some years ago, "Americans believe themselves to have a special mission in the world" (Hall and Lindholm 1999: 3), and Iraq would prove no exception. Indeed, the same logic was also often applied to Afghanistan, as Bush made clear in his last visit to the country as president of the United States in December 2008: "I am confident we will succeed in Afghanistan," he said, "because our cause is just" (*Irish Times* 2008).

What is true of war and sports is also true of business, politics, romance, education, and every other sphere of social life where we find competition. For instance, we look at Jack Welch—the successful former CEO of General Electric—as someone who, by virtue of his business acumen, must excel at many other things besides business. We imagine him to be generally intelligent, thoughtful, a careful reader of people and events. And there is little doubt that he and many others like him see themselves this way. We, along with them, are accordingly disappointed when events prove them to be incompetent in departments other than what they notably excel at. Most of us learned in disbelief about President Bill Clinton's attempt to cover up his sexual transgressions in the White House: his lack of judgment in engaging in, and then denying, the affair baffled us and probably him as well. How could someone of his political intelligence act in such an immature and arrogant manner? Public opinion polls (whether conducted by NBC, CNN, or Gallup) of Clinton dropped the most during his eight years of presidency precisely when details about his affairs with Monica Lewinsky came to light.[3] Larry Summers—an academic who had "won" in the realm of economics, not psychology or social abilities—surprised many with his direct and often socially insensitive comments as president of Harvard University. We look with amazement at Nobel Prize winners, expecting that they will prove remarkable and distinguished in just about everything they do. We are disappointed when they do not.

We could go on with other examples.[4] But the point should be pretty clear by now: we have a puzzling tendency to use the outcomes of competitive events to generalize about the competitors. The question is not whether this happens or not: it happens all the time and is indeed a major reason that draws people to compete in the first place. The question is, actually, *how* this rather strange transition from specific to general happens. Is it justified? Is it illusory? The next section examines in some detail what we may call the "logic of generalization."

The Faulty Logic of Generalization

The transition from winning something very specific to feeling as if one's understanding of the world is superior to that of the loser is puzzling. Winners never take on the entire world. Quite often, they merely face one or a handful of human beings in the context of a very specific and limited setting—a chess match, a spelling bee, an election. Even when the competitors are numerous (as is the case in war, for instance), the struggle is clearly not against the world. We must therefore understand how the transition happens.

At the simplest level, no competitive event requires skills and talents that are useful *only* in that event. A runner preparing for a marathon is doing more than training her muscles, joints, and bones. She is also planning, laying out a training program, discovering her body, encountering a sequence of challenges (running hills, running longer distances, dealing with the hot sun or the rain, and so on), thinking about the other competitors (their speed, their abilities, and so on), testing her determination, and more. A chess player is doing more than simply moving pieces according to the rules of the game. There is strategy and logical thinking. There is an enormous psychological battle with the opponent, in chess or any other competitive forum. "Your warm up begins with your *brain*," writes tennis coach and former number four in the world Brad Gilbert; "the night before a match," he continues, "I will be in my hotel-room thinking about the next day's competition . . . prepare yourself mentally" (Gilbert and Jamison 1993: 5–6). Great players have great memories: they remember past matches, mistakes, and techniques. Players must have a clear, focused mind capable of enduring hours and days of stress. At tournaments, the tension in the air is truly palpable. When the stakes are high, journalists and the media watch every move, every expression, every hesitation.

It follows that the generalization process is, to a certain extent, logical and fair. The skills and talents required to prevail are often transferable to other settings and situations in the world. Those who are good at organizing a successful political campaign, for instance, are probably quite capable of organizing many other things—such as planning for their retirement. Winners of the Nobel Prize in physics are very likely in a position to understand how a complicated piece of machinery works. Victory *correctly* suggests to a person that his or her understanding of many principles, elements, and aspects of the world and him- or herself is indeed superior to that of his or her competitors. The winner has a sound grasp of cause and effect, of tendencies, of natural laws, of what it takes to get something done—not only at the specific event in question but beyond. This is surely what many of us felt about Barack Obama when he won the presidential elections of 2008.

The generalization process also has some justification when we realize that competition often requires a significant emotional, psychological, and physical investment on the part of the competitors. Competitors feel that they must draw from their entire selves to prevail. The *whole* person, as we often hear, is implicated in the effort: "The message I've been trying to get across this week to our younger players is that when you get this far you have to be willing to sacrifice everything to take the next step," recently reflected hockey's great Claude Lemieux (Brooks 2000). When this type of investment takes place, prevailing is then seen as an indication that everything about the winner seems to be working properly. Like a car that has just been thoroughly inspected and is therefore ready to go on *any* trip, the winner often feels ready to take on the world. All systems and circuits appear to work properly: the winner is a fully functioning, sharp human being who seems poised to do well in general.

In other respects, however, the feeling of being on top of the world and the related appreciation of one's understanding of it reflect simply an unjustifiably self-indulgent and overall truly mistaken reading of one's abilities to relate to the world. This is because, without being conscious of it, competitors fall into two quite different types of illusions. Figure 3.1 outlines what tends to happen in the minds of many competitors.

First, competitors simply overestimate the extent to which the specific skills needed to win at something can help one win at something else. This is the result of a sloppy and generous interpretation of those skills. For instance, we might believe that the analytical skills required to win a political election are the same as those required to run a successful business. Yet, much evidence suggests otherwise, as the misfortunes of countless businesspersons turned politicians show us. The mistake happens, in part, because the terminology available to us to describe those skills is fairly imprecise: while those skills are quite different, we refer to them with the same name, such as "leadership," for instance, or "organizational vision." What those terms mean in each context, however, varies greatly. The mistake also happens, though, because we are simply overly optimistic or generous with ourselves. There might be an objective overlap in those skills. For instance, sending the Sputnik into space may require skills that will also help a country excel at discovering new principles of economics. The small overlap in no way guarantees, however, success in both fields. Recall here Michael Jordan's failed foray into baseball. Yet, content with the knowledge that such a connection exists, and exhilarated with our victory in one of those fields, we eagerly (and often quite unconsciously) leverage that tenuous connection to arrive at a general feeling of satisfaction with ourselves.

Regardless of why, exactly, the mistake happens (sloppy language or our generous interpretation of things), we may say that this process of generalization is being driven by *causal confusion*: believing, without solid reason, that one set of variables (what it takes

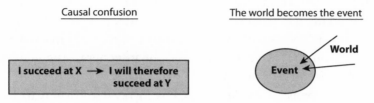

Figure 3.1. Winning illusions.

to win at X) has implications for another (our competence in the world). It is worth emphasizing, of course, that competitors are not alone in following such faulty reasoning. Those surrounding the competitors—from television commentators to journalists, parents, relatives, and others—also believe as much. Thus economists recently noted that winning the World Cup in soccer historically boosts gross domestic products by half a percentage point. Consumers somehow believe that a country capable of winning the cup must also excel at making dishwashers, cars, computers, and a host of other totally unrelated products.

Figure 3.1 also points to a second mistake. This is in some respects the opposite of the first one. While the first error consists, in a sense, in turning the competitive event into something meaningful for the larger world—"this is really the big match . . . this little thing with me and Spassky is sort of a microcosm of the whole world political situation," said Bobby Fischer as he prepared for his famous 1972 chess match in Iceland against Russian Boris Spassky—the second entails reducing the world to the competitive event itself.[5] Here, competitors are so involved in the event that they begin to think that *the outside world no longer matters.* The reasoning is that the competitive event at hand seems to encapsulate in a nutshell everything that is important and of consequence. The event becomes the world itself and whatever does not fit into it is forgotten. This happens among children when they naively loose themselves in their activities. But it also happens to adults—at the workplace, with their neighbors, with their families, and so on. As the great running back Curtis Martin—with 14,101 rushing yards, 166 starts, and 4 Pro Bowl appearances to his credit—

recently stated about football: "It's more . . . than just playing football. This has become a way, a lifestyle, a mentality" (Crouse 2006). In such a state of mind, success at one task translates into a confirmation that we are, indeed, right in general: the general is, after all, not much more than the event itself.

What happens to winners happens in reverse format to losers. Defeat tells them that their understanding of the world—of things that go well beyond the competitive event itself—is flawed. As is the case for winners, there is an acceptable logic to such self-doubt: to the extent that the competition requires skills and talents that are useful in dealing with other parts of life, the loser has reasons to question his relationship to things outside the competitive event. After failing to win an election, a politician could reasonably wonder about his overall ability to connect to people—about his "emotional" intelligence or empathy in general. Gore's inability to connect with audiences (virtual and real) in the 2000 election sent messages about his stiff personality: it was perceived to be a character flaw. But the loser also incorrectly extrapolates meanings from his or her loss. Much like winners, losers make the wrong causal connection between their defeat at a particular task and things far removed from it. And this happens, again, in the same ways as it takes places for winners. Our language and minds lead us to overestimate the relevance of the skills being tested. And we tend to see the whole world in a particular defeat. This, of course, sheds much light on how it is possible that loss can lead people to become depressed or dysfunctional, or even to commit suicide.

Reflections on Being Right

Victory and loss serve as gauges of our judgment in general—of our viewpoints about the world, the worthiness of our perspectives on things. Competition thus speaks to our insecurities about ourselves, our understanding of things, and ultimately our rightful place in this world. Its purpose is to *reassure* us, to confirm that we are indeed sound, legitimate human beings. Winning and losing are but signs of something we deeply care about. Therein lies their profound importance for us.

Curiously and importantly, the logic we use to generate judgments from competition about us as human beings is faulty. We arrive at them by either assuming erroneously that we can extrapolate from our success or failure in a particular realm or, in turn, by assuming that the outside world does not really matter—that it can all be condensed or "squeezed" into the competitive event at hand. Neither thought pattern is correct. Yet many of us regularly deploy them and take the results most seriously.

These realizations should compel us to think hard about our approach to competition. We need more introspection about what we fear and doubt. We need to ask ourselves what it is, exactly, that we wish to know and prove. And, equally important, we need to take some liberties and wonder about how matters could be otherwise. Our discussion showed us that we have put ourselves at the mercy of competition: we have decided, with little reason, that our general well-being depends on whether we win or lose at something. But competitive events could instead be our tools and servants: useful occurrences that can only improve our situation. We have made some odd choices, indeed. The next chapter probes further into what is really at stake in competitive events.

Chapter Four

THE QUEST FOR SPACE

Now all the resistance in the world cannot
stop me. I am boundless.
—Advertisement for the Advanced
Management Program at the University
of Pennsylvania's Wharton
School of Business

IN THE PREVIOUS CHAPTER, I suggested that people, organizations, and countries use competition to test the validity of their worldviews. In this chapter, we discuss another central aspect of competition. Competition offers competitors an opportunity to establish for themselves something of profound importance for their well-being: some *space*. I am talking about both physical and mental space. Human beings crave for some separation between the world and themselves. We want a buffer zone, as it were, where we are able to move and be as we wish without resistance or unpredictability. Physically, we wish to be safe from danger and have a comfortable environment around us. Mentally, we wish to be free from others and their psychological encroachments on us, so that we may feel whole, able to explore, and relaxed.

This drive for space is basic and goes back hundreds of thousands of years. Conditions have changed—we no longer live in caves or hunt in forests but instead inhabit air-conditioned offices and apartments. But our basic inclinations have remained the same. Most Americans—50 percent, according to the General Social Survey—

worry about their privacy enormously. Another 40 percent are concerned about it to some extent. Only 10 percent do not think of it.[1] My argument is straightforward. Throughout much of human history, most people struggled to satisfy their need for space. The founding fathers of the United States and waves of immigrants thereafter sought therefore to build a society that would cater as widely as possible to this drive. Most of our competitive events today are accordingly in good part about space. Winners have the chance to acquire physical and mental space. This happens both within the immediate context of the competitive event (work, business, sports, and so on) but also beyond. Losers must instead face life in far tighter conditions.

I begin with a brief history of space, and then examine how competition allows us to acquire both physical and mental space. The exercise will shed much valuable light on why we care so much about winning and dread losing.

A Brief History of Space

For millions of years, our ancestors roamed the countryside in search of space, according to current research typically in bands of about thirty individuals. Nature—wild animals, inhospitable weather, unpredictable conditions—was one obstacle. Other bands of people, themselves looking for space, were another. This was no easy way of living. To use Hobbes's famous words, life was then "poore, nasty, brootish, and short" (Hobbes 1985: 186).

The situation began to change around thirteen thousand years ago, with the domestication of a few crops, the establishment of sedentary societies, and the growth in the size of those bands (Diamond 1999). Civilized living began. But this immediately led to the imposition of stiff hierarchies—something that had not happened in the roaming groups (at least among adult males) probably because of their small size and intense need for cooperation. As cultural anthropologist Christopher Boehm put it, "The original humans were egalitarian for scores of millennia," but that quickly changed in the post-Paleolithic era, or around 10,000 BC (Boehm 2000: 81, 84).

For a very long time thereafter—namely until the eighteenth and nineteenth centuries—a few human beings (the vast majority of them men) subjugated just about everyone else. Emperors, kings, tsars, feudal lords, and the like imposed their wills on countless others acting, as it were, as gods themselves. Indeed, some thought of themselves as divine. Most of the people around them lived instead in a state of deprivation. This was true for all the major civilizations of the world: Egyptian, Mesopotamian, Indian, and Chinese (from 4000 to 1000 BCE), Greek and Roman (from 2000 BCE to 50 CE), those from Asia, Africa and the Americas (from 1000 BCE to 1500 CE), and finally medieval Europe (500 CE to 1500 CE), and all of the European colonies (from 1450 CE to 1750 CE and beyond). These were long centuries of exploitation, abuse, and appropriation. As the archeologist Susan Pollock put it in the case of Mesopotamia:

Along with the construction of impressive city walls and elaborate temples adorned with sculptures and inlaid with semiprecious stones and metals and the elaboration of artistic expression of all kinds came the exploitation of the "common" people. It was the labor of the majority that funded the trading expeditions, military conquests, and artisan expertise responsible for the great works of art and architecture that we still admire today. The proud kings who boasted of their military exploits and the great buildings and canals they had constructed were able to accomplish these deeds because they could command the labor of others. (Pollock 1999: 1–3)

We should not be surprised by this history of inequality. There is little doubt that human beings are by nature at least to some degree inclined to dominate their peers. Researchers emphasize that the three African ape species with which we share a great deal (gorillas, chimpanzees, and bonobos) form hierarchical societies. Sound arguments have in turn been put forth that the early nomadic tribes, where egalitarianism was prevalent, merely repressed humans' natural tendency to dominate (Boehm 2001: 3). A considerable body of research from psychology, anthropology, and other disciplines points to the general propensity in human beings to dominate the environment, animals, and people around them— "to our tendency to extend continuously the range of what we can control within our natural environment," as Jürgen Habermas, one of the foremost social theorists of our time, recently put it (Habermas 2003: 23).

A fundamental shift in the organization of large-scale human societies took place when thinkers such as Hobbes, Locke, Rousseau, and in the United States, Thomas Jefferson and James Madison, among others, recognized two essential facts: that most people aspire to live in peace and that, in turn, societies would truly flourish (become rich, powerful, happy places) if everyone was allowed to live in peace. By giving preeminence to individuals and their basic desires, these liberal thinkers put forth a revolution in the organization of society. The most successful societies would have as little top-down planning and intervention as possible. Citizens would not be directed toward a specific profession or told how much to produce. More fundamentally, there should be no preconceived beliefs about higher goods to be imposed on the population. Instead, people should be allowed to engage in whatever they liked, as long as they proved respectful of others as they pursued their goals. From this perspective, the primary role of governments would be to enforce the few basic principles of healthy social interactions, such as respect for the property of others, and not much more. In the more contemporary language of Isaiah Berlin and other thinkers, negative freedom in society should prevail over positive freedom (Berlin 1969).

Under these conditions, most people would choose something they were good at, work the hardest, and deploy their best skills in pursuit of their goals. This, in turn, would ensure that they would produce the most and, in so doing, bring great benefit to society. Wealthy citizens would after all stimulate the local economy with their purchasing power, generate more tax revenues, and reduce discontent and social turmoil. This was indeed Adam Smith's greatest insight: that in pursuing their own self-interest, individuals would unintentionally produce the most as a whole. His famous passage on this point is worth repeating here:

> By directing that industry in such a manner as its produce may be of the greatest value, he [the average working person] intends only his own gain, and he is in this, as in many other cases, led by an invisible hand to promote an end which was no part of his intention. Nor is it always the worse for the society that it was no part of it. By pursuing his own interest he frequently promotes that of the society more effectually than when he really intends to promote it. (Smith 1993: 291–92)

But what did these social theorists mean by living in peace? First and foremost, they meant living in a secure *physical* space. This would be a space where others cannot physically harm us, where, as Hobbes put it, we would be free from our deepest fear—that of "violent death" (1985: 186). It would be a space where human beings could fulfill what Rousseau thought to be their most basic duty: "Man's first law," he wrote in the *Social Contract*, "is to watch over his own preservation; his first care he owes to himself" (Rousseau 1968: 48). It would also be a place, however, where we are free to engage in any activity we like, provided it would not harm others in their pursuit of their goals. People could work, enjoy themselves, sleep or stay awake, read or play music, be with partners or alone, and so on. Those of us inclined to labor would probably become rich; others would become less rich but perhaps better read or rested. What, exactly, people would do in their space was not important, of course. What mattered was that they could choose what to do, which could never be the case when human beings live constantly afraid, and often under the direct domination of others. Then, as Hobbes put it, "when every man is Enemy to every man . . . there is no place for Industry; because the fruit thereof is uncertain; and consequently no culture of the Earth; no Navigation . . . no account of Time; no Arts; no Letters" (Hobbes 1985: 186).

We are talking, then, about *private property:* a piece of land that people could call their own and that the state would recognize as such and help them defend. Smith, Rousseau, Locke, Jefferson, and the others thus gave considerable thought to both asserting the importance of private property and making sure it could be safely established. Let us recall on this very point that, according to some historians, an early draft of the famous first sentence of the second paragraph of the U.S. Declaration of Independence ended not with "happiness" but with a direct reference to property: "We hold these truths to be self-evident, that all men are created equal, that they are endowed by their Creator with certain unalienable Rights, that among these are Life, Liberty and the pursuit of Property." Property was in any case at the very forefront of Jefferson's mind throughout his life: "The true foundation of republican government," Jefferson wrote, "is the equal right of every citizen in his person and property, and in their management" (Jefferson 1999: 212).

Living in peace also meant, however, having access to what we may call *mental* space. The first sentence of the Declaration of Independence of the United States now ends with happiness—a much more abstract and surely psychological state of being. People should be allowed to think whatever they wish. No inquisition could persecute a person for not believing in this or that god. No person would be jailed for holding this or that belief. James Madison, among others, wrote at length about this idea. The following passage summarizes his view. It is especially interesting because of its use of "property" to describe both physical and mental space:

This term [property] in its particular application means, "That dominion which one man claims and exercises over the external things of the world, in exclusion of every other individual." In its larger and juster meaning, it embraces everything to which a man may attach a value and have a right, *and which leaves to everyone else the like advantage.* In the former sense, a man's land, or merchandise, or money, is called his property. In the latter sense, a man has a property in his opinions and the free communication of them. He has a property of particular value in his religious opinions, and in the profession and practice dictated by them. He has a property very dear to him in the safety and liberty of his person. He has an equal property in the free use of his faculties, and free choice of the objects on which to employ them. In a word, as a man is said to have a right to his property, he may be equally said to have a property in his rights. (Madison 2006: 223)

We can rephrase the above passage as follows: individuals' minds should be allowed to *be* as they wish, free as much as possible from external impediments and interferences. Our minds are defined, separate entities with internal functions, needs, and skills. They have interests and abilities ("faculties," in Madison's words), and they should be allowed to move freely in their chosen direction. Because *others* can threaten the freedom of our minds, we should devise a society that keeps those others at bay as much as possible. This, then, is what the likes of Madison and Jefferson were after: offering every citizen of their nation the possibility to have unhindered and peaceful space, to give back a small portion of the Garden of Eden to each and every person—both physically and mentally. In the case of the United States, this was the promise of the new and vast nation, and of its Western territories and big skies.

Competition and Space

Our history indicates that we as a society have valued, from our earliest days, the acquisition of physical and mental space. A great number of studies confirm that many of us deeply care about space—in absolute terms as well as compared to other cultures.[2] My argument is as follows. Competition and competitive events provide us with regulated and safe venues for acquiring such space. Those events are therefore of fundamental importance to us. Curiously, most of us do not think of competition as being about space. We rather focus on many of its other functions, such as en-

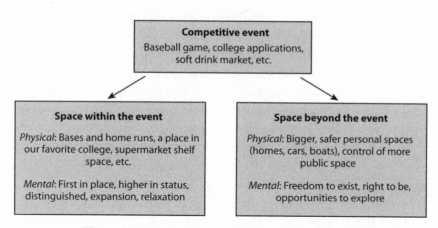

Figure 4.1. Competition and the acquisition of space.

couraging us to produce more, helping us become wealthier, or simply to entertain us. But competition is very much about space. In the next pages, I describe how this is the case. Figure 4.1 outlines the relationship between competition and space. Many of our competitive events are inherently about space. Winners gain physical and mental space; losers give both types of space up. But the spoils of victory allow winners to acquire physical and mental space well beyond the confines of the competitive event itself. Let us explore both sets of dynamics.

Space within the Event

In a very immediate sense, most competitive events in the United States are first and foremost about the acquisition of physical space, about the satisfaction of conquering space—a fact that for some reason has yet to attract the attention of sociologists and psychologists of sports.[3] The two quintessential American sports are baseball and football. In baseball, the offensive team tries to hit the ball in the way that best allows its players to run from one base to the next. A score happens when a player comes "home"; the defending team is protecting "home" and all the other bases from the incursion of the offense. The number of home runs and base hits makes up a player's resume. Home runs provide fans with some of the most exciting moments in a game. When does a home run happen? It happens when the hitter manages to send the ball across (and beyond) the entire field—a symbolic and practical dismissal of the large space that must be covered to do so. Baseball is fundamentally about the acquisition and conquest of space. It is about one's freedom to move through space unhindered, as happens with a home run and the defensive team having to watch the hitter slowly run across the bases without any possibility of stopping him. The hitter conquers space, the defense must deny itself its basic instinct to stop him.

In football, progress is measured in yards. A team has four chances to conquer ten yards. If they succeed, they have four more chances for ten more yards. Quarterbacks are evaluated on the basis of yards passed, running backs on the number of yards run. But teams ultimately win if they score more touchdowns than their opponents, which means ending up in an opponent's end zone more often than the opponent does in theirs. Weak teams usually "give up" lots of yards and let opponents in their end zones more than they should. So here, again, we see that teams fight to protect their homes from the intrusion of others.

More generally, at the pinnacle of American sports we find those highly exclusive "halls of fame" where only a very few athletes are "inducted." What is a hall of fame but a real, tangible building that creates a space where most competitors would love to be but which they cannot enter except as visitors? "Hall of famers" get a "spot" in the house: their names, records, and memorabilia are put permanently on display—that is, they take up space—while those of others are simply kept out. Visitors, in turn, make their pilgrimage to the holy site to express their admiration and devotion to their heroes.

Business, too, is fundamentally about space. In the United States, most companies compete for one thing above all: market share. Successful companies have large market shares, ambitious companies want to increase their shares. Indeed, getting more market share *is* considered by many to be the primary objective of a business entity. As Richard Miniter, former editor of the *Wall Street Journal Europe*, recently put it:

> Business leaders are gripped by the cult of size, the dogma of business. They are mad for market share. Nearly every company is mesmerized by it. Keeping it, growing it . . . try to talk to a senior executive without the subject coming up. . . . Nearly every time I meet with a CEO or senior executive, market shares come up. The reason is no mystery: Top executives know that they are measured by it, and they know that they measure their subordinates by it. . . . Market share is also an obsession among Wall Street analysts, institutional investors, financial journalists, growth-minded entrepreneurs, high-flying consultants, self-styled gurus . . . most business schools are temples to market share and churn out more acolytes every year. (Miniter 2002: 19–20)

In fact, we judge the health of entire industries and not only companies in terms of market shares. For instance, the continuing crisis of the American auto industry is one of lost market shares to Japanese competitors.

But companies are especially revered if they create a whole *new* market in the first place. Our admiration in these instances is less about how much companies actually control and more about the fact that they could make something out of nothing. In the language of this chapter, we admire those companies because they create new space. The classic example is Starbucks and its introduction of specialty coffee drinks into a country where until then demand for them was nonexistent. "We were selling specialty coffee back at a time when specialty coffee had a 1 percent market share. More people owned airplanes than espresso machines," noted recently Tom Walters, communication coordinator of the company's original roasting plant (Michelli 2007: 59). But the company changed all that. "Starbucks' mission was to change the way people drank and appreciated coffee," John Moore, who marketed the Starbucks brand for eight years, wrote recently. "When the company began, coffee was viewed only as a hot, brown liquid that was consumed out of habit and a need for caffeine. Starbucks knew that the coffee experience could be—and should be—much more than that. When done right, the subtle, rich exotic flavors of coffee, served in a cozy, relaxing environment could lead to the kind of 'rewarding everyday moments' that were missing from the American landscape" (Moore 2006: 4). The mission was accomplished, and the astronomical success of Starbucks is now the subject of business school case studies and countless articles and books.[4]

What is true for companies in the marketplace is also true for what goes on inside companies. Good personal performance leads to promotions, and these normally lead to bigger offices. The organization and allocation of space in an office setting is of basic importance for just about everyone working there. Winners at the workplace are often more secluded and have secretaries interface with others in the company. Those secretaries provide a much coveted buffer zone between their privacy and the open, public space. We learn as much by reading the opening paragraph of one of the most authoritative and popular books on how to be a professional personal assistant in American corporations: "As an administrative assistant . . . you will act as a liaison between your boss and the rest of the company. Sometimes you'll act as a buffer" (Stroman et al. 2007: 3). The secretary protects the boss's unhindered space: a place where he can now move freely. It belongs to him and no one else, though he must continue to defend it. There are exceptions, of course. Some CEOs, such as Alan Greenberg during his many years at the investment bank Bear Sterns, avoid seclusion and prefer to work right next to others in the firm (Sparks 1996). But they are likely to be the exception. More often than not, business leaders enjoy more room, better views, and more privacy.

Even politics is very much about space. National elections in the United States are about winning states, whether for Congress or the presidency, something that would not happen in a purely proportional system of representation. The map of the country is thus duly colored in red and blue, depending on whether a state supports the Republican or the Democratic Party. The fight is for states and that is how the contenders approach it: "The lesson of this election is clear," said a jubilant Senator Evan Bayh of Indiana after the Democrats' major success in the midterm congressional elections of 2006: "We won by turning the red states of the heartland blue" (Zeleny and Zernike 2006). And victory gives a candidate access to the most coveted spaces in the world of politics: Capitol Hill and the White House. Much the same can be said about state elections and the right to inhabit the governor's mansion. Losers, by contrast, are denied that access. One of the most important moments in the history of American politics was thus the day when, for the first time ever, in January 2009 an African American family moved into the White House.

In all of these cases, victory is about expanding one's presence into new spaces as opponents unwillingly make room for us. What is the increasing madness surrounding college admission in the United States really about if not about being the ones who get selected for that classroom seat and dorm room at the college of one's choice? Yet there is also a mental dimension to all of this.

Most obviously, victory gives winners the right to feel "above" the losers. Winners are in "first place," "ahead" of the losers. Chairmen of big corporations, according to more than 90 percent of the respondents of the General Social Survey, belong to the "top" of our society or near the top. Less than 1 percent of respondents viewed them as belonging to the "bottom."[5] Unskilled workers, by contrast, belong to the bottom or quite near it according to around 90 percent of respondents. We craft for ourselves an imagined hierarchy of us and others—we generate an abstract order about us and our opponents. This is precisely what happens in the yearly "ranking" of colleges by U.S. News and World Report, in the ranking of professional tennis players, or in Forbes magazine's yearly list of the world's wealthiest individuals. Hierarchy, of course, implies distance: by winning, we move further away from others and enter the "rarified"—that is, less populated— realm of those who have prevailed. By losing, we find ourselves stuck in a larger crowd—those who have failed to distinguish themselves.

In a more subtle way, victory gives competitors more "room" for their perspectives and opinions. Having been proven "right" about what it takes to succeed (the skills, preparation, strategies, and so on), winners now feel entitled not only to hold on to their viewpoints (i.e., no one has "intruded" or undermined those viewpoints) but, quite often, to elaborate, articulate, and expand on how they see things. Winners, in other words, have the opportunity to *reach beyond* their previous borders of influence. And, as they so do, others pay attention. As they provide advice, others take notes. Alan Greenspan—the purported "maestro" of the financial markets who was appointed to an unprecedented five terms as chairman of the Board of Governors of the Federal Reserve—began making speeches at the tune of more than $100,000 per occasion one week after stepping down in January 2006. In politics, concession speeches are seldom heard by anyone other than the most ardent supporters of the defeated candidate, and barely reported by the media. The winner's speeches, on the other hand, command much attention, have far more people listening, are normally reported in parts or even in full in newspapers and other venues, and explicitly address more than one's supporters. "And to those Americans whose support I have yet to earn," stated President-elect Obama in November 2008, "I may not have won your vote tonight, but I hear your voices, I need your help, and I will be your president too."[6] On winning his second term in office in 2004, President Bush thus turned explicitly to those who voted for Senator John Kerry and said:

> So today I want to speak to every person who voted for my opponent: To make this nation stronger and better I will need your support, and I will work to earn it. I will do all I can do to deserve your trust. A new term is a new opportunity to reach out to the whole nation. We have one country, one Constitution and one future that binds us. And when we come

together and work together, there is no limit to the greatness of America.[7]

And President Clinton said much the same in 1996 on winning his second term in office:

The challenges we face, they're not Democratic or Republican challenges. They're American challenges. What we know from the budget battles of the last two years and from the remarkable success of the last few weeks of this Congress is the lesson we have learned for the last 220 years—what we have achieved as Americans of lasting good, we have achieved by working together. So let me say to the leaders of my Democratic Party and the leaders of the Republican Party, it is time to put country ahead of party. (*New York Times* 1996)

In a more fundamental way perhaps, winners acquire space by quelling other voices aspiring for success. Recall that competitive events serve to separate winners from losers, to make distinctions, to distinguish. Distinction is after all what a lot of competitors crave in the first place, as we saw in chapter 2. At the beginning of the competition, there are two or more contenders. At the end, there is only one or perhaps a few winners. Winners thus carve out a space for themselves in the competitive arena: they make a claim on that space. Losers, having proven themselves less worthy, understand that they do not "belong" there. With their heads down, they quietly step side. This is the case for individual competitive events as well as for extended periods of competition. After so many victories, Bill Gates has ensured for himself a place in the pantheon of information technology greats. The same can be said of John McEnroe for tennis, for instance, or Robert De Niro for movies.

Closely connected to this is the possibility for relaxation that comes after victory. Competition tenses the mind; success allows it to *relax*, which means an expansion of sorts. This is possible because we now have a temporary buffer zone, as it were, between ourselves and others. We know that for the near future no one will bother us. We have bought ourselves moments or even an extended period of genuine peace. A powerful recent advertisement for Net-Jets airplanes on the back cover of the magazine the *Economist* and elsewhere underscores precisely this point. In it, we see a photo of Warren Buffett and Bill Gates flying on a Boeing Business jet. Sitting next to each other on a leather sofa, both have business clothes on, but they have removed their ties, unbuttoned their collars, and taken off their shoes. Though Gates's computer and briefcase are nearby, they are laughing as they are enjoying a drink, some fruit and cheese, and a bowl of jellybeans. Cards on the table indicate they just finished playing a game of bridge. The message could not be clearer: winners, even the most aggressive and predatory ones, take time to enjoy themselves, almost as kids would. It follows that we, the readers, should do the same, to the extent that we consider ourselves winners. Losers, by contrast, should not do that, since they are expected to continue working hard, perhaps engage in some introspection, and guard themselves from the criticisms and opinions of others.

We see, then, that competition brings to the winners mental space in a variety of ways. We also see that losers stand to lose space. We must conclude with a warning, however. Things are seldom set in stone. In our society in particular, we have made sure to let losers have many chances to challenge winners. No person can be president of the United States for more than two terms. In sports, title holders must often "defend" their position at some point after winning it. And the average tenure of CEOs in big American companies is only seven years and decreasing over time (Byrnes et al. 2006). Whenever something serious is at stake, there lurks "beneath" the current winner a number of incredibly hungry, single-minded people ready to devote all they have to take his place. "It is incredibly tough to stay at the top," Paul Gastonguay confided to me. Gastonguay had been Ivan Lendl's hitting partner for four years at the time when Lendl was ranked the number-one tennis player in the world, and Gastonguay himself was recognized as a formidable player. "There are many guys who give everything they have got to take your spot; if you slip just a little, they will take it." Many winners feel therefore a push to constantly defend what they have achieved—and this very fact probably accounts for a significant percentage of the anxiety that most of us feel even when we have succeeded time and time again. The pursuit of space is almost never complete.

Space beyond the Event

The image is a familiar one: the lion, king of the forest, moves with perfect calm and self-assuredness, lazily glancing here and there without worry. There are no predators that can trouble him. The land around him is his: superior strength gives him access to all that is around. Much the same happens in many animal species: strength, periodically tested with fights, decides who gets access to food, shelter, and mates. Losers accept this, as researchers Gherardi and Daniels (Gherardi and Daniels 2003) recently demonstrated in the case of the eastern white river crayfish. At first, the crayfish are eager to fight. But after their first losses, when challenged they respond with retreat. In the animal kingdom, the strong ones roam with ease in physical space.

It is no different in our society. Success in very specific areas of life—such as work, sports, or politics, for instance—translates into money and power, and those are often quickly used to acquire space (and much more, of course). We see this most clearly in the case of homes. A good year in the consulting or investment banking industries translates directly into increasing home prices in places like Manhattan. The "bonus-anticipation effect" (the expectation of large bonuses) by itself has an impact. "Part of our recent increase in sales activity," said James Landsill (senior manager at the Corcoran Sunshine Marketing Group) in December of 2006 in reference to the New York real estate market, "has been buyers trying to beat the bonus rush" (Anderson 2006). Rich people buy bigger houses with larger parcels of land than poor people. They buffer themselves from others and the rest of the world. Within their homes, they distance themselves from others who might live there (i.e., their children) or come to visit: master bedrooms thus have master bathrooms; large homes have guest suites with kitchens and bathrooms. Outside of their homes, they build gates or, with their like-minded neighbors who share their values, gated communities. Those communities are truly worthy of study, not only for their ever increasing numbers: their "walls and gates," wrote recently a scholar of urban geography, "have social and psychological as well as physical effects." They separate those in from those outside by offering a sense of security, and everything from grocery stores to lakes to fitness centers (Low 2003: 12). More importantly, by removing unwanted interferences from the outside, they "order" one's "personal and social experience" and thus hold the promise of a life of happiness (Low 2003: 10).

Wealthy people often have a second or third home, where they go to escape not so much the crowded conditions back at home (they have large homes, after all) but the boredom that comes from inhabiting the same space all year round. They escape that space by buying more space far away. Distance here is also important: the further away the second home (i.e., the more space between the two spaces) the better, though of course, one must possess the means to travel that in-between space quickly. Real winners thus have private jets to take them from their homes near work to their far away cottages. NetJets' recent high-profile campaign informs us that Roger Federer became the owner of a Falcon 2000 EX in 2004. Buffett bought his jet in 1995 (and then the entire company in 1998). These winners do not own that in-between space, but they have mastered it as much as possible—that is, they have brought it into submission. "Where am I going?" asked a Goldman Sachs employee recently when, upon entering the company's headquarters in New York City, he was handed a $1,000 discount coupon by a twenty-six-year-old model dressed in a purple flight attendant outfit as she was trying to entice recent bonus recipients into using a charter plan service. "It's your own private jet . . . you can go wherever you like" (Anderson 2006).

Cars merit attention, too. Winners have multiple, and often big cars. The goal is to make those as much of a continuation of one's private space as possible, which means equipping them with gadgets that cater to our every need—a seat that massages us, a steering wheel that warms our hands, a computer on board that remembers our preferred driving settings. Our cars must be fast too, so that they may conquer space rapidly with as little discomfort as possible. Those cars tend to be imported, of course—for that, too, is another sign of spatial conquest. It matters little that we have speed limits that do not allow us to take those cars past third gears—the potential of being able to conquer space is often enough. Hence, as the Wall Street bonuses started to come in late 2006, Miller Motorcars of Greenwich, Connecticut, was "fielding more requests for the $250,000 Ferrari 599 GTB Fiorano than it can possibly fill" (Anderson 2006). The car can go beyond two hundred miles per hour.

Even in public places, winners have more space. At the airport, airlines have reserved clubs for their preferred passengers; on the airplane, winners in business and other realms of life reward themselves with larger seats and more room for movement. It was thus with little surprise that the Government Accountability Office, which tracks the use and misuse of public funds by government officials, reported recently on the "improper" but otherwise "widespread" and largely condoned "premium class travel" by high-ranking officials in prestigious offices such as the Department of Defense and the Department of State (U.S. Government Accountability Office 2007). The rules may not formally allow it, but those at the top of the game get more space. At the stadium, as spectators winners have separate boxes. And at operas, they can walk backstage to meet the performers. Losers must instead make do with far more cramped conditions.

It is as much a matter of space around oneself as it is about moving through—indeed, mastering—space. Winners simply move in space with far more ease than losers. In our society, many of us look down on public transportation as too inconvenient, slow, and cramped. Public transportation, then, is for losers. Winners ride cars and arrive faster and more comfortably.[8] Ideally, they do not even drive themselves but instead leave the nuisance of navigating through traffic to someone else. Winners have shorter lines—whether at the airports' check-in areas or at popular restaurants. Losers are excluded from all of this and must instead wait, often in close physical proximity to others: standing or sitting tightly next to someone else, they can hear their conversations, smell them, and even feel their movements as the lucky ones whisk by before them without time or inclination to even grace them with a glance.

There is a mental dimension to all of this as well. As is the case for what happens inside the competitive events, winners generate mental hierarchies of themselves and others. Socrates observed many centuries ago that human beings compete for one of three things: power, prestige, or money (Plato 1989a). Modern economists and psychologists tell us that our sense of worth depends on comparisons with others, rather than on objective assessments of how well we are doing in absolute. As Richard Layrad, a well-known scholar of happiness, recently observed, "Many studies of happiness . . . suggest that if a person earns an extra 10 percent and so does everyone else, he experiences only 2/3 of the extra happiness that would accrue if he alone had had the raise." He then adds that "when each of us works more and earns more, this imposes a genuine loss of happiness on others. It is a form of pollution."[9] He thus considers the findings of a study where graduate students at Harvard University were asked the following:

- Which of these two worlds would you prefer?
  A. You get $50K and others get half that
  B. You get $100K and others get more than double that

The majority of respondents answered A, in line with the results from many other similar studies (Layard 2003).

What does this tell us? People use money, prestige, and power to distance themselves from others—to eliminate from their purview what Layard calls "pollution" and what we could simply call "others." Those "others" include not only direct competitors but everyone else too: the best doctor in town feels superior to (literally "above") not only other doctors but also the local janitors, clerks, and others working in less-prestigious positions. But they do not stop there. They also compare themselves to lawyers, business people, and politicians: how do they stand in their respective communities? How much money do they earn or have in the bank? The mental exercise creates imagined space. What is at stake is more than a hierarchy of how good we are at something: rather, it is a hierarchy of us as people, as whole persons. "I am a superior person," thinks the successful doctor: his whole self is higher than that of others, it moves in more rarified environments where only the few, the excellent live.

Hierarchy means vertical ordering. But winners are also rewarded with what we may call "horizontal" space: to entertain and weigh different options, to explore this or that idea, to indulge. Their minds are allowed to *wander*. This surely happens inside the borders of the competitive event itself. For instance, at work, winning buys oneself more room for creativity and personal initiative. Those at the bottom of the hierarchy have monotonous and very circumscribed jobs: they are expected to follow directions. Those at the top are expected to use their minds quite differently—they must explore, generate ideas, create. The role of the secretary, write Stroman et al. in their manual on how to be a perfect administrative assistant, is "to *relieve* your busy employer of a great deal of work, especially the *details* of office procedure and other matters that do not require your employer's personal involvement" (Stroman et al. 2007: 3, italics added). But that freedom to wander extends far beyond the realm of the competitive event.

Consider, for example, what happens on a plane. Those flying business class (successful lawyers, doctors, business executives, and others—many of whom most people would consider to be winners in one respect or another) are given an elaborate menu with many choices. Those sitting behind them in economy class are instead simply *told* what they will eat, or at most given a couple of very basic options. As the curtain separating business from economy class is pulled, they are denied even the spectacle of what goes on only a few feet away from them. The same happens back at home.

Winners have houses with more features and amenities—more TV channels, more ways to listen to music, more rooms, more showers and Jacuzzis, and so on.

Potentialities, imagination, the possibility of movement: the winners' mind has access to all of these. In a more fundamental way, we may say that the winner faces a world that is far less finite than that of losers. The beauty of money, sociologist Georg Simmel once wrote, is that it *is* infinite: any given amount is at once the hamburger, the shirt we saw in the store, the leather seats in my next car, the bottle of wine from France. The more we have of it, the greater we can dream (Simmel 1971: chap. 12). The rich man walking down the street knows he can own just about everything he sees that is for sale. His mind, that is, can go places where others cannot. Much the same happens when one gains a lot of fame or power—both by-products of winning, of course. Fame and power can make many things, almost everything, happen.

All of which leads us to one final and very important observation: the mind of winners can relax in a general sense. As we saw a few pages ago, within the competitive arena, there are moments of relaxation. But victory, especially when major, affords the possibility of a broader feeling of relaxation. The winner is entitled to a sense of overall peace, completeness, even stillness. He can face the world without the need to overcome and fight. He is alone, in a position to come and go, do nothing or work, be correct or make mistakes. He has acquired, in other words, that most cherished possession of all: the freedom to *be*.

What We Are After

We have seen, then, that competition in our society is very much about space: about acquiring that physical *and* mental space where we can finally feel secure and fully ourselves. This is a fundamental desire for most, if not all, human beings. But we saw that it is especially important, and surely taken to an extreme, in America. The history of the United States is, in some respects, a history of spatial conquest. The very birth of the country was about space—

physical and mental. The American dream continues to be about space. Many of us long deeply for some distance from others, for a buffer zone, for a place where we can simply *be* without interference from others. At the same time, we are also deeply keen to use space *in relation* to others. Space for us means hierarchy and therefore the possibility of superiority. We define and feel good about ourselves by contrasting our position with that of those below or behind us. And many of us do this every chance we get: as Kohn put it in his critique of competition in the United States, "No corner of our lives is too trivial—or too important—to be exempted from the compulsion to rank ourselves against one another" (Kohn 1986: 2).

We have now made some significant progress in our exploration of our intense drive to win and dislike of loss. Victory gives us space, a sense of identity (recall chapter 2), and proof that we are "right" (recall chapter 3). In one simple phrase, we can say that *it grants us a place in this world*. This is of fundamental importance to us. Thus we pursue it with the utmost intensity and have great fear of loss. But, as we do so, we remain remarkably simpleminded. We do not investigate our motives, our questionable logic, or what competitive outcomes really reveal about us. Fully determined, we press ahead with little doubt that matters could be otherwise. That something may be off, that we may be deluding ourselves, that we may be in great disharmony with others and much of what we do, that the results fail in most cases to satisfy us in a definite manner—all this does not occur to us. Our mission is simply to win, for, as Vince Lombardi famously put it, "Winning isn't everything; it is the only thing".

Chapter Five

POWERS AND LIMITATIONS

I think that winning is great.
Not good—*great.*
—Jack Welch, *Winning*

MOST OF US CONSIDER WINNING to be better than losing. Why?
The simple answer is that we think that winning makes us "better
off" while losing makes us "worse off." But this begs two further,
fundamental questions: *how* does winning benefit us and *how* does
losing hurt us? We have so far examined some of the most important things that are at stake during competition. We did not say
much, however, about the outcome of competition and how it
changes our relationship to whatever we win or lose. That change
is at the very heart of winning and losing. What happens, then,
when we "win" or "lose" something?

I suggest in the following pages that both winning and losing in
our society can take on remarkably different forms. Sometimes
winning and losing have to do with ownership: gaining or renouncing the right to have, use, or dispose of something. In other cases,
winning or losing are fundamentally about access: when we win,
we get access to something or someone while, when we lose, we
are deprived of that access. In yet other cases, we see that winning
and losing are about control. Each form provides the winners and

losers with specific sorts of *powers* and *limitations*. Understanding those powers and limitations can help us make sense of our deep interest in competition. It also makes clear that, despite our tendency to believe otherwise, winning and losing are not, in fact, mirror opposites of each other.

"Forms" of Winning and Losing

We have explored *what* we win or lose when we compete. We must now think about what it means to win or lose something in our society. We want to know what the actions of winning and losing entail. What happens when we "win" something? And when we "lose" it? Winning and losing *amount to a change in the position* we have vis-à-vis the prizes at stake in a given competition. For instance, victory sometimes grants competitors ownership of objects which were once beyond their reach (for instance, money or a trophy): in those cases, winning something *means* gaining the right to possess that something, transitioning from not having that right to having it. In other cases, winning something means acquiring the right to be in certain spaces that were previously closed to us. This happens, for example, when we win a seat at a basketball game, a free night in a hotel room, or a free plane ticket to Las Vegas. On those occasions, winning does not entail ownership but rather access to something: when I win something, I gain access to it.

There are several forms of winning and losing. Though apparently quite simple, each can be rather complex. And each, by virtue of what it is, has major implications for what winners and losers *can and cannot do*—their powers and their limitations over time. We should begin, then, with the simple step of identifying the basic forms of winning and losing. Figure 5.1 does so and then gives examples of what may be won or lost in each case and—to start our discussion of time and power questions—whether winning and losing concern themselves mainly with the future or the past.

We observe *four* distinct ways of winning and losing: acquiring (or forfeiting) physical ownership of something, acquiring (or forfeiting) intangible ownership of something, establishing (or fail-

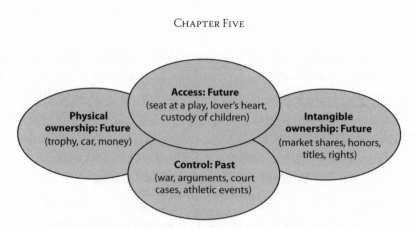

Figure 5.1. The basic forms of winning and losing.

ing to establish) control over something or somebody, and gaining (or forfeiting) access to something or somebody. We can understand each form better when we think about specific objects of victory. Physical ownership concerns tangible objects, such as a car. Intangible ownership has to do with abstract things, such as market shares or a title. Access generally has to do with spaces (a seat at symphony hall) or people (one's children). And control typically applies to events as they unfold through time (such as wars, arguments, or athletic events).

We should note that there are certainly cases where one's victory or loss can take on two or more forms. If I win a car, for instance, I acquire physical possession as well as access to it. If I win access to a cruise ship for two weeks as it travels to the Virgin Islands, I also can look forward to controlling small parts of that ship (such as my room). It is probably the case that the importance of victory and loss is greater for competitors whenever more than one form is involved. We should also note that overlaps in forms are not always possible: it is hard to imagine, for instance, how victory can give me physical and intangible ownership of something.

We should then observe that three of the four forms of winning and losing have to do with the future: that they cause a change in our future position toward something. When, for instance, victory gives me access to physical ownership of a car, such ownership begins at the moment of victory and extends forward in time. It does not mean that the car belonged to me yesterday. The same can be said of intangible ownership and access. But matters are often quite different when it comes to control. When I have won a race, for instance, this is something that concerns what has already happened: victory says something about my relationship to things in the past—namely, that I was able to control them in my favor better than what my opponents could do for themselves. Put differently, the race (the object of my victory) has already happened and belongs to the past. Victory merely states something about my position relative to that event.

Let us now analyze more closely each form and the freedoms and limitations that it gives to competitors. As we do so, we will notice something interesting: that winning something is not always the opposite of losing it, despite the fact that in our everyday lives we regularly encounter those terms as the negation of each other (I can either win or lose a game, my victory is someone else's loss, and so on).

Physical Ownership

Winning in some cases entails the coming into possession of something that before was not ours. Something that did not belong to me—such as money or a car—becomes mine by virtue of my victory. That is surely an exciting prospect. It should be clear right away that this form of winning is made possible by two facts: the existence of recognized and enforceable private property rights (people can "own" things), and the wide acceptance of the notion that things can be easily transferred from one person (or collection of people) to another. Both requirements may seem obvious to us, but we should recognize that in many societies (past and present) one or both of these may be missing. In feudalistic societies, for instance, most people owned essentially nothing and thus little could be meaningfully transferred from person to person. The same can be said of many nomadic societies and some of the communities that have embraced the principles of socialism. The birth and evolution of private property and property rights in our own society was a gradual and at times conflict-ridden process.[1]

Now, what does physical ownership actually mean? At the simplest level, it means having the *exclusive freedom to do whatever we want with something*. If I own a sweater, I alone have the right to wear it, wash it, keep it in my closet, dye it, and throw it away. No one else has those rights. But there are limitations to my rights and, according to historians of property rights, those limitations have fluctuated in their extent over time (Christman 1994: 17). I cannot use the sweater to choke somebody, for example. If I win a car, I cannot drive that car into a marketplace full of people. If what I win is something that is alive, such as a cat, my limits are even greater. I cannot beat, seriously neglect, or abandon a cat (while I may do all three with an inanimate object, such as a sweater). We should therefore rephrase our definition and say that winning, when it involves the acquisition of physical ownership, gives competitors a set of exclusive but limited rights over something. The limitations reflect considerations of others (their rights to live a peaceful and dignified life, for instance) but also agreed-upon rules and other matters.[2]

Winning something in this context, then, provides victors with a good dose of *freedom* and *power* toward the object in question, and therein probably lies most of the allure of this form of winning.[3] Victory expands one's sphere of control beyond its current boundaries; put differently, an object previously outside of it is transferred within it. The winner begins to contemplate what, exactly, she will do with the object. If it is money, for instance, how will she spend it? If it is a trophy, where will she showcase it? If it is a car, how will she look driving it and where will she drive it? This contemplation generates excitement and pleasure—though it can also be a cause of stress and tensions since new possibilities can raise doubts and concerns about making the right choices, worries about new responsibilities, and so on. We should note in any case the forward-looking nature of this form of winning. My victory implies a change toward the object in question that extends forward through time. This explains in part the pleasure of winning objects: that pleasure comes from imagining the possibilities that the future holds for us—surveying all that we could potentially do with the object of our victory.

Forward looking does not necessarily mean indefinite ownership, however. When I acquire physical ownership of an object, this can happen in one of two ways: permanently or temporarily. Both bring a special type of excitement. When money is at stake, for instance, victory normally grants the winner indefinite ownership of that money (until, of course, the winner decides to spend that money). If the winner holds on to the money, no one will ever be able to claim it again. The prospect is thrilling and surely informs the mood of winners, even if unconsciously. When ownership is permanent, objects can be said to truly belong to the winner. There are in turn cases when physical ownership is temporary—when it is clear from the start that it will be contested again, and the winner may or may not find herself in a position to own that object again. This is the case with the Stanley Cup, for instance: every year, the winner is challenged for that cup. Though perhaps not as exciting as victory unbound by time, this type of victory generates its own type of excitement. Limited ownership is often seen as a special and unique time in one's life, a time that is not likely to last for long and that should therefore be enjoyed. It also often comes at the expense of someone else, whose turn of ownership has been terminated; most competitors are likely to feel a certain pleasure in depriving others of a coveted object.

Two more observations about this form of winning are in order. What the object is matters a great deal: indeed it is the combination of the freedom and power *and* the specific item in question that is important. When I win a car, I feel excited about the endless possibilities that owning a car gives me. My excitement around winning a free soft drink would, of course, be a lot less. Second, what makes the transfer especially exciting is often its *public* nature. Winners acquire objects typically by participating in some form of organized event that can involve other competitors, referees, or an audience. More important, the transfer is made possible by the recognition of others that indeed a change of ownership has taken place. The validation is external and the transfer is first and foremost a societal occurrence, with the winner put at the very center of others' attention.

For losers matters are different and perhaps a bit more complex. In competition when ownership of a physical object is at stake, loss does not necessarily mean giving up an object; rather, it means facing the fact that *we missed the opportunity to own* that object. The sorrow that comes from loss is therefore of a unique kind: it is based on having to face the status quo when we had the opportunity of experiencing a change. The pain comes from unmet hopes. Thus, for instance, the movie *The Lord of the Rings* won the seventy-sixth Oscar for "best picture" in 2003. The other nominated movies lost. How can we describe their loss? It amounts to a continuation of the status quo despite the possibility of change.

This is quite interesting—for we are bound to ask why we should despair about the absence of change in our lives. In our example of the Oscars, nothing negative happened to the producers, directors, and actors associated with the movies that did not win. Yet they likely suffered when they discovered that their movie had lost the competition. Subtle and probably unconscious mental dynamics are at work here: we are upset because visions of a possible, imagined future have not materialized. All of this also means that winning and losing are not necessarily the *mirror opposites* of each other. While winning means acquiring ownership of a physical object, loss need not be about losing ownership of a physical object. Thus, returning to our Oscar's example for a moment, one movie director's winning of the prize does not inevitably mean someone else's loss of that prize.

Of course, there are times when loss can also mean relinquishing physical ownership of something—and in this sense losing does appear to be the opposite of winning. The bankrupt person who is unable to meet his mortgage obligations risks losing his house to the bank. Last year's champions in the National Hockey League must give the Stanley Cup to this year's winners. A gambler who bets money stands to lose it to someone else. In those instances, the loser ceases to have freedom and power over particular objects (while someone else comes into their possession). And the pain associated with this departure is probably quite close to being the opposite of the joy one gets when acquiring ownership of an object.

And certainly loss is often a public event, much like victory. Part of the pain it generates can therefore be said to mirror the joy felt by winners. Outside rules and conditions deprive the loser from acquiring the objects at stake. There are witnesses to the loser's failed attempt to make those objects their own. The losers tried to extend their range of influence and failed. This can be grounds for a sense of humiliation.

When it comes to time, losers are subject to similar time dynamics as winners. Loss can certainly be definitive—and this is bound to happen whenever the victor acquires definitive ownership of the object. And loss can also be temporary—something that is likely to happen when victory itself is temporary. The losers' feelings will mostly mirror those of the victors: sadness at the prospect of having to give up (for good or for a limited time) any hope of owning the desired object, and a certain degree of resentment when required to surrender the object to someone else. Recall, however, that losing need not mean giving up the coveted object: it may simply mean a continuation of the status quo (while someone else grabs the prize). The mental dynamics here are likely to be quite unique, as the losers must deal above all with their own image of the future rather than a real change in their actual position in the world.

Intangible Ownership

What happens when someone wins the Grammy Award in music, the most valuable player (MVP) award in an athletic competition, or the Miss USA pageant? Victory in these cases does not amount to the acquisition of physical ownership, for there is nothing concrete to possess. Instead, victory grants to the winners the *exclusive claim to those titles, honors, or whatever other abstract things might be at stake*: the ability to say that they alone are in a position to call themselves this or that. Only the winner of a town election for mayor can say "I am the mayor." Winning thus amounts to the appropriation of something abstract at the exclusion of others.[4] Therein lies the primary source of pleasure in this type of victory: the ego-driven awareness that only I can make certain claims. "Only I am the mayor," the winner is in effect saying.

Winning is also, however, a process by which one comes into possession of something abstract that did not used to be his. Abstract prizes can be owned much like physical ones. Thus women won the right to vote in the United States in the early twentieth century: they made theirs something that was not theirs beforehand. Today women are making progress in their fight for equality at the workplace: they are slowly winning that equality. The same can be said of various minorities in the labor force, prisoners in jail looking for more rights, and ambitious singers seeking fame: all are looking to win something intangible that at a given moment does not yet "belong" to them.

But what advantages or rights toward abstract prizes does intangible ownership bring to those who acquire it? If I "win" a title, honor, or fame, how does my position toward those prizes change? In many cases, victory allows me *to use* titles, honors, and fame (and many other abstract things) in certain situations to advance myself, a particular cause, attain certain objectives, or a variety of other purposes. As mayor of my town, I can invoke my title to command the respect of an audience. Or, as the winner of the "employee of the year" award, I can remind my colleagues of my title when being questioned about my performance at something. Before winning those honors or titles, I simply could not use them. What about other types of abstract prizes, such as equality at the workplace or the right to request vegan food in jail? Those prizes, though abstract, have very practical implications. Equality at the workplace means, for instance, equal salaries for the same job regardless of who is working. When I win equality at the workplace, I gain the ability to impose that equality on the workplace. The same applies for my request for a vegan meal as a prisoner in jail:

when I win the right to such a meal, I gain the ability to impose that meal on the institution where I find myself. Before winning those abstract prizes, I can do nothing with them. When I win them, I can use them to my advantage.

Almost nothing in life, however, comes without constraints or strings attached. Hence, victory of abstract objects is normally highly regulated. I should not use my title as state governor to ensure that my children get special treatment in schools. Titles come with very clear usage instructions. And, as such, at times they impose *more* constraints on winners than was the case before the victory took place—though this very fact surprisingly does not stop people from craving those titles. For example, Tara Conner, Miss USA 2006, was reprimanded for her excessive drinking, drug use, and sexual promiscuity by no less than Donald Trump in his position as owner of the Miss USA competition. She was allowed to retain her title on the condition that she enter rehabilitation and undergo drug tests, and on the assumption, in Trump's words, that she was a "good person" with "a good heart" that "got caught up in the whirlwind of New York" but can have a second and final chance to demonstrate that she is worthy of her title (Goldman 2006). Trump and many others would not have taken issue with Conner, of course, were she not the "owner" of the Miss USA title.

And, if physical ownership requires the existence of property rights, ownership of abstract things is especially dependent on others' acknowledgment and willingness to recognize such ownership. Others must accept that I own something, accept that they cannot make a concomitant claim to it, and must comply with whatever expectations and requirements my new status might impose on them—even when much of this is not mandated by law. The pleasure of winning an MVP award, for instance, heavily depends on others recognizing the title and giving the winners the respect that "they deserve." The value of the victory would be greatly diluted if other players would simply ignore the fact that the award was given out or if they somehow contest it. Concession speeches in political elections involve precisely the public recognition that someone else has won the title in question. Those speeches need not be given but are instead considered part of the election ritual.

What about time? As is the case for physical ownership, victory as acquisition of intangible ownership is forward looking. When I win a title, I look forward to my possession and use of that title into the future. Therein lie some of the most pleasurable aspects of victory: imagining and anticipating what awaits me. But, differently from physical ownership, here the distinction between temporary and permanent ownership is often blurred. For example, champions in sport must surrender their title typically after a short period of time: they must prove themselves all over again as worthy of ownership. Much the same can be said of winners of political elections, though their terms might be longer. Yet most of these types of winners retain some affiliation with their former titles: they become ex-presidents, for instance, or ex–Miss USA. This possibility of "stretching," as it were, one's claims of ownership brings real advantages. It usually commands continued respect and prestige. As such, it is a primary driver of competitors' desire to win.

Let us now turn to losers. In most cases, loss simply means that one has failed to secure ownership of something that was at stake and was not hers in the first place. One of the most publicized sports events in the United States is the NCAA Division I basketball playoffs held in March of every year. Here teams are matched against each other in brackets that eventually lead to the final game. There is no money at stake for the players. It is all about winning the title and becoming champions. What happens to all the teams that do not reach and win the final? They are barred from claiming to be that season's champions. Loss hence amounts to the *elimination of the possibility* of acquiring something that the teams do not currently own. Often the cause of despair and sorrow for some players, relatives, staff, and friends alike, loss therefore ultimately translates into the continuation of the status quo. Losers have not, in fact, lost anything that they previously had. Thus, as is the case for physical ownership, this prompts us to question the logic of loss and pain: why do many losers suffer—as many psychological studies show—when their situation does not really imply a change in their situation?[5] Unmet hopes are surely partly to blame. Yet we must also wonder whether envy—perhaps in different ways for different sorts of people and varying depending on the specific contexts—might also play a role: titles are exclusive and losers surely must feel "left behind" or "relegated" to irrelevance.[6] They nervously and hesitantly watch winners celebrate, and then quietly leave the premises with their heads down.

There are situations when loss does truly mean deprivation of something that previously belonged to someone. When a criminal loses his right to vote, he gives up something that was legitimately his beforehand. When a company loses market share, customers that previously bought their products or services are now turning to competitors. And, when the president of the United States fails to a secure a second term, he loses the title of president to someone else. In these cases, loss can be said to be really the opposite of victory (and often occurs because someone else is winning).

With regards to time, depending on the type of competition in question, loss can again be definitive or temporary. At the Oscars, a movie that is nominated but fails to win the prize will not have a second chance at it: in these cases, loss is definitive. But in many cases, loss can be reversed. A company can regain market shares, authors of books can submit their books multiple times for a particular award, and defeated candidates for political positions can run for office again. Definitive loss is sometimes made easier by the possibility of retaining some claim to the honor, title, or other prize in question: I may lose my title as governor of my state, but I will always be former governor.

Access

Winning and losing can sometimes have nothing to do with ownership. When I win a seat at the opera house, I do not become owner of that seat—not even temporarily. That seat is never mine. When, at a silent charity auction, I win a dinner with Brad Pitt, I do not become the owner of Brad Pitt himself. When I win a new friend, I do not own that person. What happens, then, when I win any one of these things? I win the right or opportunity to enter into some form of *interaction with something or someone*. This can be a rather passive matter, as happens when I win the right to sit and watch a movie at a theater. But it can also be rather interactive, as might be the case when I win a dinner with a celebrity or a contract bid to work on a construction project. If it is interactive, my victory may bring certain impositions on others or endow me with certain rights—waiters must serve me, for instance, and as a construction worker I am in a position to move blocks, dig holes, and knock down walls. Indeed, that interaction itself may be what makes victory attractive: I look forward to being served at a restaurant and to using my hands and brain to build something.

Compared to ownership, my freedom and privileges as a winner are quite often more limited. I can do a lot less with my seat at the movie theater than if that seat became mine. A ticket to the museum does not even permit me to touch the paintings and statues before me. Access normally involves a fair amount of *distance* between the winner and the object or place in question. It has more to do with having the privilege of *being* somewhere rather than of using something as I please. Why, then, is this form of winning exciting? By and large, it is exciting because it puts us into contact with something that would otherwise be *completely out of our reach*. We are excited to win because we have the opportunity to see, taste, touch, or otherwise interact with something or someone that we would otherwise never come close to us. We are now in a position to understand how books like Dale Carnegie's 1936 classic *How to Win Friends and Influence People* (Carnegie 1981) sell millions of copies and make it on the *New York Times*'s best-seller list for years (Carnegie's book sold more than 15 million copies and was on the newspaper's best-seller list for ten years).

There is also a second reason. Sometimes victory brings us access to positions of power. The president of the United States, when elected to office, wins access to the White House. When this happens, we can use those positions to shape the course of events around us—surely an exciting prospect. Much of Carnegie's book is thus in good part targeted at those interested in manipulating or having control over people. The last chapter of the book is for example titled "Making People Glad to Do What You Want," while the entire third section of the book teaches readers how, by winning friends, they can turn people to their "way of thinking" (Carnegie 1981: 113).

Time is, of course, an essential component of winning understood as gaining access. What we win is the privilege of entering a space that is normally fully closed to us. We fundamentally win time—which means that there normally are very clear boundaries around it. Sometimes access is for a few hours or days (a free movie ticket, a cruise), sometimes for a few hours per week (as when the judge awards visiting rights to parents to see their children), sometimes for a season (as is the case for a pass at a ski resort), sometimes for years (the president of the United States wins access to the White House for four years at a time). Seldom, however, is time unlimited and our access forever.

But if time is essential, so is place—victory, after all, often has to do with extending the spaces that we are allowed to enter. We are allowed to enter this or that cinema, to come close to this or that celebrity, to enter (as an elected official) the Senate or House of Representatives. It is therefore fair to state that winning, when related to access, changes our position vis-à-vis a space by allowing us *into* that space. In this regard, this form of winning is very different from the other three primary forms, none of which deals with questions of space.

Let us now reflect about losers. As with ownership (but differently from control, as we shall see shortly), losing may merely entail a continuation of the status quo. We attempt to gain access to something from which we were initially barred. When we fail, our situation does not change: we still remain barred from accessing that something. The fact that someone else wins that right of access may make us upset. In truth, however, the outcome should not upset us too much other than for the fact that our hopes—our imagined future—does not materialize. To this, we must add as well the perception that, in preparing for the competition, we spent considerable energy and resources without achieving our goals (something that is surely true for winning as ownership).

The pain is probably more legitimate when losing means *renouncing* our existing right to access something or someone. Then, indeed, we lose something we initially had, and the change in our situation can be a real cause of distress. Parents can lose access to their children; bankrupt persons can lose access to lines of credit or their own assets; companies can lose access to customers; and college students can be barred from attending classes or even graduating because of reprehensible behaviors. All these losses clearly imply a worsening of one's situation.

Intangible ownership often allows losers to still make some sort of claim on the object of competition (as the example of ex-presidents reminds us). When someone loses access to something or someone, that loss can be rather definitive: the loser gains little by boasting that she *used to* have access to this or that. Yet loss can also be temporary—as the case of a one-semester suspension from a college campus or the case of limited jail terms (when one is barred from the rest of society) suggest.

Control

Joyce Meyer is a famous preacher who devotes much of her writing and speeches to winning. She begins her best-selling book, *Battlefield of the Mind*, with the following statement: we see from the Scriptures that "we are in a war . . . our warfare is not with other human beings but with the devil and his demons. Our enemy, Satan, attempts to defeat us with strategy and deceit, through well-laid plans and deliberate deception" (Meyer 1995: 13). The passage points us toward yet another form of winning—one that has very little to do with either ownership or access. What happens when we win a war? We certainly may come into physical possession of things; yet, we do not own the war. Nor does victory grant us access to it. Much the same can be said of when we feel that we have won an argument, an athletic event, or as lawyers, a court case, or a fight against a mental problem (such as depression, for instance). This is because victory in all of these things refers to something that no longer exists: the war, argument, games, and court cases are over. Accordingly, given that they no longer exist, we can neither own nor have access to them. Nonetheless, we say we have won them.

What, then, could victory mean in these cases? The answer has to do with control: compared to our opponents (people but also diseases, mental problems, computer viruses, and so on), we were able to dictate the course of events better than they could. In the given competitive arena, we were therefore more powerful than they were. But it is more than a matter of power: it has also has to do with *what we did* with that power. If I used that power to hurt myself, this would not amount to victory; it would be a very tragic form of loss. Competitors who are indeed superior (i.e., have a greater control over events) to their opponents but "waste" their position by damaging themselves (let us imagine a soldier who, in a moment of distraction, shoots his own fellow soldiers and is now in a much weaker position vis-à-vis the enemy) are indeed "guiltier" or more deserving of scorn than those who succumbed while earnestly fighting their foes. Winners, then, are *those who are able to control the turn of events to their benefit;* winners are those who steered matters in the direction of their choosing. If we study the objectives of policymakers and generals when going to war, we thus see that most tend to speak of victory as the ability to steer events on the ground toward a predetermined, desired direction (Mandel 2007: 462). The trial lawyer who wins the case before a jury manages to have the jury vote in support of her client—she managed to direct or turn the minds and will of the jury in a given direction. The winner of a physical fight manages to control his opponent's body more than his opponent manages to control the winner's body. The winner of a foot race has greater control over his body (can make it run faster) than his opponent does. The fight is about who has more control over something.

Of course, once the event is over, our control over it ceases. Again, victory here is an adjudication of past events—and, in this regard, it is quite different from other forms of winning. This explains in part why many of us become restless after winning an event like this: we long for a continuation of our power, and thus look for the next opportunity where we might find it again. Thus political scientist G. John Ikenberry (Ikenberry 2001) recently explored in his intriguing book *After Victory* the dilemma that states face after winning major political and military conflicts. The irony of those conflicts, Ikenberry observed, is that despite their enormous costs for everyone they often leave the future quite uncertain. Winners naturally try to extend their control into the future but with little guarantee that they will continue to prove dominant. Indeed, only winners who realize that they need losers to continue to survive are normally able to retain some of their powers.

Now let us ask what powers, exactly, victory gives to the winner. We might be tempted to think that no real powers are gained: after all, victory here refers to something that has already happened and belongs to the past. We should differentiate between the short and long term. As the competition progresses and immediately after it is over, winners are effectively *imposing themselves* over the losers, forcing losers to behave in ways they did not want to, limiting their options and movements to their own advantage. This is the clear message of a recent book on winning at "office politics": the successful deployment of a "Political Game Plan" guarantees control over others and their decision-making processes ("you will be shown techniques for managing your boss more effectively"), so as to guarantee that one can "get ahead, gain influence, and gain what you want" (McIntyre 2005: back cover). The winner of a wrestling match pins the loser to the ground and thus limits his movements. In a battle, the loser cannot hide from the winner, who has the ability to kill the loser at will. In a chess match, the losers' pieces are cornered if not out of the board altogether. Or consider peace treaties, which amount to formal recognitions by the fighters in a war that one party has won and the other lost. The winner generally has the freedom to dictate the terms of that treaty, as the United States did in the case of Japan at the end of World War II when the Japanese emperor announced the "unconditional" surrender of his country, and as happened at the closing of World War I when the allies faced a defeated Germany.

In the long term, however, matters are quite different. As Ikenberry intelligently pointed out, power differentials can diminish rather quickly. With the competition over for some time, other factors play an increasingly important role in shaping the world around us. The United States had significant direct control over Japan at the end of World War II; by the 1960s that control had greatly decreased. The winner of a wrestling match ceases to have physical control over the loser immediately after the match. Even when the struggle is within ourselves (such as when we wish to win a battle against fat or cancer, for example), the powers of the winner (our bodies and mind, for instance) over the loser (fat or cancer) become null over time (years after losing one hundred pounds we do not think that we are still imposing ourselves over the fat cells that we eliminated long ago, though we continue to keep at bay new ones that could come our way).

What about losers? When it comes to control, loss means that the loser was less able to control the course of events than the winner so that, as the competition comes to an end, the loser actually often finds herself worse off than before. A trial lawyer loses a case in court when he is unable to generate arguments and evidence that prove more convincing than those coming from the other side. A basketball team loses a game when it is unable to outscore the other team. Both have experienced something negative. In this regard, we may say that losing amounts to the opposite of winning. And, much like winning, loss is more about the short-term rather than the long-term since that which is won or lost (a game, war, a court trial) belongs to the past, and thus, as time goes by, the direct consequences of having lost tend to relent (whereas, for instance, losing access to something or winning physical ownership of something else are very much about the future). Here, then, we see two special characteristics of control as a form of winning or losing. First, it is the only form that is primarily about something *that has happened in the past*. Second, control is the only form where we find a genuine and consistent *symmetry* between victory and loss—where, in other words, the terms *winning* and *losing* do actually stand in opposition to each other.

Reflections on Victory and Loss

Jack Welch wrote that winning is great because "it lifts everyone it touches" (Welch 2006: 4). But how does that happen, exactly? Victory and loss change our relationship to the world. Sometimes winning means coming into possession of something, tangible or not. But in many other cases it concerns access or control. The same applies to losing. Only sometimes does losing mean relinquishing ownership of something. In many instances, it is about access or control. Each form of victory or loss gives the winners, and deprives the losers of, a set of particular rights over that which is won or lost. It also presents them with a special set of challenges.

We saw, as well, that forms of winning and losing tend to correspond to certain objects of victory or loss. Winning a war does not mean "owning" it, for instance; winning a car can very well mean that. And each form comes with a "time" dimension. Control is often about the past, while ownership and access are very often about the future. Finally, we learned that winning and losing are often not the mirror opposites of each other. Loss can often mean a continuation of the status quo while victory almost inevitably brings about a change in one's conditions in life.

Our everyday, matter-of-fact polarized language hides a great deal, then. Much of it is of great consequence. Thus, as we proclaim that we "must win the peace in Iraq" or that we wish our children to grow up to be winners, we ought to become cognizant of all that we are really saying. Our words are truly pregnant with meaning, implications, and expectations. We ought to use them carefully indeed.

PART 3

Our Beliefs

Chapter Six

TYPES OF WINNERS AND LOSERS

I don't have anything else to prove.
—Lennox Lewis, 2004 World
Heavyweight Boxing Champion

WE HAVE EXPLORED the structure of our competitive events. We learned about the prizes, powers, and limitations that come with victory and loss. Something of great importance became clear. We are deeply unsure about our proper place in the world, are largely unaware of our doubts and logic, and thus continue fervently to pursue victory and shun loss. Simmel inspired our analysis. It was a study of how competitive events are set up: what is at stake, and how victory and loss change our stance toward the world.

In the next four chapters, we turn to our *beliefs* about winners, losers, and the world around us. Who, in our minds, is a winner? Who is a loser? What do we believe a person must do to earn those titles? Moreover, what do we believe about competitive events and the world in general that allows for the existence of winners and losers as well as their importance in our culture? Weber taught us that most things in society are pregnant with meanings and significance—that they are at least in part the outcome of our minds. We "make" winners, losers, competitive events, and the world around us. What, then, do all those things look like? And what do they say about our compulsion to compete?

In this chapter, I focus on the making of "definitive" winners and losers. Temporary winners and losers are, for the purposes of this book, less interesting. We are eager to know what, in our collective imagination, makes a person into a real, permanent winner or loser. As it turns out, there are several, sometime contradictory types of those winners and losers. One becomes any given type by doing or not doing certain things—by following certain paths—and thus by displaying to us particular personal traits. I will examine first those paths. I will then discuss the types of winners and losers that result from each path.

Paths to Eternal Victory

As a society, we recognize several, partly contradictory paths to becoming a definitive winner. Four are predominant. Each reveals the qualities of a definitive winner. Figure 6.1 identifies the paths.

Let us discuss each in turn. In the *Consistent Victory* path, a person becomes a definitive winner to our eyes by virtue of her continued winning over time. She is a winner *because she has demonstrated* her status of winner time and time again. Closely related, she is a winner because, by virtue of her achievements, *she understands what it takes* to assert herself at every turn. The notion of consistency is crucial here: the competitor delivers a superior performance systematically even though her environment, opponents, and even herself (her mood, emotions, mental and physical conditions) are never the same and, in fact, vary dramatically from instance to instance. The world around her is constantly changing and hurling new, and typically bigger, obstacles in her path. Her body and mind may at times feel exhausted, sluggish, or simply not interested in performing. Past victories raise expectations and weigh heavily on her: "It's hard when you're on the top and not winning matches . . . now I'm expecting more from myself," reflected Svetlana Kuznetsova in 2004, a year after stunning everyone by winning the U.S. Open tennis tournament (Robbins 2005). Most people eventually succumb, as Kuznetsova basically did (she did not win an important match for eighteen months after winning

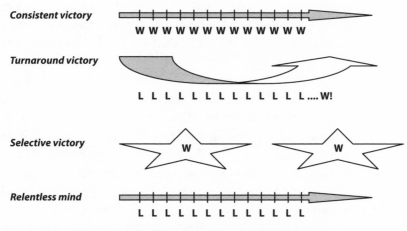

Figure 6.1. Paths to becoming a definitive winner.

the U.S. Open title). The consistent winner, by contrast, delivers over and over again, proving thereby that her mind is subtle and sophisticated enough to understand and overcome whatever may come her way. Of course, as psychologists have pointed out for some time, these sorts of people are rare, for they require at once single-minded determination with highly flexible and sophisticated cognitive and physical skills (Suedfeld and Rank 1976).

Here, then, is the real essence of the consistent winner: she inhabits a different world than most of us, for she seems free from those ties and considerations that limit us. While we live in the "everyday" world and are therefore affected by it, consistent winners "float" above it, manage to escape it, and thus acquire a mystical aura. Max Weber had a term to describe those sorts of people who manage to escape the repressive nature of normal life, who appear to have "repudiate[d] involvement in the everyday routine world" (Weber 1978b: 245): charismatic. "The term 'charisma,'" Weber wrote in his famous passages on the subject, refers to a "certain quality of an individual personality by virtue of which he is considered extraordinary and treated as endowed with supernatural, superhuman, or at least specifically exceptional powers or qualities" (Weber 1978b: 241). Repeat winners are precisely so—exceptional—and thus command our admiration and awe.

Now, we should emphasize that the title of definitive winner does not actually apply to one who keeps on winning but to one who has already won so many times that no further victories are necessary. This person may continue to compete and win; however, to be a definitive winner what matters is what came before, for the term *definitive* is conclusive and therefore not concerned with what may come in the future. Thus, when we say that this or that person is a true, real winner, we are—whether we realize it or not—expressing a judgment that draws from the past and not the present or future. And thus in this sense many competitors appropriately stop reaching for more when they know they have achieved the definitive winner status: with nothing more to gain and their skills potentially on the decline as time goes by, they prefer to leave their record spotless and avoid looking like a "shadow" of their previous selves. Consider, in this regard, the recent words of baseball star Craig Biggio from the Houston Astros on announcing his retirement: "For me to be able to walk away now, on top, on my own accord, I'm very happy with that. I'm in a good place. I think I've done everything that I was supposed to do on a baseball field . . . I just didn't want families bringing their kids to the game and saying, 'He's just not the same guy we used to watch or the guy we really love and respect.' . . . I didn't want to be a player that played the game too long" (Lozano 2007).

The interesting question is *how many times* a competitor needs to win in order to achieve the status of definitive winner—in order for her past to be projected into the future. There is no simple answer. Would General Electric's Jack Welch still be considered a winner had he retired from General Electric in 1998 instead of 2001, after seventeen years at the helm? Under his leadership, the market capitalization of the company increased by $400 billion dollars. Would $300 billion have been enough? Surely, Michael Jordan did not need to win six NBA titles and five MVP awards to become a definitive winner. But would three titles have been enough? It seems clear that definitive winners tend to win *more* than the standard winning records of otherwise very successful competitors. And it is surely the case that *what* is being won (an

NBA title versus the title of best player in a local 40+ basketball league that plays on Thursdays only) matters. But we cannot pinpoint the breaking point between normal and definitive winner.

We can say with certainty, though, that consistent winners can be found in just about any sphere of social life. In business, they are those executives that quarter after quarter and year after year increase their companies' profitability or market shares. In the legal field, they are those who consistently convince juries of the correctness of their arguments and who have therefore never lost a case. In sports, they are teams and individual competitors that go undefeated for very long periods of time. In academia, they are professors who have published consistently in the very top journals of their fields. We find definitive winners even in religion—indeed, especially in religion: they are those followers of Christ who, having won their earthly battles against temptation, win for themselves a seat in heaven. In the words of preacher Joyce Meyer, Jesus taught us how to "win the victory over the lies of Satan" so that "your total victory will come, but it will take time because it will come 'little by little'" (Meyer 1995: 19, 40).

But winning consistently is only one of several paths to definitive victory. A second and rather counterintuitive one involves those who have established traditions as losers (typically because of limitations of their own but also because of broader circumstances beyond their control) but who manage at one point to turn their situation around and clinch a victory. Those who do so are not automatic winners, to be sure. Two conditions generally have to be met for the *turnaround victors* to be regarded as permanent winners. The first is that what they had to overcome has to be sizeable. Consider the case of a failed politician, for instance, who has lost election after election by large margins. Undeterred, he continues to fight and run in elections. Or consider the case of a businessman millions of dollars in debt after many failed business ideas who persists and eventually builds a highly successful company. The second condition is that the victory be of some relevance. We are not interested in the dropout kid who cannot get good grades at school and has no friends but at some point manages to become

101

assistant manager at the local gas station. Rather, we are interested in the rejected kid who, after habitually failing, builds a business empire or writes a best-selling novel that captures the imagination of the nation.

Let us be clear about what is at the heart of this winner. What we admire is clearly not their ability to win over and over again. Rather, we are impressed by their ability to turn something negative into positive. More to the point, we are impressed by something in their minds that did not let them give up—as many of us would have probably done. We appreciate their spirits. And in this sense our appreciation is far less outcome-oriented and much more about the competitors' character. "You lost four [games] out of seven. And they started to, like, write you off, right?" said President George W. Bush to the Indianapolis Colts after they won the NFL championship in 2007. "Some of these sports writers started to say, you know, well, they don't have what it takes, they can kind of do okay until it comes to the big one, and then they just don't have the character necessary to make it work . . . don't have what it takes to win . . . so this is a victory for good hearts—good hearts off the field and good hearts on the field. And we congratulate you. Thank you for winning . . . that heart will take you a long way" (Bush 2007: 512–13).

We must quickly note here, however, that there is a big difference between our appreciation of turnaround and consistent winners: we are in awe of the latter, but not necessarily of the former. Turnaround winners command above all our respect, instead. And that respect has to do with their transition from a poor state of affairs (one that we ourselves do not belong to and thus invokes a certain amount of pity and perhaps even distaste) to a more normal condition. We appreciate the decency and sense of aspiration of turnaround winners. Of course, if the victory is truly sizeable and puts the winner into an exalted position (as happened to the Boston Red Sox in 2004), then we may develop a sense of awe for that person. But even that awe will not be the same as the one we feel for consistent winners, who indeed appear to belong to another world.

We should not underestimate the importance of turnaround winners in the American imagination. The obsession with consistent victory is certainly widespread. But the notion of the weaker person emerging from oblivion to take on the world perhaps resonates with many people in a more profound manner and, as such, is often the material of success stories in a variety of settings and spheres of society. We may indeed say that it is part of the mythology of the country. The "comeback hero" who fights against the odds is often the central character of many Hollywood movies. This is the story of Rocky or Rambo in Sylvester Stallone's movies, who prevail only after coming close to complete defeat. It is also the story of Rudolph the Red-Nosed Reindeer, who is at first marginalized among his peers for his glowing nose but is eventually chosen to lead Santa Claus's sleigh. It is, more generally, the story of the transition from rags to riches and, therefore, of the millions of immigrants—starting with the first settlers—who came to the United States precisely as losers eager to become winners once and for all. And it is at the center of what it means to attain the American dream: that is, not to be born wealthy with a wonderful family and house, but to work and achieve those things. "Upward mobility," as *Business Week*'s Aaron Bernstein put it a few years ago in an article, "is one of America's most cherished values" which, until recently at least, shaped the hopes and visions of "most Americans" as they took low paying jobs knowing that they "would gradually climb into the middle class" (Bernstein 2003).

Definitive winners can become so through a third venue: by winning one or a few times only and otherwise competing at an average level or simply not competing at all. Compared to the consistent and turnaround winners, the *selective winner* has less of a grip on the collective imagination. But it does exist nonetheless. Pulitzer Prize winners offer good examples. Administered by Columbia University since 1917, the prize honors journalists, musicians, and book writers annually. In the case of books especially, winners are sometimes quite unknown to the general public. The award catapults them into the status of definitive winners who in effect need not write ever again to prove their worth. Much the same can be said of recipients of the Presidential Medal of Freedom, one of the two highest civilian honors (along with the Congressional Gold Medal). While many of the recipients are known figures (Colin Powell, for instance), many others are not. Indeed, the awarding of the medal is quite often intended precisely to bring some overdue recognition to individuals who have been ignored for highly valuable feats they once performed. Those recipients can thus finally reasonably claim to have gained the status of definitive winners. A third example comes from the quadrennial Van Cliburn International Piano Competition, which takes place in Fort Worth, Texas. Here young pianists—many of whom do not make enough money playing and must thus practice in the evenings and on weekends— vie for their chance to win first place and literally acquire instant and life-lasting fame among classical piano lovers in the United States and beyond.

What, then, makes selective winners definitive winners? Consistent victors impress us with their performance and otherworldly qualities. We admire the tenacity and determination of turnaround victors. When it comes to selective winners, it is above all the magnitude of their victories that matters. They become definitive winners because they have managed to win something extraordinarily important—something highly prestigious and widely recognized that only a very few people can ever get. And, because we assume that extraordinarily important prizes must reflect extraordinary feats, those people become definitive winners by virtue of the fact that what they did, once or a few times, was truly outstanding. Here, then, we see what really sets these winners apart: their intensity, exceptionality, brilliance at something—all of which, though deployed perhaps only on one occasion, forever shape our perception of the winner. Thus, by definition, the dimension of *time* is not important in the case of selective winners. Their transformation into definitive winners happens not because of their track record but because of the intensity of something that they did once.

There is one final way of becoming definitive winners. Unlike the others, this one does not involve any actual victory in the practical sense. Instead, in a curious departure from considerations of outcomes, it focuses only on the mind of competitors. Here phrases such as "trying is what matters" or "winners never quit" come to mind. Extended losing streaks are required, for what counts is one's unabated effort against continuing disappointing results. What makes these people definitive winners, then, is their unfailing spirits and determination in the face of repeat failure at achieving the desired results—in one word, their *relentless minds*. A great number of psychological studies have shown how losing streaks can sap in a devastating way competitors' confidence in themselves. But powerful examples tell us it can be otherwise. Christopher Reeve was once Superman. An accident confined him to a wheelchair, paralyzed, from 1995 to 2004. He could have resigned himself to a secluded, depressive life of inaction and self-pity. Instead, he famously chose to "go forward," to live his life to the fullest, and in the process, to work hard to help those who suffer from paralysis. His mentality was that of a winner and we, the audience watching and hearing, undoubtedly viewed him as such—definitively. Reeve himself was pretty vocal about the path he chose, inspiring many others never to give up, regardless of circumstances. The following statement captures his mentality:

> When the first Superman movie came out, I gave dozens of interviews to promote it. The most frequent question was: What is a hero? My answer was that a hero is someone who commits a courageous action without considering the consequences. Now my definition is completely different. I think a hero is an ordinary individual who finds the strength to persevere and endure in spite of overwhelming obstacles. They are the real heroes, and so are the families and friends who have stood by them. . . . What I do is based on powers we all have inside us; the ability to endure; the ability to love, to carry on, to make the best of what we have—and you don't have to be a "Superman" to do it.[1]

The spirit of perseverance makes the person, who is de facto losing, into a winner. But let us emphasize one important caveat: in the absence of tangible positive outcomes, this venue toward definitive victory depends on a fairly good dose of sympathy from those around the competitor. The compliments comes from supportive friends, family members, associates, and coaches who know how hard the person has been trying and are willing to let go of actual outcomes and focus only on effort. We may also say that a reasonable amount of hypocrisy is involved: after all, the initial preoccupation with practical outcomes is dismissed or put on hold in favor of something that in the first place counted for very little. Indeed, put differently, those willing to call someone a definitive winner despite his continuous losses in no time would shift back and pay attention to outcomes should the person start to win. We may thus say that the possibility of the mental winner emerges *only* when the other three venues to definitive victory are exhausted, as we shall see in fuller detail in chapter 7.

This does not mean, however, that we should dismiss this type of definitive winner as irrelevant. Its spirit is very closely related to that of the all-American turnaround winner. Recall that what is fascinating about the latter is, in part, the determined spirit that is willing to fight to remedy an unwanted situation. Indeed, that spirit above all is at the very heart of the American spirit and popular imagination of what it means to be American (victory, when it happens, merely helps us celebrate that spirit, since it justifies its worth with practical evidence). The very root of both types of winners is similar, then: a determined, indefatigable, optimistic mindset that never relents regardless of conditions.[2]

Paths to Eternal Loss

As is the case for winning, we recognize more than one path to becoming a definitive loser. Each leads to a very particular kind of definitive loser. Figure 6.2 identifies the three primary paths.

The most obvious path is to be a *consistent loser*. The careful reader will have noticed that this path appears to be identical to that of those who become winners because of their relentless minds. But the dynamics at hand are quite different. The relentless mind is

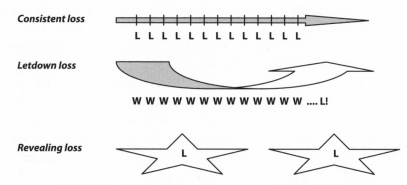

Figure 6.2. Paths to becoming a definitive loser.

winning "material" because, despite almost always losing and never bringing home a victory, he exhibits an impressively determined and optimistic spirit. In judging those with that sort of spirit, we thus put aside their performance and focus on what is happening in their heads. In the case of the consistent loser, by contrast, our attention is mostly on the performance. Indeed, we believe that the performance tells us something about the competitor. What could it tell us?

First and foremost, repeat loss can be a sign that the competitor tried in several ways to achieve the desired objectives without success. The resulting failure points to the incompetence of the competitor. We reckon that something must be wrong with their general perspective on things. After a number of attempts, we conclude that the apple is essentially rotten. The competitor is accordingly dismissed—in our minds or, more concretely, from their job or post. He has failed to perform when given ample opportunities. Importantly, note that we would not think of someone who did not want to try and succeed (and failed) as necessarily a definitive loser. Put differently, definitive losers in this first case must be those who, *eager* to win, are *incapable* of achieving the desired results. We judge those competitors, then, on the basis of their aspirations *and* failure to achieve them. They are definitive losers because they keep on failing to achieve what they want. We shake our heads at their foolish aspirations and, in so doing, actually brand them essentially as the opposite of the consistent winners, whose performance we take as a sign of their impressive abilities to get what they want time and time again.

The vicissitudes of Defense Secretary Donald Rumsfeld illustrate this type of loser rather well. After an apparently conclusive victory against the regime of Saddam Hussein, Rumsfeld failed spectacularly to secure the peace in Iraq. It was certainly not for a lack of effort on his part. Rather, it was because of an incompetent assessment of what that task would require, who the enemy was, and how the people of Iraq would react to a U.S.-led invasion. As the casualties, bombs, and chaos took their toll, calls for his resignation grew exponentially over time from not only the public but also politicians, diplomats, and, more problematically for Rumsfeld perhaps, military leaders. The problem centered on Rumsfeld's perspectives on things, his understanding of reality on the ground. In the words of Mortimer Zuckerman, editor in chief of *U.S. News & World Report*, Rumsfeld committed a "sad litany of failures," he "misjudged the strategy, tactics, and resources required for success in Iraq and obstinately held to his dictums to the military leadership that have led to today's calamitous scenario" (Zuckerman 2006). Rumsfeld resisted calls for his resignation, arguing that his radical approach—calling for fewer troops than normal military doctrine would require, focusing on "surgical" operations to eliminate the "few" insurgents that were causing trouble—would eventually start to produce results. He was accordingly slow at making changes. As the bad news kept mounting, Rumsfeld came under more and more pressure. Approval ratings by the public reached record lows by 2006.[3] His resignation on November 8 of that year—the day after the Republican Party suffered humiliating defeats in midterm elections largely because of Iraq—was widely welcomed across the political spectrum and the public. With this final defeat, for many observers Rumsfeld walked into the pantheon of definitive losers.

But repeat loss can also be symptomatic of another problem—one that is bound to generate scorn and dislike but in a whole different way than in the previous situation. Sometimes we learn that the competitors are simply not interested in succeeding. They compete for one reason or another. But they do not try hard. In this case, we the audience find fault with the competitor. We detect a certain degree of laziness (as opposed to incompetence, as might have been the case in our previous example), indifference, and in general the wrong sorts of values. The competitor is not eager to excel, to stretch herself, to pursue dreams and improve her lot. Though surely preferring victory over loss, she is not preparing properly for the competition. She prefers to do other things. What makes poor people poor? According to the vast majority of Americans (around 75 percent) who answered the General Social Survey, loose morals and drunkenness do much or at least some of the explaining.[4]

Here, then, is a question of will or intention: the competitor seems to *choose* mediocrity—and this very fact cannot be easily accepted in a society where ambition is a way of life. Our judgment will be all the harsher when we know that the competitor has the potential to excel. Then, our judgment of the person will be all the harsher, for many of us believe that anyone with potential *ought to* capitalize on it. Sloth, after all, is one of the seven deadly sins. From this viewpoint, trying becomes a matter of responsibility out of respect for those who do not have the same potential (and would give so much to have it and fulfill it), and out of respect of potentiality itself, the competitor should work hard to succeed. As their failure to do so and willingness to accept loss after loss is not readily accepted, the person turns into a definitive loser.

Now, we should note that consistent loss can lead to definitive loser status in just about every sphere of life—from work to personal romance—as the vast number of books, videos, and seminars dedicated to breaking losing streaks suggests. But we should also observe that tolerance for loss is higher in some spheres than others. In business, repeat loss is generally accepted a few times at least, especially among entrepreneurs. Aspiring authors of fiction manuscripts wishing to be published know that a string of rejections in no way means their work is worthless. The same cannot

109

be said of trial lawyers, who generally understand that several losses in a row can be highly problematic for their careers.

Definitive losers can become so through a second, and quite counterintuitive, venue: after winning time and time again, the person loses once. Though isolated and clearly not indicative of a mind that does not know how to win, the loss amounts to a major *letdown* and brands the person conclusively a loser. Consider this recent passage by *New York Times* journalist Mark Leibovich (2006):

> As a general rule, it can be an unpleasant career move for a Democrat to run for president, streak to primary victories, win his party's nomination and, ultimately, fall short. For his troubles, he will automatically be consigned by large sectors of his party to a distinctive Democratic pariah status— his campaign ridiculed, second-guessed and I-told-you-so'd endlessly by insiders and operatives who bemoan how "winnable" his election was and "unlikable" his personality is. They will reflexively lump the runner-up into the party pantheon of losers and hope he stays away.

This was certainly the story of Al Gore when he failed to win an election that was in the eyes of most observers his to win. Though possibly in the process of redeeming himself by winning the Nobel Prize for Peace, Gore became a definitive loser among Democrats and Republicans alike for many years and could possibly remain so for the rest of his life (Corn 2001). It was also the story of Pete Rose, an idolized baseball champion who precipitously fell from grace after admitting in 2004 to betting on baseball games (though not those involving his own team, the Cincinnati Reds). During a career that spanned from 1963 to 1986, Rose garnered achievements without equal: to date, he is the all-time major-league leader in hits, games played, times at bat, and outs. He won three World Series rings, three batting titles, two Gold Gloves, one MVP award, and the Rookie of the Year Award. Finally, he made seventeen All-

Star appearances playing in an unequaled five different positions. Yet, after admitting to betting, he was permanently banned from baseball. Shortly after that, the Baseball Hall of Fame formally decided that no permanently banned players could be inducted into its ranks (beforehand, informal agreements among the voters had prevented those players from being inducted). Rose had hoped that his confession would free him from his "prison without bars," that his admission of guilt after years of speculations would finally allow him to "come clean" and receive what he felt he deserved (Rose 2004). He was wrong.

How are we to make sense of this second path to becoming a definitive loser? How is it possible that countless accolades and past successes can be so quickly tossed aside and deemed irrelevant? The most obvious factor has to do with the magnitude or importance of what is being lost (much as was the case for the selective winner, who became a definitive one by succeeding at something very important). A series of modest victories are easily overshadowed by failure in the pursuit of something big. But this by itself cannot turn the person into a permanent loser, since we could easily respect the person who ambitiously reaches out a bit too far and does not succeed. What is more critical is that the failure be somehow profoundly embarrassing—which in turn means that the loss reveals something negative and new about the person. When, then, does a major loss become embarrassing? Let us recall the Gore and Rose examples. Gore lost something major (the presidency) that he should have won. And victory was within reach not so much because people thought that Gore had the necessary requirements to win the elections but, instead, because of the popularity of the Clinton-Gore team and the perceived weakness of George W. Bush as an opponent. The victory, in other words, *was there for Gore to take.* All he had to do was not mess things up. As it turned out, Gore failed miserably to take it—most memorably in the three nationally televised debates in which he came across at once as snobbish, overbearing, and stiff. What made the difference, then, was the *juxtaposition* of the *ease of victory* and

Gore's *inability* to take it. In the mind of many observers, such inability—in the context of such an important race—obliterated whatever claims Gore could make about being a winner.

Pete Rose's story differs greatly from Gore's. Here the embarrassment comes from having done something *illicit*, something that goes beyond the boundaries of acceptable social and moral behavior. Of course, had the local barber or college professor bet on baseball, no one would have called them losers. What matters, then, is that Rose had achieved greatness by performing extraordinarily well and legitimately in the game of baseball. When he revealed his illegal betting habits, the *juxtaposition* of his great, clean records and his dirty deeds destroyed him. This is, of course, how the careers and reputations of many great politicians and public figures come to an end. The story of New York governor Eliot Spitzer—the morally indignant, Harvard-trained, high-flying prosecutor who in 2008 got caught frequenting a high-end prostitution ring—comes immediately to mind. The same can be said of Marion Jones's admission of steroid use in 2007. Admissions of transgressions or, better yet, independent discoveries of transgressions can single-handedly obliterate achievements accumulated over a lifetime. And, importantly, note that the transgression need not be about doing something illegal: it can be about doing something unacceptable given the circumstances. Recall, for example, how Howard Dean's impressive campaign for president (which we could say amounted to a series of impressive victories) began to fall apart when Dean launched his now notorious "scream" during a rally celebrating his impressive and fully unexpected (as of a few months or even weeks earlier) third-place in the Iowa primaries. The "un-presidential" behavior—perfectly legal but socially and politically unacceptable—was replayed by the media incessantly (CNN eventually apologized for it), led to a withdrawal of support from the public and campaign officials, and virtually put an end to Dean's hopes for the Democratic Party nomination.

If the first two paths to definitive loser status depend to some degree on what came before, the third path—that of the *revealing loser*—concerns a single or a few events which, by themselves and without references to a track record of victory or loss, contain in our view all the necessary information to produce the most definitive of judgments on the person in question. Consider, for instance, the example of a father who is dearly loved by his wife and children. By all accounts, he has been a model member of his family—faithful, hard working, and devoted. One night, two thieves break into the house when the family is asleep. Hearing some noises, the father wakes up and quickly realizes that someone is in the house. Paralyzed by fear and uncertainty, rather than confronting the thieves directly, the man lies still in bed. The thieves first proceed to take all the valuables in the house. Then, stumbling into the children's room on the way out, they shoot one of the children who had just woken up and made eye contact with the thieves. When asked about what happened, the father does not have the courage to tell the truth. He claims instead that he had not realized that someone had actually broken into the house. When further probed, he later admits to having been overtaken by a sense of panic. Despite her attempts to understand and forgive her husband, the wife irreversibly changes her opinion of him. Part of her thinks of him as a coward, a loser who in the moment of truth could not stand up to protect his family and, when asked about it, could not own up to his behavior.

The person in question need not be always someone other than ourselves. Most of us have approached certain important or telling moments and events in our lives precisely with the idea that we should behave in one way and not another because of what our choices would reveal about who we are (to ourselves and potentially to others). I recently read a story about a woman, Leslie Rogers, who realized one night that she was witnessing a man brutally beating a woman on a street in Philadelphia. She reacted by running toward them, taking her cellular phone and dialing 911, and yelling—so the man could hear, "a man is beating a woman at 15th and Pine!" The man fled and the woman survived the attack, albeit severely injured. Rogers reflected afterward about why she acted so admirably: "I remember, while I was running, thinking maybe this isn't the smartest thing to do. But I didn't want to wake up the next morning and not be proud of how I handled it." She realized, in other words, how defining her actions would be, for herself but also for those who would hear about it. The journalist reporting this event opened the article with this pronouncement about Rogers's character: "Leslie Rogers, a waifish 23-year-old artist and waitress who dyes rainbow streaks in her hair and wears $3 thrift-store little-house-on-the-prairie dresses, is a lot tougher than she looks" (Dribben 2007).

What do stories like this tell us? A single event can serve as a powerful test of a person's true dispositions and character. The event gives the person the opportunity to "rise to the occasion" and display who they really are. Everyday life is full of routines, established patterns of behavior, and clear guidelines. It surely challenges us at times, but in ways that do not reveal our deepest tendencies, emotions, potential or character. Occasionally, however, we find or put ourselves in situations which allow others and even ourselves to discover our innermost qualities, what "we are really all about." Isn't such discovery often what drives people to take on truly daring challenges?

Now, those innermost qualities of a person are the least likely to change. They lie at the core of that person's being. They define the person more than what we can observe about them in everyday life—which we could say ultimately engages highly socialized aspects of ourselves and thus exposes very little of ourselves to the world. Recall on this point the cutting words of sociologist Robert E. Park:

> It is probably no mere historical accident that the word person, in its first meaning, is a mask. It is rather a recognition of the fact that everyone is always and everywhere, more or less consciously, always playing a role. . . . It is in these roles that we know each other; it is in these roles that we know ourselves. (Park 1964: 249)

Park is correct but not completely so. There are indeed times when the mask is removed and people's truer selves—that which has not been affected by pretending to be something we are not in the first place—are exposed. We learn then something fundamental about people and, depending on the information thus gathered, use the resulting information to make conclusive judgments about their nature. These are rare moments in one's life, and indeed, most of us would probably prefer that such testing moments never come our way. But come they do at times.

Types of Winners and Losers

The preceding discussion is about paths to victory and loss. But, as the reader must have realized, paths matter not only as ways to get to the final outcome but also because they shape what definitive winners and losers are, in our minds, all about. *How* we become definitive winners and losers is therefore critical for the type of definitive winner or loser that we will be. Can we be a bit more explicit, then, about those types? Surely, all definitive winners share by definition one trait: they no longer have to demonstrate that they have asserted themselves in the world. Their position is therefore conclusive. Yet our perception of the consistent winner differs much from that of the turnaround winner, for instance, or that of the relentless competitor. Let us close this chapter by identifying the key characteristics of each definitive winner along with the types of emotions or feelings that they inspire in those around them.

Table 6.1 makes clear one fundamental fact about definitive winners: they can be dramatically *different* from each other—so different that we should wonder whether one single word (*winner*) should be used for all of them. The consistent winner, after all, is ultimately about the consistent domination of the world (and himself). The selective winner is about something completely different: genius, the magnitude of a single accomplishment that is so big that no further achievements are needed. The relentless mind has nothing to do with practical outcomes but everything with mental effort and attitude. Finally, the turnaround winner is about dramatic change from bad to good. Each type elicits different reactions from

TABLE 6.1
VARIETIES OF DEFINITIVE WINNERS

Type of definitive winner	Qualities	Audience perceptions
Consistent winner	Focused, overwhelming	Untouchable, ethereal
Turnaround winner	Overcoming, redeemer	Hero
Selective winner	Brilliance, depth	Awe
Relentless mind	Tenacity	Respect

those around it. And, indeed, when asked to specify which type they would rather be, most people show a preference for the consistent winner, followed by the selective winner, the turnaround winner, and expectedly last, the relentless mind. This was, for instance, the ranking for nearly 75 percent of respondents in a class of twenty-three undergraduate students of mine.

Much like definitive winners, definitive losers share one important characteristic: they have failed to assert themselves in the world. Their failures tarnish them forever, even if later successes might help their image a bit. Yet again we see that there exist rather different types of definitive losers. Table 6.2 identifies those differ-

TABLE 6.2
VARIETIES OF DEFINITIVE LOSERS

Type of definitive loser	Qualities	Audience perceptions
Consistent loser	Incompetence, foolishness, laziness	Dismissal, distaste
Letdown loser	Weakness	Disappointment
Revealing loser	Fundamentally flawed, rotten	Rejection

ences. By itself, the consistent loser can really come in two varieties: the incompetent fool who tries to achieve over and over what he cannot get, and the lazy person. Both might be losers, but for completely different reasons. Thus we will dismiss the first as silly and instead feel some anger toward the second. But we do not see in either type what we see in the revealing loser—a fundamentally problematic character—or in the letdown loser—those limitations that prevent them from reaching further. These are quite different sorts of losers, as suggested by the responses of people when asked about which type they would really prefer not to be: the majority—around 60 percent in my class of college students—pointed to the revealing loser.

We should keep this perplexing variety of definitive winners and losers in mind. It clarifies the impetus behind so many people's efforts to continually compete and win. It helps us understand our otherwise puzzling statements about how proven winners can suddenly fall from grace, obvious losers can become winners, and much more. And it sheds light on the strange twists of logic and reasoning we deploy every day to judge ourselves and others.

Chapter Seven

PROCESS VERSUS OUTCOMES

He went down fighting, I know he did.
—Lyzbeth Glick, wife of 9/11 victim

By and large, we attribute the labels of "winner" or "loser" to people based on practical outcomes. But, curiously, that is not always the case. Sometimes our attention is focused on the process of competing or, more specifically, on our attitudes as we try and reach for something. We alluded to this fact in the previous chapter when discussing the case of those who lose all the time but then, somehow, we decide are winners anyway. The truth is that we believe that we can be winners and losers when it comes to our attitudes, *regardless* of outcomes. "He went down fighting, I know he did," said Lyzbeth Glick proudly. Her husband Jeremy Glick called her on the phone before taking on the hijackers on United Airlines flight 93 on September 11, 2001, which crashed into a field in Pennsylvania. "Jeremy and the people around them . . . decided that if their fate was to die, they should fight," said his uncle, Tom Crowley (Kennedy 2001). It is clear: Jeremy Glick died a winner. But this begs the question: How can someone who fails to get something he desperately wants (in this case, living) be considered a winner?

The answer has to do with the fact that in our minds we *distinguish* between the process of pursuing something and the actual outcomes. When outcomes are positive, we tend to mesh the two together. But the moment outcomes are negative, we are quick to differentiate between our pursuit of something and our ability to actually obtaining it. We approach competitive events with strong beliefs about how a competitor should behave in the pursuit of her objectives. And we judge competitors based on those beliefs. In this chapter, I explore how all of this happens. I also ask whose interests we have in mind when evaluating their performance: theirs or society's?

What Process?

We often hear it: coaches, friends, and supporters of various kinds comforting the loser of a competitive event by praising the way he struggled. "I am very proud of the effort that they put in tonight," said Greg Ryan, head coach of the U.S. Women's National Team after being trounced by Brazil 4–0 in the semifinals of the 2007 soccer World Cup in China. "The game didn't go our way, but I'm very proud of all of our young women who put in the last two-to-three years of their commitment, time, dedication, to come out and give their best tonight."[1] It often seems a bit contradictory, if not hypocritical. After all, had the loser won, everyone would be talking about the outcome. How the person secured her victory might also be a subject of discussion, but very much with the positive outcome in mind. People would note how this or that move or reaction was critical, efficacious, or instrumental in clinching the victory. A significant body of research shows that winners in competitive events are much more prone than losers to attribute their success to their skills, abilities, and so on (Zientek and Breakwell 1991). Even if the victory was "ugly," people would enjoy thinking about how a less-than-impressive performance could generate a positive outcome: "It was not pretty, but they got it done," they would reflect. Success, psychologists tell us, makes it pleasurable to go back and think about what we did to earn our victory

119

(Riess and Taylor 1984). But a loss is by contrast altogether different: competitors and especially supporters alike are tempted to forget outcomes and search for encouraging signs in the process.

What does this mean? It means that, when it is convenient, many of us *readily admit* that we view the process and the outcomes as quite different things. In the case of victory, we are happy to mesh the two together. But in the case of loss we sometimes choose to ignore one phase (outcomes) and focus our attention on the other (the process). The latter comes under scrutiny in and of itself—as a whole and self-contained world that we can subject to what we hope is a positive judgment. We ask ourselves if the person is a winner or a loser *based strictly on what happens in the process*. That is precisely the spirit behind coach Ryan's words. We will examine later how we evaluate the process. Our duty for now is to understand better the "process" itself. What is it?

In terms of time, the process is everything that happens up to the end of the competition. More specifically, it refers to that phase of an event when competitors mobilize to pursue their goals. Now, that phase is made up of two sorts of things: the *actions* a person takes to obtain the desired results and the *mental attitudes* behind those actions.

Examples of actions include playing piano in a music competition, buying stocks as a professional investor, or giving speeches during a political campaign. They are undertaken for the express purpose of winning whatever is at hand. As it turns out, though part of the process, usually these are not of interest to us as we consider how we can rescue our beloved competitor from the status of loser. Why? The major reason is that actions are very often intimately connected to the outcome. This is so because either they directly lead to the outcome (a series of bad political speeches or musical notes, for instance) or, by virtue of perhaps being fine in terms of quality but not superior to the competitors, are ultimately insufficient to ensure victory. Hence, we would never really celebrate the poor shots at goal of the U.S. team against Brazil or even the few good shots they managed to take. Instead, if, like coach Ryan, we are interested in discovering the winner in those who have lost the competition, we are likely to simply try to forget *what* actually happened during the competition and encourage others to do the same.

Our attention will instead turn to mental attitudes: the way competitors, *in their minds*, approached the competition. We will inquire about their thought processes, reactions, tendencies, and more. How motivated were they, for instance? Did they let some setbacks distract them from their mission? We will examine in detail in the next section what, exactly, we are bound to ask in most cases. What we should recognize here are three important characteristics of mental attitudes.

First and foremost, mental attitudes can be easily *divorced* from the outcome. This is because, unlike actions, they are from the start a couple of steps removed from outcomes: loss reflects most directly (or, put differently, inevitably) actions but only sometimes mental attitudes. In a basketball game, for example, the losing team is almost by definition outplayed in the court by the winning team. But the mental attitudes of the losing team can easily be of equal, if not superior, merit to those of the winning team without leading to victory. One can try very hard—harder than the competitor— and still come up short. The possibility of separation presents us with an opening of immense value: we may now pronounce judgments about the loser's attitudes that do not take into consideration the negative outcomes of the competition.

This would be very difficult to do in the case of actions. But we may do so when it comes to attitudes, provided that we have independent standards with which to evaluate them. We can summarize our discussion so far in graphic form. Figure 7.1 shows the "process" in competitive events as being composed of two major elements: actions and attitudes. It indicates the indirect connection (via actions) between mental attitudes and outcome and then suggests that mental attitudes can themselves be used to generate independent judgments about the competitor. In this case, the outcome was negative (the person lost the competition) but the judgment about the person's approach to the competition was positive.

Our propensity to see mental attitudes as quite separate from practical outcomes is not particular to competitive events only, of course. It is instead something that runs deeply in our culture. Our

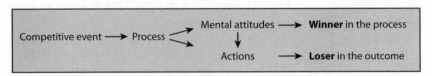

Figure 7.1. Separating attitudes from outcomes in case of loss.

moral systems, for instance, distinguish between intentions and consequences. Some of us believe that the former do not matter: "The road to hell," goes the famous saying, "is paved with good intentions." But for most of us intentions are at least somewhat important when it comes to judging people: we hope for those who have erred that they "meant to do well" or that they simply "did not mean" to do badly. The hype and outrage surrounding the Enron trial, for instance, had certainly much to do with the scale of the debacle but also with the extent to which executives Jeffrey Skilling and Kenneth Lay knew about the financial strategies of their company and chose to act mendaciously. The demise of Enron, wrote *Fortune Magazine*'s Bethany McLean and Peter Elkind in their book on the topic, is a story "of people drunk on their own success, people so ambitious, so certain of their own brilliance, so fueled by greed and hubris that they believe they could fool the world." Their book, accordingly, "explores the motives, thoughts, and secret fears of a fascinating array of characters" (McLean and Elkind 2003: back cover)—or, in the language of this chapter, the state of their minds.

We find the same distinction between the mind and practical outcomes in our criminal system. Thus killing somebody by accident is an entirely different thing than doing so willfully. This is the difference between involuntary manslaughter and murder. These are distinctions that we have made for centuries. Aristotle, despite his strong interest in consequences, recognized the independent nature (and therefore importance, from the point of view of judgment) of intentions. Indeed, considerable sections of the *Nicomachean Ethics* are devoted to an analysis of voluntary versus nonvoluntary actions. Thus, for example, he urges his readers to distinguish between the bad actions of a drunk and those of a sober person. Both are certainly culpable, but to different degrees (though the drunk, Aristotle says, is also culpable for something that the sober person is not: allowing himself to get drunk) (Aristotle 1976: 113). Much later, in the eighteenth century, Immanuel Kant proceeded to put intentions squarely at the very heart of Western morality with his categorical imperative by asking us to act so that we are ready to have our reasons for acting become universal laws (i.e., reasons that anyone can use).

Even—perhaps especially—in Christianity we find this split between intentions and outcomes. The notion of repentance, so important for salvation, is about mental states: it entails a reversal of the original intentions behind our bad deeds. The born-again Christian is someone who conceptually embraces the word of Christ and vows to live a life that embraces his teachings (which means "trying" more than "succeeding" in every instance to follow those teachings). Sin, after all, is as much an action as it is a state of mind. "The first word of the gospel," preacher Richard Owen Roberts tells us, "is not 'love.'" It is not even "grace." The first word of the gospel is "repent." Repentance, he adds, is an "urgent and indispensable theme that is kept at the very forefront of the gospel message" (Roberts 2002: 23). Roberts is correct, of course: Jesus' first words appear in Matthew 4:17: "Repent, for the kingdom of heaven is at hand."

A second, crucial feature of mental attitudes has to do with *potentiality*. For any mental attitude that we observe, there is another that could have been expressed but was not. The competitor who demonstrates determination is not devoid of the ability to be distracted. Our appreciation of any given attitude thus very much hinges on our belief that, had things gone differently, that attitude might have not been out there for us to see. In recognizing, for example, that John gave everything he had in his tennis game, we also implicitly acknowledge that he *could* have instead played halfheartedly. This, too, is of much importance for us: it would be harder for us to speak well of John if there was no chance that he could have played with little passion.

We hold, then, a basic view of people as multifaceted beings endowed with a set of fairly incoherent (and sometimes simply opposite) tendencies. From this perspective, competitors are "open-ended" persons carrying within themselves a multiplicity of possibilities. As they engage in a given contest, they can realize those possibilities or leave them "dormant" and, in many cases, engage in a process of "discovery" of their many abilities and limitations. Those possibilities are at times in conflict with each other: we can be lazy but also hardworking, driven or indifferent, focused or distracted. This means, in turn, that our view of competitors is in part informed by a sense of internal tension. Competitors are not necessarily fully at peace; they must examine themselves, and then overcome some of their own tendencies. Is this not the key message of those business, sport, religious, and self-help gurus whose books and videos occupy so much space in our bookstores? Consider the fact that in 2007 alone, the popular preacher Joel Osteen published four books, titled respectively *Become a Better You*, *Your Best Life Now: 7 Steps to Living at Your Full Potential* (also available in Spanish), *Your Best Life Now for Moms*, and *Starting Your Best Life Now*. To top it all, he then released a calendar to aid readers on their self-improvement journey.

As is the case with the split between attitudes and outcomes, our view of competitors as complex beings with conflicting multiplicity and potentialities also resonates strongly with our cultural system. We all recall, for instance, the U.S. Army's recruiting slogan for twenty years, until 2001: "Be All that You Can Be." The message was clear: we can live our lives one way (fully) or another (only partly realized), and the army would make sure we did the former. We sentence criminals based on the assumption that they *could* have acted otherwise. This explains the common attempt on the part of defense lawyers to present their clients as mentally incompetent—that is, incapable of knowing the difference between this or that and, therefore, of not deserving punishment. And we send our children to college with the hope that, with the help of their professors and peers, they will cultivate their more positive qualities while learning to control their more negative ones. Thus, according to its mission statement, Dartmouth College offers an "inspirational setting" where students can develop an appreciation for "integrity," "responsibility for each other and for the broader world," and "independence of thought."[2]

All this leads us to the third characteristic of mental attitudes: *choice*. The process of competing is, in our view, fundamentally about choosing. Competitors must make a choice between this or that potentiality, this or that path. Potentialities are important but only because ultimately they turn into reality. Faced with the option of giving up or continuing to pursue their goals, what did the competitors choose to do? Did they fight until the end or give up early? Did they hold on to their ambitions or did they renounce their dreams? For many of us, the answers to these kinds of questions are fundamental for our assessment of the persons before us. Rather than outcomes, we turn to the choices people make in the pursuit of that outcome to assess their characters. Put differently, all competitors are similar in the menu of options they face; they differentiate themselves on the basis of how they go after those options.

Needless to say, our belief in choice in competitive contexts is again part of a broader cultural system. The idea that individuals can and do choose as they go through life is a fundamental building block of our society. Nearly 86 percent of Americans believe, according to the General Social Survey, that "what happens to me is largely my own doing," while only 14 percent think they have little influence over the course of their lives.[3] According to the World Values Survey, Americans are fourth in the world when it comes to believing that they enjoy freedom and control over their lives.[4] Freedom and personal responsibility are fixtures of our economic system, which is founded on the principle that individuals should be allowed to produce and consume what they wish. It is part of our criminal system. Consider, for instance, California's "three strikes and you're out" law (Proposition 184), according to which a person convicted of three felony crimes (however minor) stands the chance of being sentenced to life in prison. Rather than concerning itself with the practical consequences of the crimes, the law seeks to punish those who choose to ignore prior warnings (and, in parallel, seeks to convince other criminals not to commit a third offence). And it is a key aspect of Christianity, wherein embracing Christ is seen as an act of volition—as a choice between light and darkness, good and bad, heaven and hell.

Making the Judgment

We evaluate competitors partly on *how* they pursued their objectives and, specifically, on their mental approach to the competition. Both losers and winners can be subject to this. But, as already noted, we are more likely to embark on it in the case of losers as a way of rescuing them from purely negative judgments. What standards, then, do we use to evaluate those losers? And why are those standards so valuable to us?

We participate in all sorts of competitive events—political, business, athletic, intellectual, and so on. Yet, most of us seem to care about four basic sorts of issues when we think about how losers approach those events. First, did they know and remain unequivocal about what they wanted? Second, did they give it all they could? Third, did they ever lose hope? A fourth set of questions normally concerns the player's attitude well after the competitive event is over: did they take advantage of this opportunity to learn? If the answers to any of these questions are positive, we may have grounds to rescue losers from their status and turn them into partial winners.

Why, then, do we rely on these specific standards to evaluate losers in their pursuits? Most of us would say that adherence to those standards can make competitors happy—either in the moment or at a later time. But this may be only half the story. A more subtle and perhaps powerful explanation may have to do with what *benefits society the most*. From this perspective, we value those standards (without necessarily knowing it) because they push competitors to behave in ways that, though possibly harmful to them, are most likely to yield a positive result. Let us consider each standard in turn.

Clarity of Goal

Many of our movie heroes are determined, unwavering characters. John Wayne never hesitated. Bruce Willis's firm, cold glance leaves no room for doubt: he is like a wolf ready to attack. We teach these values to our children and students. No business school in the United States has a curriculum that does not include teaching students how to draft a business plan. Companies without a goal, the mantra goes, are bound to fail. Thus corporations spend billions of dollars every year hiring management consultants to help them articulate a vision. With a vision, they can then spend more money crafting strategies.

A major standard by which we judge how competitors pursue something, then, is the clarity of their goals. We want to know a few things. First, do they know, among many possible objectives, what they really want? Or are they instead confused in their heads about things or perhaps desiring several things at once without really being upfront about it? A Google executive recently reflected at a conference on why the company had, from its start, the right approach: "At the very early days, we already knew what we want and that is to organize the world's information and make it universally accessible" (Estavillo 2006). Such clarity is by itself a virtue. And lack of clarity is by contrast a problem. According to Dennis Ross, chief Middle East envoy in the first Bush and Clinton administrations, a major fault of the George W. Bush administration's approach to Iraq was its "confusion on objectives": Was it disarmament? Or was it regime change? (Ross 2007: 116). Our advice to the young, ambitious entrepreneur who wishes to start a new coffee chain that will take on Starbucks is to stop for a moment and really find out what they are truly after: Is it money, or is it fame, or is it really the desire to satisfy in a different way or perhaps change people's tastes for coffee? We praise those with clear goals, even if they fail. We dismiss those who are confused.

We also ask competitors whether they really understand what they are after. An athlete may have no doubt in her head that she wants to run a marathon. Our question to her would be whether she understands what that means or whether she holds in her head a faulty image of it. We praise those who embark on something when they have a solid understanding of what they are after. Failure may set them back but will not prevent us from complimenting them.

Finally, clarity of goal is also about time. As we pursue our objectives, we must not allow other matters to distract us. Do we stay true to our initial mission? Or do we lose our focus and instead "drift" toward other attractive things? As we run a marathon and our muscles begin to ache, for instance, the idea of stopping, getting some water and perhaps a massage sounds incredibly tantalizing. Or, as feedback from polls start to tell us that we will lose the election race, do we start thinking of other things we could be doing with our time? In the heat of competition, priorities in our minds change. What we ask competitors is to view those changes as *illusory*—as not reflecting our true preferences. We ask them to resist the temptation and "stay the course" (a phrase that won President George W. Bush much respect in the earlier phases of the Iraq war). We view negatively, by contrast, those who waver over time—those who run after one thing now and something else later on.

Overall, then, we approve of those who keep their goals clear in mind *even* if they lose. We tell them and ourselves that winners do have clear goals. Losers are confused. But where does our judgment come from? Why do we value clarity so much?

The most obvious answer is that we believe that clarity of goals, even if it is associated with a loss, is a necessary condition for attaining positive outcomes in general. Confusion over goals, Dennis Ross notes, creates confusion over means (Ross 2007: 116). "Success results more from certain mental traits and personal characteristics known as *attitudes* than from any other single factor," writes Walter Staples in his book *Think Like a Winner!* "Winners are not born," he adds, "they are made" (Staples 1993: 30). And one of those attitudes is to have clear goals, as training and education guru Robert Mager tells us: "Exactly what should we do to accomplish our important goals? The answer is that 'There is no way to decide what action to take until we know what we are trying to accomplish'" (Mager 1983: 1). So, then, we want competitors to be clear about their goals so that one day, should they fail this time or another time, they will eventually achieve what they want.

But there might be a subtler and perhaps more troubling answer as well. What if, as Freud suggests for much of what we consider our "virtues," clarity of goals happens to advance the interests of society as a whole (of "others") at significant cost for the individual himself? What if, in order to function properly, society asks us to repress what otherwise would come rather naturally to us—in this case, the desire to change our mind, the freedom to hesitate in front of, and wonder about, the complexity of things?[5] Asking competitors to come up with a clear and unequivocal idea of their goals may make them into highly effective pursuers of goals *while*, at the same time, preventing them from engaging—for their own evolution and growth—in a good amount of introspection and discernment of differences between one thing and the next. Society benefits when people set themselves an unambiguous goal and do not deviate in their pursuit of it. It is not clear that individuals do to the same degree.

This is probably the case with young people, whom parents, coaches, and others increasingly expect to be unwavering in their aspirations. As the young high school student pursues with feverish determination acceptance to an elite college, for example, he is likely to have thought too little about what type of education he wants or person he wishes to become. Doubts and other temptations may come along. But he knows better: what he must do is get excellent grades and fill his resume with countless activities. Hesitation would not be welcome. What is then learned at a young age continues through adulthood, as one is socialized into professional careers and circles. The ideal employee is someone who is fully dedicated at excelling at their specific job in the company or organization where they find themselves. He is not someone who wonders too much about pursing alternative career paths or simply changing employers.

Uncompromising Effort

I have often looked at the motivational posters in gyms or the workplace with puzzlement. They assert with no doubt the goodness of some *thing* but say absolutely nothing to support their position. Many praise "effort." One such poster, picturing a kay-aker in the midst of a turbulent waterfall, says: "Effort: Live Each Day Like It's Your Last." The message is clear: we should give all that we have when we pursue something. We should hold nothing back.

Effort is thus an extremely important yardstick. We look positively on the person who tries his best. According to the General Social Survey, when respondents were asked to think about the most desirable qualities a child should have, "trying hard to succeed" was seen as extremely important by 27 percent of the respondents. 53 percent deemed it very important, and another 18 percent as fairly important. Only 2 percent thought of it as not too important and a stunning 0 percent thought it was not important at all.[6]

We are impressed that they directed all their talents and energies toward a desired goal. From this perspective, it matters little that they may have failed to achieve their goals. We see this clearly, perhaps, when people praise fallen soldiers and police officers. Their effort is sufficient to earn them the highest honors. "A hero is one who gives until there is nothing else to give," Monsignor Francis Feret said recently during his homily for Philadelphia police officer Gary Skerski, who was fatally shot one Monday night while answering a robbery call at a bar (Stoiber and Schiavo 2006). We feel quite different about those who hold back something. The idea here is one of relative depletion: what matters is not *how much* in absolute terms competitors spent in their efforts but whether they spent *all* that they could. That is the sign of a virtuous competitor.

But effort is also about determination. This is the message of countless self-help books and motivational speakers. A winner is someone who, when knocked down, finds the strength to get up again and keep going. We are interested, then, in the inner drive of competitors. We want to know whether there is a force inside of them that allows them to continuously direct their talents and energies toward the fulfillment of their objectives. Their effort has to be uncompromising. Winners do not sway as they pursue their objectives.

There is, finally, an important moral dimension to all of this. Depletion and determination count for very little if we are not *earnest* in our efforts. The effort has to be clean: it has to come from our true selves and not involve in its origin or unfolding anything "foreign" or external. The doping scandals in sports make this obvious. Marion Jones might have won five Olympic medals in 2000, but we have now learned that she took a performance-enhancing drug to achieve her feat. Those of us who marveled at seeing her sprint on the track now look on the same images— images of struggle, of overcoming—and shake our head. Her pushing herself to the limit is no longer impressive, since it availed itself of something other than what was hers naturally. The result was that, in the full glare of the media, she voluntarily returned her medals with tears in her eyes by saying "I have betrayed your trust"—that is to say, I have led you to believe I was earnest when in fact I was not. Jones then added, "I hope you can find it in your heart to forgive me" (Tresniowski and Dowd 2007).

Thus earnestness means, as well, respect for the norms of the game. The problem with Barry Bonds's homerun statistics, or of other impressive feats by a number of baseball players, has to do with cheating. Bonds's alleged use of steroids has led many baseball fans to doubt or outright dismiss him: that is to say, not to deny that he hit so many baseballs outside of the field but to strip those achievements of their place in the game's history books. The result, again, is that his efforts—his hitting the ball—is no longer cause for marvel but of distaste or, as long as the truth is not known, of doubt.[7]

The question, then, is why we care so much about effort. Again, our answer would be at first that we believe that effort will eventually be rewarded. We may lose one time, or a few times. But effort will eventually lead to some results. Besides, effort makes winning all the more rewarding. Thus, again, we may have the competitor's interest in mind when urging them to push themselves. A motivational poster with a football player pointing his finger to the sky states "Work Hard" and then, below, quotes Theodore Roosevelt's claim that "Nothing Worth Gaining Was Ever Gained without

Effort."[8] Still with the best interest of the competitor in mind, we sometimes urge people to give their efforts out of a conviction, Puritanical in nature, that working hard is good in and of itself—that it has a cleansing effect on our minds and spirits. As Thomas Jefferson put it, "A mind always employed is always happy. This is the true secret, the grand recipe, for felicity" (Jefferson 2003: 6). Here we truly take no account of the outcome of one's efforts and instead really praise effort for its own sake.

Yet, in the end, there may be one major and quite basic reason for why we deem those who try hard to be winners: because we as a society benefit the most if people push themselves as hard as they can, even when this may hurt them in various ways. People who try hard are likely to work harder, generate more goods and services (including entertainment for us), create jobs, pay more taxes, and much more. It matters little that, after squeezing themselves for a long time, those people will "burn out," or that, by fully dedicating themselves to one task, they will neglect other aspects of their lives, their loved ones or friends, or their other interests and passions. From the point of view of the "system," people are expendable and replaceable resources—and, given what is needed at a given point in time, they should be exploited to the maximum. This is especially the case if they happen to be self-motivated, if they learned from a young age—as we try to ensure through our school system and other venues—to embrace our love of effort. Even our emphasis on earnestness may have a darker side: cheating may benefit a competitor but *not* society as a whole, since the respect for rules is fundamental for the smooth functioning of any collective entity. We ask for clean efforts not so much because of our noble instincts or a sense of ethics, or even a belief in what is good for a competitor but, rather, out of what may serve the whole. Of course, we do all this in most cases without actually knowing it—a fact that is at once interesting and problematic.

Relentless Optimism

According to yet another intriguing motivational poster, Thomas Edison once said that "I have not failed: I have just found 10,000 ways that won't work." We may not get what we want, but people will look favorably upon us if, while failing, we kept a positive attitude. Winners do not think negatively, in other words. A host of books on "optimism" in our personal lives and workplaces makes this clear.[9] "Optimists," corporate culture guru Price Pritchett reveals in his very first paragraph of a recent book on the topic, "get paid more, are healthier, win more elections, and live longer" (Pritchett 2006: 9).

But what, exactly, does it mean to think positively? Above all, it means continuing to believe in the possibility of victory until the very end. Concession speeches in politics represent major turnarounds in how candidates speak about themselves and their hopes. Until conceding, the expectation is that they will speak as if they are bound for victory. Now, everyone knows when this no longer sounds realistic. But a true competitor is nonetheless expected to play the part: only to speak of victory and the good things to come. Those who die of illnesses but fight until their last breath are winners. Those who give up early on cannot be called the same.

Thus we teach our children and we expect our friends and colleagues to "never give up." Setbacks can, of course, be acknowledged. What matters is that we interpret them as temporary deviations from the path to victory. "Americans regard failure—even bankruptcy—as a stone in the road rather than a dramatic verdict," a journalist for the *Economist* noted recently (*Economist* 2007). Indeed, regardless of what may happen along the way, we must never accept that loss is inevitable. On the contrary, we must always believe that the outcome will be in our favor. John F. Kennedy once famously reminded his fellow citizens that "the American by nature is optimistic. He is experimental, an inventor and a builder who builds best when called upon to build greatly. Europeans ask, 'Why?' Americans ask 'Why not?'" (*Economist* 2007). Thus nearly 85 percent of Americans report in the General Social Survey that they are "always optimistic" about their future, most believe that the future holds promise for newborns, and most agree that there are things that are worthwhile doing in life.[10]

Such optimism is rather interesting, for it can easily amount to a distortion (or at least rather loose interpretation) of the facts. Objectively speaking, a dire situation does not call for optimism. The same can be said of even a mixed situation. The glass is both half empty and half full at once, and stating that it is only one or the other is simply erroneous. Nonetheless, that is precisely the view we subscribe to when we judge how someone behaved during a competitive event. Those who gave up in the midst are losers (regardless of outcomes) and those who stayed positive displayed the traits of a winner.

We must therefore ask what explains our perspective. Helen Keller once famously said that "nothing can be done without hope and optimism." So, as was the case for effort, one explanation might be that optimism is often a necessary (though not sufficient) condition for victory. This is because we think optimism helps us see new things: it "reveals possibilities that are hiding in the shadows"; it helps the positive-minded person find "benefits and creative solutions the pessimist overlooks" (Pritchett 2006: 10). Moreover, it is because there is always the odd chance that they can still win—that nothing is over until it is over. Unexpected turns of events can change things dramatically. So, a distortion of reality may prove practically beneficial to us. And those who are willing to adopt such a perspective deserve the title of "winner"—for they show an understanding of what is required to become a winner.

At the same time, it is quite difficult to justify optimism in the face of clearly negative circumstances. Would it not be better for competitors to give up and devote their resources to something else? Thus, again, we must wonder whether we really have the welfare of the competitors in mind. Is it possible that we are deluding competitors above all for the benefit of the whole? Society bears little of the costs of that delusion (surely, people in dire situations could stop and make better use of their resources, but the learning curves involved with switching, the new array of start-up costs, and other factors make that option not very attractive on the whole) and reaps many of the benefits (when a few people, propelled by their optimism, keep going and eventually succeed they tend to produce things that others can truly benefit from and which outweigh the waste of energy and time on the part of those who fail). I posit that a reevaluation of our instinctive embrace of optimism is in order.

Willingness to Learn

The fourth standard we use to turn losers into winners has to do with their openness of mind as they pursue their objectives. In terms of time, this normally extends beyond the actual competitive event. Once the event is over, we ask whether the competitor is willing or eager to reflect critically on how he performed. What is required here as a starting point, then, is an admission of less-than-optimal performance. If the competitor did not perform to the best of their abilities, we ask him to investigate why this happened. Where did he let himself down?

But even if the competitor performed to the best of his ability, we wish to know whether he was willing to think in theoretical terms what he could have done differently to ensure a more positive outcome. In any case, the truth is that we never think that someone truly competed to their fullest potential. Thus, even in situations when it looks like they could not have performed any better, we assume that there is some room for improvement: this assumption drives our curiosity.

All of this means, then, that we are willing to grant someone the status of winner precisely when, in the face of defeat, she proves capable of accepting responsibility. The winning spirit has to do with having the strength to look straight at reality without illusions (and thus let go of any unjustified optimism it held on to during the competition) *and* with having the acumen to gather whatever information is needed to ensure a better outcome in the future. We may rephrase the previous sentence by saying that one becomes a winner by demonstrating courage as well as intelligence. Why, then, should we look so favorably on this idea of learning from one's loss? Here, the interests of the competitor *and* those of society might actually be aligned. A willingness to learn certainly benefits competitors and, *as it does so*, also society. Learning is a sure step toward more self-knowledge and, as a result, further refinement of one's skills and proper deployment of future resources. "The true art of success," we read in a recent book on how to deal with negative outcomes, "is learning how to cope with failure" (McAlpine and Dixey 2003: 60). This is bound to improve individual performance—with obvious benefits for the broader community. At least in this case, then, our language and inclinations appear to be whole and fair.

Process and Outcomes

We have seen that losers can also be winners if they approach the competitive event at hand in the "right" way. This happens when we rescue losers from poor outcomes by focusing on their attitudes. This requires that we view the process of competing *as altogether separate* from the outcome of the competition. We have a set of beliefs about what is commendable and what is deplorable in one's pursuit of victory. We judge competitors on the bases of those beliefs. Openness to learning, uncompromising effort, and optimism become important. As we judge, regardless of what may think, we do not always have the competitors' best interests at heart. Sometimes, we are advancing the interests of society and hurting those of competitors.

Matters are complex and tricky, then. Our commitment to the language of winning and losing is obviously great: we rescue losers not by encouraging them to forget about their failures and all that happened, but by turning them into winners anyway. We do this quickly, with a good dose of hypocrisy, and without much thought. Indeed, we fail to see that our efforts may ultimately harm those we are trying to help. What a puzzling mind-set this is. Alternatives abound, of course. For instance, we could be far more explicit about the differences between process and outcomes, and decide that we should use different terms for identifying successful or unsuccessful persons in each phase of competition. Or we could simply look out for the best interests of competitors, whatever that might mean for the well-being of society. Or we could even decide that processes in and of themselves really do not matter, after all—that outcomes only are important and processes should only be taken into consideration strictly in their relationship to outcomes. Options abound.

Nietzsche said many times that we must embark on a merciless analysis of our values. In his book *Daybreak* he wrote that we must "tunnel" into the foundations of our beliefs to investigate and "dig out" the very premises of our worldviews (Nietzsche 1997: 2). Socrates, with his incessant investigation of people and what they held to be good, thought as much. We have made good progress in shedding light on "winning" and "losing" in America. The next two chapters will help us further. We examine the role of our minds in making competition both possible and profoundly meaningful.

Chapter Eight

INJECTING VALUE

Man is an animal suspended in webs of
significance he himself has spun.
—Clifford Geertz, *The Interpretation
of Cultures*

EARLIER IN THIS BOOK, we learned about some of the most important prizes that are at stake in competitive events, such as "being
right" or feeling superior. But are these prizes naturally part of any
competitive event? What is necessarily at stake in competitive
events and what, by contrast, do we "inject" into those events? In
this chapter, I discuss this injection. To do so, I introduce the concept of the "prize ladder." At the bottom of the ladder, we find the
most obvious things one wins or loses in any given competition:
the demonstration of great physical or mental ability, money, trophies, and so on. As we move up the ladder, we find things that are
more and more removed from the competitive event. For the most
part, these are introduced by us into competitive events. We should
probably care the least about those prizes. They are often the most
abstract and artificial. Yet, curiously, we instead choose to infuse
them with extraordinary significance.

We should take time to understand this process. It is a fundamentally mental affair. And, as we proceed, we should also ask why

the injection of such artificial but important prizes occurs in the first place. Why do we inflate the importance of competitive events to such great extent? We can identify a few important reasons, ranging from the ability of mass media and other interested actors to magnify the significance of competition in our lives, to the channeling of otherwise destructive drives into safe and controlled environments, to the need and search for a meaningful life in an otherwise dull and routine-driven existence. The reasons might vary, but all suggest that competitive events somehow *become*—rather than naturally are—highly charged events. This realization should lead us to question our otherwise uncritical acceptance of those events as important and, at times, life defining.

The Prize Ladder

If a group of extraterrestrials landed in the United States, they would likely marvel at the intensity with which Americans immerse themselves in competitive events. Why do millions of viewers spend countless hours every day watching amateur talent competitions such as *American Idol* on television? Why does half of the United States come to a standstill during the Super Bowl and watch very large, burly men throw a leather ball around and inevitably fall on top of each other every few seconds? Why do political candidates sacrifice, for weeks and months, most of their hours and days to run for office? Indeed, it would not take an extraterrestrial to be greatly puzzled. Any outsider unfamiliar with the necessary cultural and other types of references required to *understand* what is at stake in those competitive events would also be rather puzzled. The thrill of victory and the desperation that comes with loss often *transcend* what the competition is most obviously about. Anyone unequipped with the required tools to know what lies beyond the veil of the obvious is bound to miss the point. After all, as Clifford Geertz has often reminded us, human beings live in rich and complex webs of cultural symbols that endow otherwise banal and mundane occurrences with great significance. The challenge for outsiders is to see and access those webs. Insiders navigate through them "spontaneously and with ease" (Geertz 1975: 45). Those not of the same culture are instead faced with the difficult task of having to interpret those webs.

We should begin our discussion, then, by distinguishing the sorts of things that are naturally at stake in competitive events and those that are injected into them. To do so, I introduce in figure 8.1 the prize ladder.

At the bottom of the ladder, we find things that are directly related and intrinsic to the actual, objective competitive event at hand. Piano players compete to see who can play the piano better (i.e., make a sequence of pleasing and accurate sounds in the eyes of judges). Basketball teams work hard to put the ball into the basket (following certain rules in a given period of time) more times than their opponents. Candidates for political office are after the highest number of votes. Children in the Scripps Spelling Bee prepare for months to spell more words than their opponents. The player who wins a game of Monopoly ends up with more paper money than the other players. And chess players strive to checkmate each other's king. At stake in all of these is one's ability to succeed at what the competition most immediately demands and asks for. For our alien or cultural outsider, these prizes are probably the easiest to understand. Basketball players are obviously running and pushing to get the ball into the hoop, while chess players are obviously interested in something having to do with each other's pieces. As it turns out, however, these are important prizes but, on closer scrutiny, they are normally the least valuable from the perspective of competitors and audiences alike. As Huizinga put it in his seminal study of play and competition, "There is something at stake" in competition, "but this 'something' is not the material result of the play, not the mere fact that the ball is in the hole" (Huizinga 1955: 49).

A second type of prize normally provokes a bit more interest and emotions. Some of these have to do with all the skills and talents required for competing in the event at hand. At stake here is

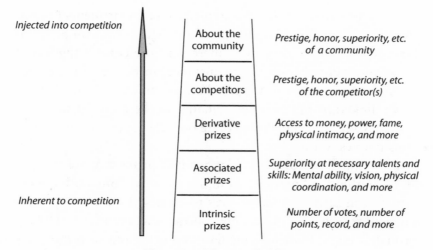

Figure 8.1. The prize ladder.

one's ability to claim that he or she is better *at those skills and talents* (both physical and mental) than the defeated opponent. Thus winning a piano competition, for instance, puts a pianist in the position to claim that his or her technique, understanding of music, range of emotional expression, and even determination and practicing skills are superior—as they concern the specific music played on that event, of course, but also the world of piano music in general as well. Beating someone at basketball puts one in a position to claim that her shooting, dribbling, and jumping skills in basketball (along with her mental concentration and poise) are better than those of the opponent. Winning an election enables a candidate to say that his ability to speak to and persuade voters is superior to that of his rival. From this perspective, competitive events serve as testing grounds for a given set of skills and talents—discrete and bounded events that competitors engage in to generalize about their abilities in particular realms of life.

The other prizes on this step of the ladder are those explicitly tied to the outcome of the given competition. They include trophies of various kinds, money (for example, the $1.6 million at stake at the 2009 U.S. Open tennis tournament for men's and women's singles), and free use of luxury goods, such as apartments (as happens, for instance, to the winner of the Miss USA competition). These prizes are certainly not inherent to the competitive events themselves: victory at chess, for instance, in no way implies as a rule that one is awarded money. Yet, to the extent that they are directly linked to superior performance at the required skills and tasks, they fall within the immediate boundaries of the competitive events in questions.

On the third step of the ladder, we find prizes that we may say are still within the "natural" boundaries of the competition itself. Winning can often give one *access* to money (by way of sponsorship, paid speeches, book writing contracts, and much more), fame (through a larger audience, media interviews, and so on), professional and personal connections, and even opportunities for romance and love. Though not necessarily guaranteed (the winner must know how to take advantage of these prizes) nor explicitly discussed by the organizers of the competition, these prizes are in effect at stake during the competition and result quite naturally (insofar as they reflect the appreciation of a large number of people for the feat that has been achieved) from the outcome of that competition. These are often very valuable prizes and, as such, explain much of the joy that winners feel when clinching their victory. Thus victory in high-profile political elections or for high-ranking nominated government positions—such as the race for president of the United States, or the position of secretary of state or Supreme Court justice—almost guarantees individuals lucrative contracts later in life for speeches at a variety of outlets (clubs, universities, etc.), books, attractive jobs (at think tanks, for instance), and more. Days after stepping down from his position as Federal Reserve chairman in 2006, for instance, Alan Greenspan received $200,000 for a speech at Lehman Brothers and, earlier that same day, $100,000 for a consultation with Japanese investors (*Economist* 2006)—altogether significantly more than his yearly salary at as Fed chair. Similarly, winning coveted prizes in sports makes it much easier for athletes to attract valuable endorsements, or become television commentators or coaches after retirement. These are indeed very important components of the competitive event.

Prizes found in the preceding three "steps" of the ladder can all be said to be "reasonable": those belonging to the first two types are an intrinsic component of the competitive events themselves (and, as such, generally all that is at stake in the minds of young children as they compete), while those belonging to the third type often reflect the large number of people who find the events worth following. Competitors value those prizes, especially as we move from step one to step three. Matters are different as we move up the ladder. On the last two steps we find prizes that seem to have been *injected* into the competitive event. These are brought into the competition from the outside in rather artificial fashion: there is no obvious reason why they should be at stake. Yet, they are constructed, built, and thrown into the competition with much force and impetus. Often, they are not even the products of the competitor or the members of the audience at any given point in time but, instead, the inheritance of ancestors and times gone by. As Geertz puts it when discussing symbols and culture more generally, "from the point of view of any particular individual, [they] are largely given. He finds them already current in the community he is born in, and they remain, with some additions, subtractions, and partial alterations he may or may not have had a hand in, in circulation after he dies" (Geertz 1973: 45). Their importance, oddly enough given their status as things from the outside, is great: it is for these prizes that competitors suffer the most, work the hardest, and feel the most responsibility.

What, then, are these prizes? Here, we are entering the world of ideas, images, and notions. More generally, we are stepping into the world of meanings that are attributed to victory or loss. We believe, with much anxiety, that a competition's outcome tells us quite a lot about ourselves. In one word, we may say that it tells us something about our *worthiness*, not only when it comes to the competitive realm in question but, crucially and more generally, about us as *persons* in general. Was not our discussion earlier in this book about differentiation, "being right," and mental space in a sense all about worth? That discussion can be expanded to include the following "prizes":

- significance: Are we relevant and unique persons deserving to be in this world?

- superiority: How do we stand relative to others (siblings, neighbors, foreigners, etc.)? Are we better human beings?

- beauty: Are we attractive people, both physically and psychologically, that merit admiration from others?

- legitimacy: Do we deserve to exist and live in our community and the world? Is there a reason for our existence?

- honor and prestige: Are we fair, courageous people with noble qualities?

- destiny: Is there a grander design for us, charted perhaps by a divine or superior being or our lineage, ancestors, fate, the universe?

- our relationship to some divine being: Are we on God's good side?

- freedom: Are we in control of ourselves and the world around us?

Thus winning a prize for best employee of the year, for instance, gives us an overall sense of significance and legitimacy. We feel good about ourselves not only as workers but as human beings: fulfilling one's duty is an admirable thing to do, a sign that we are indeed good citizens of our community. The prize confirms to us our standing in society: that we are giving, caring, and dedicated people—people with a conscience, people who know how to put the collective good before their self-interest. When recognized with the prestigious Federal Employee of the Year award for 2006 by the Partnership for Public Service, for instance, colleagues and observers alike described Nancy Cox—who is chief of the Influenza Division at the Centers for Disease Control and Prevention (CDC)—not as a self-centered doctor eager to advance her career but as a warrior eager to fight for the public interest. "Nancy Cox represents the best of what CDC is about," stated CDC director Julie Gerberding, "world-class scientists serving on the front lines each and every day to protect America's health." In keeping with her image, Dr. Cox herself duly accepted the award by distancing herself from her achievements and instead emphasizing that it should be seen as "a reflection of the excellent work done by many, many people who've worked on influenza at CDC—both in the present and past—and have helped build our influenza program into what it is today" (*CDC News* 2006). Employees of the year, Dr. Cox's example reminds us, are not opportunistic—they do not take advantage of situations or of those around them but instead serve as role models for the community at large.

Some of the most important prizes have to do with God. According to the General Social Survey, more than 75 percent of Americans believe that God plays a role in shaping one's success or failure in life.[1] With victory, thus, comes the belief that God was instrumental in shaping our performance and, by reflection though seldom acknowledged, in punishing our opponent with defeat. We then reason that God's favorable treatment of us must have a reason. We consciously or subconsciously assume that God must be rewarding us for something that we are doing right, not in the particular realm in question (politics, a sport, etc.), of course, but in life and as people in general. We must somehow be worthy of God's grace. We must be living a virtuous life that is in line with God's desires. We have won because God sees in us that we are good Christians or Muslims, good fathers and husbands, honest and hard-working people (indeed, we must not only be doing well on those fronts, but also better than our competitor). The doctrine of Manifest Destiny, which did so much to shape the early history of the United States, was rich with these sorts of ideas. Many of our present-day politicians hold on to the belief that the people of the United States as a whole succeed—indeed, are bound to succeed—in their endeavors because God is on their side. Individuals in turn believe the same for themselves. Hence when New York Yankees' Aaron Small was called in 2005 from the minors to bat for the most famous baseball team ever and performed outstandingly, his thoughts immediately turned to the skies: "I just felt a little weak in the legs, I guess you could say. I'm just so thankful for it. I appreciate the Yankees giving me this opportunity, and I thank God for the opportunity. He's blessing me" (Rhoden 2005). Of course, God's blessing of Small must have come at someone's cost—someone, this line of logic would suggest, who obviously did not enjoy the same good standing with God as Small himself though, curiously and importantly, losers are probably less likely to see loss as a sign of God's negative judgment on them and to openly give interpretations of outcomes by making reference to God.[2]

Gratitude to God is another sign of one's moral rectitude in life. Accordingly, those who believe that positive competitive outcomes reveal something about one's relationship to God go to great lengths to express loudly and clearly their awareness of God's power and benevolence. Behaving otherwise would be inconsistent and potentially damaging to them. People therefore thank God effusively and not only for single events but entire careers. "I thank God," Jerry Bailey—perhaps the best jockey in U.S. history—said recently when announcing his retirement in 2006, "for not only the talent he has blessed me with but for also keeping me in relatively good health" (Drape 2006). Competitive events reveal to us how we are faring in the eyes of God—not as players, of course, but as people. When the outcome is positive, we are careful to acknowledge God as we contemplate not our destiny on this earth but beyond.[3] And as we do so, others approve: according to the General Social Survey, most Americans approve, for instance, of pro athletes thanking God during sports events.[4]

In yet other cases, the prize at stake is a sense of "belonging" to one's community—not the community of competitors but of neighborhoods, towns, or even American society in general—despite what others may believe. At stake, then, is one's place in society and, in this sense, victory speaks most clearly to marginalized or otherwise disadvantaged members of our communities. We often

observe that immigrants rely on their successes in business, politics, education, and other competitive areas of social life to demonstrate to themselves and others that they, too, have those key
traits (such as determination, courage, respect of the law, or mental and physical abilities) that are associated with the "American
spirit." The impressive school performance of children of Asian
immigrants is accordingly often praised in mainstream media both
for what it is—success at math, for instance—but also as a way of
gaining acceptance (or even becoming leaders) in American society. It is then compared to the performance of children of other
minorities to show how those minorities lack one of the right pre-
requisites to be American—they are, in a word, not legitimate.
Legal victories in court for physically handicapped persons have,
in turn, been hailed by many as major steps forward not only in
the specific realm of law in question but, more generally, in the
overall effort to establish that physically handicapped people are
legitimate and normal members of our society.

Perhaps the most common, high-stake prizes, however, have to
do with honor. The dynamics here are twofold. On the one hand,
by virtue of having poured so much into preparing for the competition, competitors feel that they are putting their entire selves at
risk. At stake are their will and determination, their concentrated
minds and precious time. Winning becomes a matter of principle:
having set for themselves the goal of succeeding, the competitors
want to settle for nothing less. Are they able to fulfill their promises to themselves, to deliver to themselves the promised satisfaction and goods? If not, they will have to face themselves in the
mirror and explain to themselves how they could not live up to
their expectations. The reverse of honor is probably shame, and
losers are certain to feel some extent of that. In some respect, nothing could therefore be dearer—for at stake is ultimately one's relationship to herself. These dynamics are especially at work in cases
where the preparation for the competitive events takes much time
and effort: applying to college after four years of study and extra-
curricular activities (this applies to the students but also at times to
parents, who often feel that they too have heavily invested in the

preparation phases, as is often the case when their children attend private high schools), running for high-profile political elections, competing in sporting events such as marathons, and more. But they are also at work in other types of situations (the overweight person who is determined to lose weight but fails to stick to his dietary regimen).

On the other hand, competition as a *public* event brings honor to the winner and, depending on the circumstances, honor (if the contender fought well and those witnessing it recognize and focus on this) or dishonor to the loser. Competitors are after all performing in front of people and, as such, are interested in demonstrating something to them, winning their hearts, and gaining a place in their memory. "History," wrote recently Harvard Business School competition guru Rosabeth Moss Kanter without the slightest hesitation, "is written by the victors—and not just because losers often disappear into oblivion" (Kanter 2004: 88). This understanding of competition is not new for us but, rather, has been part of our civilization for thousands of years. Indeed, honor was almost all that was at stake in the great physical fights and athletic competitions recounted in Homer's tales of Greek heroes. In the *Iliad,* for instance, Hektor responds with compassion, but negatively, to his wife's plea not to go and fight for Troy against the attacking enemy ("Father and mother—I have none but you, nor brother, Hektor; lover none but you! Be merciful! Stay here upon the tower! Do not bereave your child and widow me!") by stressing that he could not do otherwise: "Lady, these many things beset my mind no less than yours. But I should die of shame before our Trojan men and noble-women if like a coward I avoided battle . . . long ago I learned how to be brave, how to go forward always and to contend for honor. Father's and mine" (Homer 1974: 155). Hektor *had* to compete for his honor, that of his father and, as he makes clear a few passages later, that of his son. And, similarly, public honor was all that was at stake in the exciting and moving races held for the funeral of Patrokos described at the end of the *Iliad* in which Odysseus— by now older than many of the warriors around him—finds himself competing. With the help of Athena, Odysseus sprints to victory before a cheering crowd. And as Antilokhos observes, after graciously accepting his defeat, "Every man here knows, but anyway I'll say it, friends: the immortals honor the older men as much as ever" (Homer 1974: 560).

We could go on. The main point should however be clear at this point: in the words of Huizinga again, "The object for which we play and compete is first and foremost victory, but victory is associated with all the various ways in which it can be enjoyed . . . [such as] honour, esteem, prestige" and all other prizes that make us feel special, significant, important—in a word, worthy of being in this world (Huizinga 1955: 52). What we should now emphasize is that this important, though quite artificial, attribution of meaning can happen at two different levels, as the prize ladder indicates. First, it can occur at the level of the *competitor:* the prizes, with their powerful implications, reveal something about the competitor or competitors, as our examples of the employee of the year and the athlete thanking God suggest. As members of the audience, we learn much about those competitors; the competitors themselves, in turn, enter the competition eager to discover and prove something to themselves.

But, quite often, the outcome can also say something about a larger group of people, a *collectivity*, who is in fact *not* competing in the event. Our preceding discussion of minorities provided us with an example. The collectivity can be an entire family, a town, a state, a political party, the nation, an entire race, and so on. What happens here is that the competitor or competitors are seen as a representative of that larger community. In the case of presidential elections, the collectivity is the millions of people who support the given candidate. In the case of international sports competitions or military conflict, the collectivity is the country as a whole. These collective types of prizes belong to the last step of the ladder: this is less because of their incredible significance for large groups of peoples and more because they are ultimately the most "artificial," or constructed, prizes of them all. Simply put, they are the most removed from the competitive event itself and require, for their existence and significance, significant mental attributions, connections, and projections. How else can the performance of one or a few people become a gauge for the overall worthiness of great numbers of people who have, in the last analysis, objectively speaking very little to do with the competitors themselves? The injection of meaning in these instances is the most aggressive and, logically speaking, unnecessary. It is, therefore, often the most perplexing. [5]

There are many telling illustrations of this remarkable and rather widespread tendency to view the performance of competitors as something specifically indicative of the overall worthiness of a larger community. At the national level, according to the General Social Survey, more than 75 percent of Americans feel proud to be American when their country does well in international sports.[6] President Obama's victory in the presidential elections of 2008 was seen, at once, as a triumph for all African Americans in the country, minorities of all sorts, Americans in general, and even foreigners who disliked the Bush administration. Or consider the case of golf champion Tiger Woods, in whose case the collectivity is Thai and African, but especially multiracial, Americans who feel that Woods's incredible success has helped establish those races as legitimate contenders in a sport traditionally monopolized by whites but also as legitimate participants in the American dream more generally (though his recent marital troubles have probably weakened the impact of his achievements). "I am Cablinasian," Woods has said on a few occasions, thus crafting a new term for being a mixture of Caucasian, black, Native American, and Asian. As the *New York Times*'s Larry Dorman put it when Woods became the youngest person to win the golf Masters at the Augusta National Golf Club, the event, though athletic in nature, carried enormous "social significance" (Dorman 1997).

Psychologists and sociologists have in turn shown how marginalized migrant communities rely on the successes of their children at sports or academics to feel that they finally belong to American society. In one such study, researchers showed the importance of persistent victory at field hockey—a sport traditionally associated with white suburban America—by the girls' team at a Southern

Californian high school. With a population of more than 50 percent Hispanic and only 30 percent Anglo, a good portion of the town's residents were poor, recent immigrants from Latin America, or second-generation Latinos. Thanks to a very capable coach and the continued support of parents and friends, the team won ten straight league championships and two California Interscholastic Federation (representing all of Southern California with the exception of Los Angeles and San Diego) championships. Some of the players were even considered for national and Olympic teams. How were these victories interpreted by the community at large? Parents, friends, local politicians, journalists, the players themselves, and citizens of the town saw in those achievements evidence of Latino, female, and working-class competence not solely in field hockey but life in general. Thus parents, at first suspicious of the sport, came to see "hockey as an activity of effort and physical sacrifice" (Heeren and Requa 2001: 422). Fathers proved willing to miss work to attend important games. And the local paper, in turn, wrote article after article on the team's accomplishments.

These reflections bring us to our next point. We must ask why this artificial injection of meaning, which is of great consequence for members of our society, occurs in the first place. Why do we infuse our competitive events with so much meaning—making them so important and consequential for those directly involved but also for those who, watching from the sidelines, feel as if their sense of worth is also on the line? The next section proposes some explanations.

Explaining the "Injection" of Meaning

Once on a visit to England, the shah of Persia reportedly turned down the invitation to attend a horse race because, he said, he knew quite well that one horse would run faster than the others (Huizinga 1955: 49). Competition is interesting not because of what is objectively and practically happening but because of the meanings we give to it. The shah simply "refused to take part in a play-sphere that was alien to him" (Huizinga 1955: 49): he found the event uninteresting, in other words, because he did not have the reference points that made it significant. We must wonder why the injection of meaning takes place in the first place. As with every complex social process, there are many reasons. But a few are critical and deserve our attention.

To begin, we must recognize that competitive events have been central to social life for thousands of years. "Contests in skill, strength and perseverance," noted Huizinga, have "always occupied an important place in every culture whether in connection with ritual or simply for fun and festivity" (Huizinga 1955: 195). The advent of modern mass media, financial interests, and the professionalization of sports and other forms of competition have all worked to push those events further into the spotlight. Recognizing the financial potential of competitive events, investors along with competitors and their partners (such as team owners, special interest groups, the media, and so on) have capitalized on technological advances to bring those events into the living rooms of millions of people. The best way of doing so has been to infuse into those events meanings that, objectively speaking, are not there. Thus we see that a simple football game between two Midwestern universities is advertised weeks in advance as a major showdown between two rival schools with great legacies, or that Apple founder and CEO Steve Jobs is introducing a new and exciting technological product not as strictly that—a remarkable advance in the field—but as a way of taking revenge against his archrival Bill Gates. Once widespread, such practice of artificially infusing meanings into competition becomes widely accepted. Its positive results (for both those pushing it and the audience, who feels more intensely entertained) induce others to replicate it. The result is that little Michael playing for the local baseball team approaches the mound to pitch and, with his parents' help, feels an enormous weight on his shoulders. It could hardly be otherwise: Michael has watched countless times grown women and men fall to their knees in the throes of winning something and cry in utter despair when faced with defeat. He has heard countless times reporters, friends, and family members raise winners to the status of semi-gods and dismiss losers as headed for irrelevance. It is now his turn to show the world what he is about.

There is then a darker possibility. In his *Civilization and Its Discontents*, Freud claimed that our society is built on the repression of powerful, dangerous instincts, such as the desire to kill or destroy. Civilization," he wrote, "obtains mastery over the individual's dangerous desire for aggression by weakening and disarming it" (Freud 1989: 84). Yet those instincts cannot be eliminated. Instead, they can be repressed and then expressed in harmless—and quite valuable and productive—ways in society. This process is called "sublimation" and is fundamental to the creation of various societal institutions in the realm of culture, economics, politics, and beyond. Considerable current social scientific research confirms Freud's view of society as a place of "pacification" and self-restraint (Atkinson 2002: 48; Dunning 1999).

If this line of reasoning is accepted, we can easily see the function that the injection of meaning into competitive events can play: highly salient and charged (emotionally, psychologically, and so on) issues that would otherwise need to be addressed in a destructive fashion are addressed and settled in a harmless (and indeed quite entertaining) manner in highly controlled environments (Dunning 1999). Hence, for example, we do not try to find out whether we are superior to our neighbors by violently attacking them, or by burning down their houses before they burn ours; instead, we meet them in a soccer field with referees (or, better yet, we send our children there as our representatives) to see who is the better player. Alternatively, if we believe that we all have a destiny and wish to discover what ours might be, we do not hire mercenaries and start conquering land and people but, instead, set up a business, work hard, hire employees, and do our very best to succeed in the marketplace. A positive outcome will tell us that good things are in store for us, while a negative one will provoke us to pause and reflect.

In all of these cases, what we are doing is taking drives and instincts (along with their accompanying anxieties, questions, emotions, and so on) that would otherwise "naturally" find quite different forms of expression and addressing them in regulated, largely innocuous settings. The strategy works: in most cases, people feel their needs have been sufficiently met. The result is a perpetuation and reinforcement of this practice to the point where we automatically turn to competitive events for the purposes of learning more about ourselves.

There is a third possibility. Following Max Weber and his insights that meaning structures shape social life, Geertz stressed that "the imposition of meaning on life is the major end and primary condition of human existence" (Geertz 1973: 434). Human beings do not simply live through experiences; instead, they have to interpret and make sense of them. At a broader level, their lives must have an overall meaning: a direction or set of directions that justify waking up in the morning and living through the day. If we accept these premises, we quickly see that modern-day life poses significant challenges to people. Recall how, according to the General Social Survey, most Americans find their lives either "dull" or "unexciting,"[7] and how, according to the World Value Survey, compared to other nations we are especially concerned about the meaning and purpose of our lives.[8] Less than 50 percent of us, in turn, find our jobs "very satisfying": most of us are only moderately satisfied with them or are simply dissatisfied.[9] Weber himself had talked about the risk that modern society would become a place of "specialists without souls, hedonists without heart" (Weber 1978a: 171). This was certainly described at great length by Karl Marx, as he spoke of alienation from work, labor, the products of our work, and ultimately our fellow human beings and human nature more broadly (Marx 1978). Much current social scientific research confirms those predictions (Dunning 1999).

With this in mind, we can see that competitive events have impressive potential for the production and consumption of meaning. As such, we readily take advantage of this opportunity to infuse those events with far more meaning than they otherwise would have. In other words, we—members of the audience and competitors alike—rely on those events to make our lives meaningful. Recent research suggests that, in turn, this exercise seems to be working quite well. In the case of audience members for instance, psychologist Daniel Wann showed that there is a strong, positive link between identifying with a sports team (in the language of this chapter, assigning meaning to the team by way of making it an extension of ourselves) and general psychological well-being. To account for this, he highlights the fact "that many traditional connections to society (e.g., religion and extended family) appear to be declining . . . identification with sports teams may serve to replace the traditional but declining social ties as members of society attempt to reestablish and maintain their social connectedness" (Wann 2006: 88–89).

But these reflections prompt us to ask what makes competitive events such excellent spaces for the production and consumption of meaning. In the first place, as already pointed out in this book, competitive events are marked by uncertainty or unpredictability. We do not know the outcome ahead of time. This contrasts sharply with many other aspects of our lives. More is therefore at stake, in a sense: those events can serve as "tests" for things we otherwise would never find out. Yet, a second factor is quite important: by and large, most competitive events are also perfectly safe. No lives are in danger and competitors on the whole stand to lose very little (i.e., they tend not to be much worse off if they lose compared to when they started) if things do not go their way. This makes it easier for us to inflate those events with additional layers of meaning. We "play" with meanings, in other words, because we can afford to do so. This applies to the competitors and also the members of the audience, who are indeed in the position to safely attribute extraordinary meaning to competitive events without any real and practical implications on their lives.[10]

Reality is complex, of course: these alternative explanations for the injection of meaning need not be mutually exclusive. It is likely that a combination of factors accounts for our propensity to load competitive events with prizes that do not intrinsically belong to those events. Competitive events may have had a privileged position in the history of our society precisely because they are at once places to release in a safe and regulated manner drives and instincts that are otherwise repressed in civilized communities *and* because,

155

as our society becomes ever more automated and mechanical, we increasingly see those events as ideal forums for the production of meaning (especially if these meanings are somehow related to darker and subconscious forces within us). Whatever the specific combination of factors might be, however, we see that in most cases competitive events *become* charged with highly valued prizes for reasons that transcend the intrinsic nature of those events themselves: we may say that those events accidentally become highly significant.

Our Strange Logic

We inject meaning into competitive events. The most coveted prizes are those that do not belong naturally to competitive events. Oddly, we care the most for those things that we make up. We believe that they tell us something about our worth. We think that they reveal much about those around us, even if these had nothing to do with the event at hand. Somehow, a victory by Tiger Wood becomes a victory by thousands and even millions of people of African and Asian descent. A promotion at the workplace becomes a sign that God loves me. My daughter's acceptance into Princeton signifies that she is "meant" for great things. We saw, as well, that we ascribe such deep and wide-reaching meaning to victory and loss almost automatically: we are not really aware of it. We are happy to jump levels of abstraction without a moment's hesitation. We arrive at profoundly consequential, but highly illogical, conclusions fully convinced that this is how things are. Indeed, others confirm it for us.

We observe, then, a mix of great intensity (when it comes to our emotions, how much we care, etc.) and simplemindedness (when it comes to how little we wonder, how much we simply accept). It is a peculiar state of mind—one that deserves attention and study. It is also a state of mind that raises some uncomfortable questions. Are we truly satisfied when we "win" the highest prizes or do we still feel a sense of doubt—a continued thirst for more confirmation, perhaps even a certain void or emptiness? Does victory provide us with the answers we so desperately want? If we go ahead, on the other hand, and remove the most important prizes from competition and do not let the outcome of competitive events define our worth as people and human beings, where else should we seek information and data about ourselves? If less is at stake in competitive events, what else will keep us amused and energized during our weekends and evenings when we watch television or go out for the night? Our relationship to competitive events would also need redefining: why should we engage in them and what should we take away from the outcomes? What, in sum, should we do to be truly satisfied human beings? We continue with our exploration of competition and the mind in the next chapter.

Chapter Nine

AWARENESS AND COMPETITION

It was wonderful to finally hear my name.
—Debra Messing, on winning the Emmy
Award for her role in *Will & Grace*

ANIMALS SEEM TO COMPETE. But, as is the case for everything else
that they do, they are not truly aware—in the way humans are—
of what they are doing. The lion chases the zebra on a pasture.
Whether it succeeds or not, neither the lion nor the zebra reflects
on what has happened. For them, there has been no competition.
After the chase, the lion is either without its prey or eating it, while
the zebra is either still standing and going about its day or feeling
pain as the lion kills it. That is all. Nothing more is added to the
experience. Neither animal is thinking about what it could have
done differently, whether it tried hard enough, whether it is a loser
or a winner, or even what it has gained or lost. Animals do not
make objects of their experiences.

We, humans, work quite differently. As we just learned in the
previous chapter, though in a very different context, our minds
matter. We distance ourselves from our experiences and, after
doing so, find ourselves in a position to analyze them. Of course,
we differ from each other on how we do so. In some cultures,
people see eating as a profoundly social, refined, and pleasurable

event. In other cultures, by contrast, it is thought of primarily almost as a chore, almost as something that must happen simply in order to satisfy a bodily need. These differences are important. But they merely confirm, rather than undermine, the point that human beings everywhere have made themselves, their actions, and the world around them the object of reflection.

Americans hold very particular views about competition. We have discussed many of those views throughout this book. My argument in the following pages is that without a strong sense of *awareness* our competitive events *would neither exist nor be very significant*. We have created something called "competition," "competitors," "winners," "losers," "effort," "us" and "them," "honor" and "shame," and so on. We have endowed those terms with great significance. And we have then become greatly cognizant—that is, aware—of those terms. That awareness is a fundamental *prerequisite* for both the normal functioning of competitive events in our society and for the importance that they hold in our society. It also highlights the fact that we could approach competition in more than one way. I discuss these ideas in detail in the next pages.

One Step Removed: The Birth of Awareness

The *American Heritage Dictionary* defines "aware" as "having cognizance or knowledge" of something. That something can be outside (an apple) or inside of our physical bodies (my lungs). It might even be inside my head, as is the case for example of a particular fear I may have. Regardless of where it exists, one thing is clear: we approach the object of our awareness as if it existed separately from our thinking minds. There is our mind and then there is the object. We hold the object before our very eyes—either physically or virtually. We sense a distance between us and it.

In many, if not all, cases, we then assume that the object of our awareness exists more or less independently of us. When I notice that there is a cat in my backyard, I am simply becoming conscious of what I consider to be reality out there: the cat is there, and I am merely becoming aware of it. I do not wonder whether the cat might not be there—whether it is somehow the product of my brain. Nor do I wonder how my own modes of perception (sensitivity to certain light waves, sounds, smells, and so on) might shape what I am actually noticing: I take as fact that the cat exists in the way that I perceive it.

We may rephrase these observations as follows: in our everyday lives, we accept as real and matter of fact much of what we become aware of. As sociologists Peter Berger and Thomas Luckmann put it in their classical book on social life *The Social Construction of Reality*, "The world of everyday life is . . . taken for granted as reality by the ordinary members of society" (Berger and Luckmann 1967: 19). We simply go about assuming that this or that exists as we see it—that the cat is black and white, that I am now hungry, that I see that my sister is in a hurry to get somewhere, that the job of vice president at my firm is quite attractive, and so on. We do not question whether we play a role in shaping the very objects of our awareness. The truth, however, is that perhaps we should.

Physicists, philosophers, and sociologists alike have pointed out that the objects of our awareness are not there as we perceive them. Rather, they are products of our senses and cognition as they respond to stimuli. Berger and Luckmann stressed that reality is "a world that originates in their [people's] thoughts and actions, and is maintained as real by these" (Berger and Luckmann 1967: 20). Immanuel Kant's magisterial *Critique of Pure Reason* starts with the premise that, though "we believe ourselves to cognize things in themselves," any given "object remains unknown to us" (Kant 1998: 186–87). Countless other observers have made similar points. Thus when I notice that there is a cat in my room, I am aware of something that my mind has produced for me. We are not aware of the cat as it "really" is. This is not to deny the independent existence of the cat or anything else we become aware of: rather, it is to underscore the fact that there is a difference between what we perceive to exist and the objective nature of those things. Thus a dog would perceive the cat quite differently in terms of colors (and smell), and a bat would be aware of the cat without having an image of it. Quantum physicists have argued something similar when they have postulated that the act of measuring a quantum system affects what we come to know about that system (including where it is).

The same observation applies to our awareness of nonphysical things. When I am aware of my love for someone, I sense the existence of that love. But can we really say that such love exists independently of me, of my thinking mind? The truth is that the mere recognition of that love is an important step toward its making. It would be quite difficult to imagine what our love for someone would be like if we deprived ourselves of our awareness that we love that person. Now think of Christmas. Can we say that Christmas exists independently of our awareness of it? Put differently, if all of us this year forgot what Christmas is, would there be Christmas on the Twenty-fifth of December? The answer is no. Our awareness of Christmas—of Santa Claus, of the Christmas tree, of the sharing of gifts, and so on—makes Christmas into Christmas. Similarly, think of our calendar and the division of time into years, days, and hours. If none of us were aware that today is May 4, 2008, today would not be May 4, 2008.

If, then, much of what we are aware of depends on us for its existence, we should also recognize that different "things" "exist" in different societies. For instance, the feeling of guilt may be recognized in one society (and indeed be a central element of it) and not in another. In one society, people may celebrate winter solstice (i.e., they identify it and spend energy and time to embrace it) but not in another. Even ambition is sometimes present and sometimes absent (Greenfeld 2005b: 330). Examples abound, of course. We are not interested in explaining why these differences exist, but only in noticing that they are there. For such differences tell us something: that things need not be one way or another, and that alternatives are possible.

We are now ready to see something fundamental about our approach to competition: competition and all that goes with it (winners, losers, the competitive event, the rules, the glory, vindication, relief, the memories, etc.) would not exist without our awareness of them. We—competitors and audience members alike—*come to competitive events with a strong set of convictions that a number of things exist.* We do not subject those convictions to much scrutiny but instead take them for granted. Those convictions, in turn, make competitive events possible in the first place in two important respects.

First, they permit those competitive events to unfold, provided that others share our perspectives—that, in the words of Berger and Luckmann, our "natural attitude to the world corresponds to the natural attitude of others, that they [others] also comprehend the objectifications by which this world is ordered . . . that there is a correspondence between *my* meanings and *their* meanings in this world, and that we share a common sense about its reality" (Berger and Luckmann 1967: 23). Events simply could not take *place if we had not subjected their various components to objectification and then our awareness.* The scheduling of a track meet between two colleges' athletic departments depends on coaches, players, and staff embracing in the most taken-for-granted manner similar views about time and punctuality, the proper sequence of events, what behaviors are acceptable or not, the exclusivity of victory (it is impossible that both teams win the meet), and much more.

Second, our convictions make competitive events into tremendously important occurrences, feared indicators of our worth, and major sources of entertainment and meaning. This is true for both those who are currently involved or witnessing a given event and others who will hear about it in the future. When Debra Messing rejoiced about hearing her name during the Emmy Award ceremonies, what made her joy possible? It was her awareness of several things: that there was a huge audience also hearing her name, that the Emmy Award is a prestigious thing, that others will admire her for winning it, that other candidates for the prize did *not* win it, that she will now be known and referred to as "Emmy Award–winner Debra Messing." Much the same can be said of any other competitive event. The excitement that surrounds any given event is purely awareness driven: if no one thought those games to be important, they would not be. *Awareness of significance is a precondition* for that significance.

We would benefit a great deal, therefore, from knowing how, exactly, our awareness contributes to the making of competitive events. What do we take for granted about competition? How does this contribute to the making and importance of competitive events in our society? What would alternative constructions of competition look like? I answer these questions in the following pages. Before I proceed, however, let me remind the reader once again that I do not intend to speak on behalf of each and every one in American society. The object of analysis in the coming pages is a dominant set of convictions that, in one version or another, find their home in many of our minds.

The Making of Competition

We approach competitive events aware that certain things exist. In the words of Gordon Fellman, we approach competition with a particular mental "paradigm" (Fellman 1998: 5). Most of us do not question things. We simply assume them to be real, matter-of-fact aspects of the event. As just discussed, our assumptions make the event both possible and highly significant. What are we aware of, then?

Ourselves, Our Opponents, and the Audience

We can begin by talking about the actors in question. We approach competitive events with three sorts of actors in mind: ourselves, our opponents, and the audience.[1] What are our beliefs about each of them? What are we aware of? When it comes to ourselves, we are profoundly conscious of *boundaries* and *separateness*. We believe we "enter" a competitive event much like we walk into a store and come out. We temporarily submerge ourselves in them to get what we want. We are hence different from the event itself: the competition may affect us but in no way does it become a part of us. We may become quite intimate with our opponents—sensing their sweat, their mental and physical exertion, their effort and frustrations. But we do not connect with them in any real sense. Indeed, we often avoid direct glances or acknowledgments of their existence. Hence, when it comes to our opponents, we are aware of them primarily as *obstacles* on our road to victory, much like a fallen tree in our path as we climb a mountain.

Thus, related to that, we perceive ourselves to be on a mission. The best coaches tell us that we should not respond to provocations: this would divert our minds and energies. In the words of Phil Jackson, coach of the Chicago Bulls when Michael Jordan was on the team, and of the Los Angeles Lakers with Kobe Bryant on the squad, "anger interferes with concentration and ultimately backfires" (Jackson 1995: 132). We must stay focused on the task at hand: "*Awareness is everything,*" Jackson writes (1995: 119). We see ourselves as agents for ourselves: deployed to obtain something that we do not have. It follows that we conceive of ourselves as "politicians," "businessmen," "soldiers," or "musicians"—that is to say not full human beings but leaner and more pointed agents. When I envision myself at a chess competition tomorrow, I do not think of my interest in music or passion for wine. I instead see myself as the chess player that I will be. Being a chess player implies not being asleep or at the wheel of a car. Put differently, as I enter competition, I create an image of myself in action: I separate myself from myself or, rather, create a duplicate of myself that is finely tuned for its mission. After the competition, I will then evaluate my performance: how well the "I" that was on the field performed—and my sense of self-worth, as studies have shown, will depend to a good extent on the image of myself that emerges.[2] It is indeed with this knowledge of a future performance that we enter into a competition.

All of this means that our approach to the competitive event is above all *instrumental*: we see and then use competition as a tool to advance our causes and, in the process, never assume ourselves to become so intimate with it that we turn into an inherent part of it. Our opponents do the same, and the event unfolds itself on those grounds: as a temporary place of conflict among parties whose interests clash head on. It is in this context that our awareness of the audience comes into place. What is the audience for us as competitors if not a third party that is eager to see how this antagonistic event turns out, to witness who will prevail and use the event for their own advancement?

We conceive of the audience in the same way in which gladiators in ancient Rome must have thought of their audience: present to see who among the fighters is left standing, to witness the scathing of one competitor and the triumph of the other. The audience may include our parents, the media, our friends, our spouses, even our children. We compete with the knowledge that they will reflect on our performance as we understand it.[3] Thus, in the words of Huizinga, the winner "is doubly delighted when somebody is watching him. In all games it is very important that the player should be able to boast of his success to others" (Huizinga 1955: 50). This explains Debra Messing's disarmingly direct and simple statement about the joy she felt on hearing her name. Had there been no audience, she would not have felt such joy. The joy, in turn, comes from knowing that the audience *understands* the award to be a recognition of distinction, of separateness.

But matters could be otherwise. We could, for instance, conceive of the opponents before us or the competitive event itself (its rules, say) as being somehow connected with us. Georg Simmel argued as much in his classic piece on conflict in society—in courts, sports, business, and beyond. Conflicts are made possible, he wrote, by much sharing. Lawyers arguing before a judge are at once opponents and partners: one could not exist without the other, all subscribe to the rules of the game, one's success is predicated on the other's loss. Conflict, moreover, makes the relationship possible— it is that which brings together the competitors. Thus competition creates some sort of *unity* out of otherwise unrelated individuals (Simmel 1971: chapter 6). Adopting such a perspective would dramatically change how we spend our time and energies, the sorts of emotions we feel, and what we would get out of competing. If this seems like an impossible stance to take, we should recognize that it already happens at times in our society and that many of us would welcome it when we see it.

Consider, for instance, how presidential candidates Hillary Clinton and Barack Obama decided to behave after an escalation of tensions and accusations over race and gender in January 2008 during their efforts to win the Democratic Party's nomination. They chose to emphasize what brought them together, their shared values and aspirations, their common visions for the future of the country—ultimately, how similar reasons have driven them to compete against each other. We may doubt the sincerity of their new language and consider the new tone part of an agreed-on (at least implicitly) strategy to keep Democratic Party members happy, but we must nonetheless recognize that the audience—the voters themselves—were obviously eager to see both sides acknowledge what unites them. Thus Clinton released a statement calling for "common ground" and then stated that "when it comes to our heroes—President John F. Kennedy and Dr. King—Senator Obama and I are on the same side. We all believe in civil rights. We all believe in equal rights" (Helman 2008). She then added: "We may differ on minor matters, but when it comes to what is really important—we are family." For his part, Obama called the recent spat "unfortunate" and recognized that both Hillary and Bill Clinton "have historically and consistently been on the right side of civil rights issues" (Saul and Kennedy 2008).

We will reflect more on alternative approaches to competition in the final chapter of this book. For the moment let us emphasize the fact that our current approach shapes how competitive events unfold *and* what we get out of them. On the latter in particular, it is worth emphasizing that our typical awareness of competition—how we conceive of competition—leads us to taking rather than giving (if we are successful), to losing rather than taking (if we fail), to see that at stake is our will against that of others, to view our success as causing the dismissal of our opponents. Some of these are causes of pleasure, but of a particular kind: a self-centered, atomistic (me, alone) pleasure that may satisfy us but perhaps not fully—for any detachment from the group is bound to please us and also make us feel isolated or lonely. When we win we disconnect ourselves from others, place ourselves higher—as our previous discussion on space in chapter 4 made clear.

The Pursuit

We enter competitive events with the clear awareness that we are in pursuit of something. We wish to have something we currently do not have. This state of mind is, therefore, one of acknowledged *deficiency*: we are short of something and, in the present moment, our life is less than complete or perfect. Candidates for political office speak openly about their desire to be in power. College applicants dream of a better future ahead of them. Job applicants wish to improve their lot. Of course, the pursuit of something costs time, energy, and often money. This suggests that the perceived deficiency—the gap between what one has before and what one wishes to have after the competition—is often substantial.

Such sense of deficiency explains much of the determination competitors often have and provides the raison d'être for the competitive events themselves. The fight would be a lot less intense for everyone involved if both competitors were happy with their situation going into the competition. But in most cases the competitors believe in the urgency of an improvement. Sometimes such urgency may be entirely justified. An unemployed single parent with two children to feed has reasons to want to beat other applicants for a job. On many occasions, however, that urgency is practically fabricated: the deficiency has to be created. We have all witnessed this when we hear of coaches of successful athletic teams assert that they are not "satisfied yet," that "more" remains to be achieved, and that a fire is accordingly still very much burning in everyone. Successful CEOs herald the end of one great fiscal year by reassuring shareholders and everyone else that much hard work lies ahead: the time for celebration is short, for much more remains to be achieved. Universities that are richly endowed complete their multiyear fundraising campaigns and new building constructions by announcing the start of new campaigns. All are asking that some deficiency be recognized, that there be awareness of that deficiency.

We see, then, how important our awareness of deficiency is for competitive events. At the same time, it is interesting to note that many of us recognize that the *pursuit of something*, regardless of outcomes, holds *meaning in and of itself*. This recognition, too, is very important for the making and significance of competitive events. To see this, let us read closely and reflect on this passage from an article in the *New York Times* describing the state of mind of some Red Sox fans after their team finally won the baseball World Series after eighty-six years of disappointing failures:

> [They] didn't take long to go from ecstatic to existential. . . . Having waited 86 years for a World Series championship, Bostonians found themselves on Thursday swirling with elation, but also scratching their heads. What are Red Sox fans to do when the angst of being one of the world's greatest underdogs is gone? "I'm having trouble dealing with it," said Mike Andrews, who played second base for the Red Sox in 1967, when they lost to the Cardinals during one of their many close-but-no-cigar face-offs. "You're just kind of caught saying, 'What's next?'" said Mr. Andrews, who now leads the Jimmy Fund, a cancer organization in Boston that is the team's principal charity. "I don't want to say it's a letdown. But it's certainly something you let become part of your life and it's gone now, and we need to come up with something new." (Belluck and Zezima 2004)

We see, then, that there is disappointment in no longer having the "angst" of being one of the greatest underdogs in the world. How can this be? Part of the answer is found in the passage itself: habit. We become accustomed to a particular situation and feel uneasy when it is over. But this cannot be all. Becoming accustomed to something means feeling comfortable with it, and this can only happen if there is something positive in the situation at hand. None of us grows accustomed to sitting in small, cramped economy-class airplane seats for several hours at a time. None of us feels comfortable about having a dentist drill holes in our teeth, no matter how many times this happens. There must be a pleasure, then, in being the underdog and, more generally, in fighting for change. What is that pleasure?

Pursuit involves imagination, hope, and the excitement that comes from anticipating success. Biologists and psychologists tell us that the brain produces sensations of pleasure well before the actual experience comes about. The brain is an "anticipation machine," something that is always busily "making future" (Gilbert 2006). Economists calculate in their utility equations for consumers (which describe the pleasure those consumers will feel from purchasing something) the positive sensations generated by planning for and looking forward to the purchase. It follows that, if we are generally to be dissatisfied with the status quo, any action that promises relief is bound to produce good feelings in us. This is how we come to value pursuit in and of itself and, in so doing, make it an important object of awareness and of competitive events in general. We celebrate competitive events, in other words, because they allow the opportunity to pursue something.

But the passage above about the Red Sox highlights something else of great importance. We hear the profoundly unnerving question of "what's next?" This simple but terrifying question can only be asked if one believes that the pursuit of any given thing has less to do with the actual thing at hand and more with having a sense of direction—whatever that might be. Put differently, what seems important is less the actual obtainment of what we are after and more the fact that we are after something—that we are in movement, that we are stretching ourselves, that we are not standing still. We are taught from very early on that aspiring for something is good in and of itself. The important thing is that we are going, not necessarily where, exactly, we are headed. We learned about this in chapter 7 when we reflected on the importance of "effort." But this apparently positive mind-set, this embrace of movement, has a negative side to it. It is a rejection of something. Of what, then?

I suggest that many of us in the United States are always in movement because *we have a profound fear of having nothing to do.* We reject a mentality of satisfaction, of completion. We embrace grand ambitions and great dreams. We must always have something to achieve. Consider, for instance, the fact that, when asked in the World Values Survey what they find important when it comes to their job, 84 percent of Americans mentioned the possibility of achieving something. In France, that figure was 50 percent, in Germany 54 percent, and in Great Britain 58 percent.[4] I was recently examining the Internet site of Swarthmore College, one of the finest liberal arts colleges in our nation. This is what one can find in the section "About Swarthmore"—presumably a section of the site designed to attract students and parents:

> Swarthmoreans are CEO patent-holders who bring technology to underserved markets, investment bankers looking for alternative forms of energy, lawyers who become college presidents, doctors who serve in Congress, winners of the Nobel Prize. A Swarthmorean founded the first liberal arts college in Ghana. Another led the team that developed the Hubble Space Telescope. Swarthmoreans invented hypertext and helped women win the right to vote.[5]

The message is clear: "Swarthmoreans" are achievers of breathtaking feats and not navel-gazers or contented individuals. If you join us, we promise that you will develop a burning desire to change the world. Do not worry, then: you will not sit idly. You will work hard and after you graduate you will have the resources to sprint toward a great future.

And let us now read the stunning biography of thirteen-year-old Evan O'Dorney, the 2007 National Spelling Bee Champion, which can be found on the organization's website along with those of the other fourteen "top finishers":

> Last summer Evan was chosen as an onstage contestant for *The 25th Annual Putnam County Spelling Bee,* but the judges

could not outsmart his spelling skills and resorted to making him spell out of order and giving him non-dictionary words. Evan is dedicated to Tae Kwon Do and has earned a first degree black belt. He loves to play piano: In addition to taking lessons at the San Francisco Conservatory of Music, he accompanies his church's children's choir. This year he began attending the Berkeley Math Circle and achieved success in various math competitions: He earned a perfect score in the American Mathematics Competition for 10th grade, the American Invitational Mathematics Examination, and the Bay Area Math Olympiad. He also placed fifth in the Northern California Mathcounts competition. His parents are Jennifer O'Dorney, his home school teacher, and Michael O'Dorney, a Bay Area Rapid Transit train operator.[6]

Little Evan is not alone. According to one important study of American families with children aged three to twelve, parents have mercilessly "overscheduled" their children—depriving them of "unstructured" free time and imposing on them instead "structured" and "goal-oriented" activities. Between 1981 and 1997, free time decreased by twelve hours per week, playtime decreased by three hours per week, and unstructured outdoor activities fell by 50 percent. In the same time period, structured sports time doubled and study time increased by nearly 50 percent (Hofferth and Sandberg 2001; Anderson and Doherty 2005: 6). These changes "have increasingly led to time-sensitive, hypercompetitive activities" (Anderson and Doherty 2005: 655).

Our fear of having nothing to do explains why we often fabricate our belief that we are somehow deficient, why we take pleasure in anticipating what the future might hold for us, why many of us always aim to be on the move. We must therefore wonder if there might be a completely different way to approach competition. Could we—would we—compete if we were fully content with the status quo? Could we be happy with loss if it came our way? Could we see competition as a way of getting something "extra" rather than something we desperately need? I suggest that the answer to all of these questions is "yes" but, at the same time, that our approach would have implications for how intensely we are willing to fight for something and for the impact that the outcome would have on us. We would probably, on the whole, be less driven: less willing to sacrifice everything, to give up all that we have, to push ourselves to extremes. We may thus be less likely to win. On the other hand, we would be on the whole happier—for our state of initial contentment would reduce the negative impact of a loss as well as the more unsettling implications of victory.

The Event

At a very basic level, competitive events could not unfold in normal fashion without our awareness of the basic rules for those events. Those events are highly regulated. Political campaigns have formal rules (on fundraising, on how to vote, on how to count votes, etc.) and informal ones (what is fair to say, that losers should concede and congratulate the winner, and so on). Sports have usually rather simple objectives (in football, for example, a team must strive to bring the ball into the opponent's end zone) and lots of rules to limit how one pursues them. In business, countless regulations specify how products and services should be produced, and internally how companies should treat their employees. It is important to understand that rules do not only constrain actors but also make competition possible—they give it its competitive character. If there were no rules to how lawyers argue their cases in court, there would be no court cases as such. If we see all this, then we can understand that our awareness of rules—formal and informal—is a fundamental prerequisite for competition to happen: without that awareness, there would be no competition as we know it. It follows that transgressors are punished: their breaking the rules amounts to an affront to the existence of competition itself.[7]

Yet, at the same time, competition is much more than the rules. It is also about intensity, pressure, our ability to stay focused, to appreciate that there is a beginning and end to any given contest, that falling behind in the early phases means something quite different than being behind at the end, and so on. All of these things make competition interesting. But their existence and impact is almost always predicated on our awareness of them. Consider for instance the difference between the beginning and final phases of a company's yearly performance. Company executives, investors, and employees talk rather differently about a loss (for instance their failure to win a new contract with a client) if it happens in the opening months of a new calendar or fiscal year as opposed to the closing ones. In the former, they see the company as being "off to a bad start"; in the latter, depending on what has happened in the previous several months, they may see it a continuation of a bad trend or a temporary setback. Isn't all of this made possible or given its significance by our (and everyone else's) awareness—of the calendar year, of the "importance" of starting a new year well, of whatever happened in the previous months? Similarly, "being behind" a runner during a race is only meaningful to the extent that we see it, that we understand that that can happen, that we see or know about the runner ahead of us. To be clear, I am not disputing the objective distance between the two runners, but only emphasizing that our perception of it is just that: a product of our awareness.

Our awareness of things may also be important for making possible another crucial aspect of competition: generating winners and losers. If a minimum level is required for things to take place as normal, a highly developed sense of awareness or, alternatively, an understanding of the sorts of things that we should be aware of at different points in the competition may sometimes be the key to victory (and, if not the key, a very important component of it). Is it not the job of advisers and coaches to increase or redirect competitors' awareness of what is happening around them, given that so much can change over time and that what ensures victory at one point may prove less useful later in time? And, if so, could we not say that competitive events are, to a good extent, battles of awareness?

On this point, it is interesting to learn about the research of two psychologists on the mind-set of revolutionary leaders. They discovered that the successful ones—those who gained power *and* managed to hold on to it—exhibit very different sorts of awareness over time. In the early phases, their minds focus almost exclusively on the goals before them and what needs to be done to succeed. This is a rather narrow but deep type of mind-set. Other issues— such as world events, the economy, alternative perspectives—are largely ignored. Once in power, however, the leaders' mental horizons broaden and they became aware of more around them. Now the state of the economy is important, for instance, as is what other political leaders elsewhere in the world are saying about their revolutionary successes. Now what representatives bring to the United Nations Security Council becomes noteworthy. Power brings new challenges and responsibilities. To stay in power requires an understanding of all of this. And it is this ability to move from one mode to another other that ensures the leaders' success. "Successful leaders were indeed those who exhibited a high degree of single-mindedness and complete dedication (i.e., conceptual simplicity) during the revolutionary struggle," wrote Suedfeld and Rank. "With a change to more complex functioning after grasping power . . . [there is] a necessity for different problem-solving characteristics to meet these changing demands" (Suedfeld and Rank 1976: 173).

Outcomes

We can start again with a simple observation: our competitive efforts are fully informed by the knowledge that there will be an outcome—that something will be decided. We enter a competitive event with the awareness (and thus assumption) that some sort of *resolution* to the question of "who is better" will occur. Our expectation is routinely confirmed by the absence of ties in most competitive situations in the United States. We solve potentially undecided situations by using overtimes (sports), rankings by experts (which is the "best college" or set of colleges in the country? Which college has the best football team?), voting (who deserves to be president?), dollar amounts and valuation (what are the top companies in the United States? Who is the richest person in the country?), number of viewers for a given show (what is the most popular sitcom in the United States for the 2007 season?), simple numbers (what was the best-selling book in the United States last year? What is ranked #1 on Amazon.com?), grade point averages (who is the valedictorian of our child's high school this year?), and more. Occasional ties are tolerated but also pointed to as evidence that a new measurement system is desirable.

Thus, related to this, we are aware of the exclusivity of prizes. Whatever is at stake will only belong to the winner. The loser will not be in a position to make any claims—as a recent book, *Winner-Take-All Society,* makes clear (Frank and Cook 1995). Only one person can win presidential or state gubernatorial elections. Indeed, competition is the process by which exclusive ownership is decided. Anyone who might think otherwise is bound to be sorely disappointed. It is this exclusivity—or more accurately stated, our awareness of it—that propels us to fight hard.

We are also motivated, however, by our awareness of many other things. How many times have we tried to win something? What will having won something do for us going forward? When golfer Phil Mickelson finally won his first major championship—the Masters Golf Tournament in Augusta, Georgia—after so many years of near misses, these were his words: "'Having come so close so many times, to have it be such a difficult journey to win my first major, makes it that much more special, sweeter. . . . The reason it's so special is that now I get to be a part of this great event for the rest of my life. I'll be back here every first week of April, and I will look forward to this tournament every year for the rest of my life" (Anderson 2004). The victory was made pleasant, then, by Mickelson's awareness of the past efforts, of future joys, of disbelief ("I cannot believe this is happening," Mickelson said putting on the green jacket of the winner), and of having earned the right to show up again and again.

Yet perhaps the most important is our awareness that others value those prizes greatly: if we did not know that others cared for them, *would we care ourselves?* Moments after winning, Mickelson grabbed his daughter Amanda and said, "Daddy won. Can you believe it?"[8] Winning is almost always a public event: victory is sweet because we know we are acquiring something that others—starting with the loser—would surely like to have. This attitude may seem rather infantile, but it is something that applies to just about every one of us. If victory merely entailed acquiring a prize without consideration for what others thought of that prize—as happens almost certainly with all animals—it would be a far less significant issue in our lives.

Indeed, the truth is subtler than that: the pleasure of victory stems from our awareness of others knowing that *we* are the ones who won that which they themselves want. It is not only a matter, then, of having something that we know others want. What is especially sweet is that we—in front of everyone—happen to be the ones to get it. Thus victory is ultimately about us: about how others see us and, above all, our awareness that others see us in a way that we find desirable. How else to interpret the words of Debra Messing, after winning her Emmy Award? "It was wonderful to finally hear my name," she confessed to reporters. "I can't imagine it being more sweet, I really can't. It's so amazing. I still can't believe it. I just can't."[9] The pleasure came from Messing's own awareness that others were hearing *her* name. We encounter this logic over and over again. Boxing heavyweight champion Lennox Lewis recently summed up his entire career with these startling words: "They [people] are going to remember me for what I achieved. That's what's most important to me" (Rafael 2004).

We are now in a familiar place. Once again, we discover that we long for the admiration of others. Why do we wish to be the object of others' admiration or outright envy? The answer is a familiar one as well: we are driven by a desire for distinction, for space, for knowing that we are right. With some reflection, most of us would probably find these rewards less appealing than they otherwise are. The problem is that in most cases we simply do not stop and recognize what is at work in our drives and motivation. We do not know what we are really after, or why we desire it. Our culture merely tells us—incessantly—that we must win. Without thinking, we follow our master's orders. And we stop only when we are finally convinced that we have made our point, until we feel that we have nothing left to prove, that we are missing nothing. Unfortunately for most of us, that moment never seems to come.

The Beauty of Awareness

A European social scientist once told me that, on his way to Europe from the United States, he caught a bit of the Super Bowl on television at a bar in the airport. He shared his confusion with me. He could not understand why Americans found the game so exciting: "I saw a bunch of huge men running for a few seconds and then falling on top of each other. Then they would get up and do it again. After a few times, commercials would come on for some minutes. Then the pileups would resume. Why is this exciting?" My answer had everything to do with awareness: what the players and us as audience were aware of (what was at stake, the history and reputation of the two teams, what the rules were, that companies spend millions of dollars for a thirty-second spot to launch their new advertising campaigns, that millions of Americans were watching the event, and much more) and, of course, what he was not aware of.

Awareness makes competition, then. We have explored this idea in detail in this chapter. In the process, however, we noted something of great importance: that "making" implies some degree of choice or freedom. This is the attractive aspect of awareness. We *could* think of competition rather differently. Our approach is highly instrumental, antagonistic, rather dependent on others, and quite eccentric. There is nothing inherently wrong with that. But it does have certain drawbacks. The biggest perhaps is that it goes against something that we, as human beings, also highly value: the desire to be part of a great whole. The fact of the matter is that competitive events bring us together. Others see us. We become part of each other's present and past. By playing together, we are making something. Victory earns us a space in other people's minds. We could make these things objects of our awareness, but we choose not to.

A second major drawback concerns the angst we carry within ourselves before, during, and after the competition. The angst is the result of the significance we attribute to those events—above all they say something fundamental about us and tantalize us with the possibility that victory will dramatically improve our otherwise less-than-perfect situation. We could however approach many competitive events as something utterly positive: the status quo is good, a loss will merely continue the status quo (and not make us worse off), and a victory will bring additional and unnecessary (but surely welcome) goods. We are taught not to think in this way. But a change in approach might do us a great deal of good. This is the subject of the next chapter.

PART 4

Conclusion

Chapter Ten

OUR RESTLESSNESS

It is important . . . to realize
one's true nature.
—Lao Tzu, *Tao Te Ching*

TOCQUEVILLE DETECTED a certain restlessness in the United States. Americans constantly appeared to aim for something better, different, and grander than their current state of affairs. He thought they were after perfection. Our analysis in the preceding pages zeroed in on one particular strand of this restlessness: our intense—and rather unique when compared to other countries—desire to win and avoid loss. Inspired by the insights of Simmel on how to investigate social things, we dug deeper into the structure of our competitive events to see what sorts of things are really at stake. Guided by Weber's idea that we ultimately construct, with our minds, the social world around us, we took apart our beliefs about winners, losers, and what surrounds them. Our findings offered us interesting insights into our love affair with competition. To be clear, as I stated in chapter 1, these are not insights that apply to *all* of us. Rather, they are observations about a dominant set of concepts in our society that mold our environment and therefore shape how many of us live.

What, then, did we learn? The primary lesson had to do with why so many of us care so much about winning and losing. Our liberal and self-assured use of those terms suggests that we simply love "winning" and hate "losing." But the truth is far more complex. Winning and losing are not endpoints but *gateways* to something of profound significance to us. In chapters 2, 3, and 4 we saw some of the most important things that are really at stake in our competitive events: differentiation from our closest peers, a license to claim that our worldviews are correct, and the acquisition of physical and mental space. If we put these "prizes" together we see that we are fighting for something of profound importance: *our proper place in the world.* We do not have or know that place. Through victory, we hope to find it. Loss sends us mercilessly back to the drawing board—unsure, once more, of who and what we are. Oddly, however, any conclusion we come to is really shaky. This is because we use very questionable logic when we interpret the content and outcomes of competitive events, as all of the previous chapters showed. And it is because we ultimately "inject" and make up what really matters in competitive events, as chapters 8 and 9 discussed.

Matters are further complicated by the fact that we are rather ignorant about what we are doing and why. Uninterested in any introspection, we prefer to devote ourselves fully to the task of winning and avoiding loss. For many of us, it is a simple matter of fact that, in our schools, workplaces, businesses, and everywhere else, there are winners and losers. We can either win or lose our war against fat, the peace in Iraq, recognition as best employee of the month, custody of our children, our lover's heart, and in the words of Newt Gingrich in his recent book, even "the future" (Gingrich 2005). That, as we saw in chapter 5, winning and losing can empower or limit us in dramatically different ways is of no concern to us. That we entertain, as we learned in chapter 6, multiple and sometimes contradictory beliefs about who is a winner or loser is of no relevance to us. That, as we saw in chapter 7, as convenience dictates we shift our focus from outcomes to the process of competing so as to rescue in rather hypocritical fashion some losers from their fate, does not worry us. We are intense, determined, ready to sacrifice ourselves and those around us—all in the dark.

Such a mind-set—combining great intensity with deceptive terms and ignorance—must clearly be questioned. We should take some time, then, to evaluate it: what does it give us, what does it cost us, and how could we do things differently? This will be a normative chapter. Assessments are often best done with comparisons in mind. I begin, therefore, by turning once again to Denmark. I proceed to depict the American case as the opposite of that. I continue with a discussion of its advantages and disadvantages. And I conclude by offering an outline of an alternative approach to competition—one that relies on mental clarity, self-discovery, and a mindful engagement with the world.

Winning and Losing in Denmark

At the very start of this book, we learned about Jante's Law. After reading its ten principles, one might wonder whether Danes compete at all. Competition, after all, serves to distinguish the competitors—precisely what Jante's Law warns against. It is therefore hard to imagine a Dane embracing or at least identifying in part with the law and still wanting to win. The suspicion is justified. Competition is not as ubiquitous in Denmark (or the Scandinavian countries more generally) as it is in the United States. And it does not hold nearly the same importance. "The "Danish way," observed recently two psychologists, "is not to rise above others" (Nelson and Shavitt 2002: 454). According to the World Values Survey, only 13 percent of Danes fully agree with the idea that "competition is good" for society: the figure is lower in only five other countries in the world.[1] In Denmark, competition is not embraced. Rather, it is kept at a distance, whether in the private sphere among family members and friends or in the public sphere (school, work, etc.).

Many social places are simply not organized in a competitive fashion. The public sector is enormous and market-oriented solutions for its problems have traditionally been shunned (Christiansen

1998). Shops that wish to stay open beyond the state-regulated maximum amount of hours have annual revenue caps (lest their aggressive stance deprive others of money). Wages and working hours for most professions are centrally regulated by labor and professional associations (Jørgensen 2005). Until 1998, the state explicitly followed a philosophy of "control" of the economy. Very few organizations motivate their workers with discretionary awards, prizes, or honors. In schools, the Ministry of Education informed me that students are not graded until eighth grade,[2] a practice that is part of an overall very relaxed educational assessment culture (Egelund 2005).

The current conservative government, in power since 2001 and led until recently by Prime Minister Anders Fogh Rasmussen, has tried to introduce reforms to increase competition in the economy, public services, and even education. This has resulted in part from participating in the European Union, which directly and indirectly pressures the member states and their culture in certain directions (Kurzer 2001), and in part a realization that things could be much more efficient. If there has been movement in the economic sphere and elsewhere, it has been in favor of competition (Campbell and Pedersen 2007), with the introduction of more deregulation, for instance, heavier reliance on the private sector, and support for entrepreneurship (*Economist* 2009). But any comparison with many other countries and the United States especially will dispel any notion that competition drives most aspects of life in Denmark. According to a recent report by the Organization for Economic Cooperation and Development, the country continues to have "significant anti-competitive restrictions" in several key sectors of the economy and the public sector (Jørgensen 2005: 5, 2). These include housing, retail, wholesale, professional and financial services, gas, construction, and even taxis. The state remains intimately involved in most industries—providing an array of services, funding, coordination, and much more. Plans to reduce the tax burden—which became the heaviest in the world in 2008 (overtaking Sweden for first place)—have been difficult to implement, since public expenditures remain extremely high.

Danes are at best lukewarm about competition. At the same time, they do compete. Sports are very popular. Danish businesses have transformed themselves radically to be able to compete in the global marketplace. Elections generate winners and losers. Entrepreneurs succeed and fail. Danes are fiercely proud of their country and support it strongly in every sort of international competition. For us, then, the question becomes how they conceive of competition. How do they talk about it? What function do they assign to it? What do parents and teachers tell their young children after a soccer match when one team is jumping for joy and the other is heartbroken from defeat? Three beliefs seem to be especially important. They concern participation, hierarchy, and order.

First, Danes are taught from an early age that the important thing is to participate. Note that it is not even to try hard. Rather, it is to take part, *to be part* of the event. Competition is an occasion to connect people with people. "We are a tribe," a former, high-ranking state official told me. "When we compete, we do it together. I know it sounds strange, but that is how we see it." A kindergarten teacher expressed a similar sentiment: "Competition is really about being together. We tell our children that it does not matter if they come in first or second." Tellingly, in a comprehensive cross-national evaluation of school systems across thirty-two countries carried out in 2000 by the Organization for Economic Cooperation and Development's Program for International Student Assessment, Danish children performed relatively poorly in science, mathematics, and reading. On the positive side, however, many students reported a strong "sense of belonging" that was unmatched by students in most other countries, including the United States (OECD 2000: 9; Egelund 2005: 210).

A comparative study of kindergartens in Denmark and the United States revealed, in turn, that Danish teachers emphasize learning in the context of free play and interactions with peers, while their American counterparts push their kids to learn reading, writing, and arithmetic on an individual basis. The result is that Danish children appear to have more advanced social skills while their counterparts are more likely to be egocentric and have difficulties participating in group activities (Broström 1998). Later in life, according to a 2009 recent report by the Ministry of Education, when the time comes to choose a profession, most students in higher education go for "welfare-oriented" careers—such as teachers and nurses—and not economics or law.[3] Now, of course, outcomes matter; if they did not the Danes would simply not hold competitive events. But the extent to which they matter is not very significant. Attention goes instead to other aspects of competition—above all, how competition brings people together in structured environments where they have the opportunity to interact with one another and belong to something bigger than themselves.

Second, though failure is not liked, victory is also looked on with suspicion. Winners are expected not to use their success to distance themselves from others. In Denmark, note three social scientists who have analyzed the country's culture, "you must not see yourself as outstanding: an outstanding person stands out above others, and such stand-outs may be outcasts" (Thomsen et al. 2007: 450). Indeed, winners are closely watched. "Danes," according to recent studies of Danish culture, "look down on conspicuous success and braggarts" (Nelson and Shavitt 2002: 440). As the kindergarten teacher mentioned above told me, "It is not good to stick out; you do not want to do it. You better not be boastful." Thus, while Americans report an unusual tendency to view themselves as unrealistically better than others (the term in psychology is "self-enhancement"), the Danes, according to a recent study of self-enhancement tendencies in both cultures, are by far more modest (Thomsen et al. 2007)—indeed, in a curious twist of logic, they are quite proud of their love for modesty.[4] Any *hierarchy* that may result from the competition must be rather flat. This applies to both winners and losers.

Victory does not license the winner to turn away from the group. Consider that in the central square of Copenhagen, one of the biggest advertisements is for Carlsberg beer—a trademark Danish product. It is a sign that states: "Carlsberg: Probably the Best Beer in Town." A very similar slogan appears also on the international website: "Carlsberg: Probably the Best Beer in the World."[5] The word *probably* would simply never be used in an American ad. Comparisons with lesser rivals should be made very carefully. We may say that victors are expected to celebrate their achievements as proof of their competencies not so much in relative terms ("I am better than the rest") but in absolute terms ("I am good"). Again, we observe as much in the education system where students who are tested with compulsory evaluation exams take computerized adaptive tests—which are designed to present students with easier or more difficult questions depending on the students' real-time performance. The result is that no two students are likely to have taken the exact same test and that direct comparisons are impossible to make (the data is, in any case, deemed private and is not publicly available) (Mortimore 2009: 53).

All this means that "others" are not rejected but, if anything, invited to come along and celebrate what a member of the group has achieved. Modesty toward others is thus highly prized: "Of course, you feel great when you win," a former entrepreneur and now public sector employee told me, "but you should never use it to feel superior to others, to put others down. We are together, that is what matters." It is therefore common to hear qualified experts in their fields—whether politics, business, medicine—preface their comments on television, on the radio, or in writing with a disqualifier: "Let me premise what I will say by stating that I do not know as much about this as so and so . . ."

But losers must also be kept close to the pack. One way of doing so is to quickly integrate them back into the very system where they failed. This is precisely what happens to people who lose their jobs (the state pours enormous resources into retraining them and finding new job opportunities), criminals (rehabilitation rather than punishment is the function of jail time), underperforming students, and others. An extremely generous welfare system ensures that practically no one is left behind. The poverty rate in Denmark in 2007 was around 4 percent—tied with the Czech Republic for lowest in the world (Cohn 2007: 16). The Danish government spends more than 4 percent of the country's GDP on labor market programs, the "most of any country in the Organization for Economic Cooperation and Development and more than twenty times what the United States spends on worker-training programs" (Cohn 2007: 14). Those who lose their work can expect payments of up to 90 percent of lost wages for years to come. And schools have extensive programs for children with learning disabilities (but virtually no initiatives for especially gifted children) (Thomsen et al. 2007: 450).

This is done, in part, with a perceived sense of generosity and decency: most Danes would simply not feel right about seeing another Dane struggle to make ends meet, or be homeless, or somehow experience great distress. But more selfish motivations also play a role. At stake, aside from having overall excellent public services, is the integrity of the group as a whole (Cohn 2007: 16). High levels of social distress would undermine the group, the "tribe" which a great number of Danes truly love. When asked if he minded paying such high taxes, the former entrepreneur replied: "Oh no, quite the opposite. I love it! I do not mind it at all. I know I put in more than I get back. Others benefit more than I do. But that is OK with me. It is a question of solidarity. We want everyone to be well. I could not stand it to see others suffer. We are a mono-culture, you see. You must have heard other Danes say that we all belong to the same tribe, no?" Like winners, losers thus also pose their own threats to the social order. For that reason, they are closely watched and taken care of. One simply cannot fall too far in Danish society.[6]

Third, competition should pose no challenge to the social order, to the status quo. "It is okay to compete, but the important thing is that whatever happens does not undermine our world as we know it. We do not want to rock the boat too much," an academic told me. If people enjoyed too much success, that would be seen as a threat to the system. The function of competition is not to produce a new order of things—whether in business, education, family life, or elsewhere. It is certainly a means to encourage people to push themselves to do better, but not for the purpose of changing the world. This is ultimately a very conservative understanding of what competition can and should do for society. And much of it makes sense when we consider the fact that the "system" is quite good: Denmark ranks high in all sorts human development and economic indicators (education, health care, homelessness rates, and so on), and most Danes in turn are very happy with the way things are. On the one hand, they are proud of their public services, for instance, along with their businesses, education system, daycare system, and much else. On the other hand, they are happy with their own, personal conditions.[7] According to the World Value Survey, 45 percent of Danes are indeed "very happy" with their lives (the number for the United States is 39 percent).[8] According to researchers at the University of Michigan who direct the survey, Danes in 2008 were the happiest people on earth (the United States came in sixteenth place).[9]

It is thus quite rare to hear Danes speak about their aspirations or apprehension about the future. Americans place much importance on goal setting and achievements (and consequently have great fear of failure). The same cannot be said of Danes: they are far less likely to emphasize future goals and the need to achieve them (Nelson and Shavitt 2002). Most Danes are quite comfortable with the present and simply hope it will continue. Many simply "wish for a family and a modest amount of money and success" (Nelson and Shavitt 2002: 454). As a university student told me: "What do I aspire to? To continue to be comfortable, really. I do not need much. I would say this is true of most people I know. They just like comfort." Another student told me that on weekends most families enjoy staying at home, baking bread together, and simply being: "Most Danes," he added, "put a lot of effort into making their homes into nice places." Indeed, the best way to compliment the host of a dinner party is to say that you had a cozy time (the Danish term is *hygge*). Hence, as anywhere in the world, politicians argue. But unlike what takes place in most countries, most Danish politicians agree that things are good. Their differences lie in what should be done to maintain the existing order.

Now, as is usually the case, reality is complex and the Danish picture painted above is made possible by the combination of several factors. Denmark is a small and, ethnically speaking, highly homogeneous country. According to government data, of the roughly

5.3 million people in the country, more than 90 percent are of Danish ancestry. Fewer than 10 percent are or descend from immigrants. In 1980, those figures were 97 percent and 3 percent respectively (Statistics Denmark 2009). Until very recently, then, virtually all Danes lived next to Danes only. The "other" was a Dane, not a foreigner or a child of foreigners. Systematically and over time, the Danes have chosen to help each other do well. All this must be seen in the context of Denmark in the international arena. Challenges coming from "the outside" (whether wars in Europe, globalization, or other things) and loss of territory have been answered by efforts to strengthen the "inside"—by ensuring a highly educated population, a highly trained workforce, universal healthcare, an even distribution of wealth, and so on. The country's defeat to Germany in 1864 in particular is seen as a moment of "national regeneration" (as the Danish Ministry of Foreign Affairs states on a webpage fully dedicated to the war) and consensus building,[10] as a key moment in the shaping of modern Danish identity.[11] The result is that Denmark today is arguably the most egalitarian society in the world—as the United Nations Development Program's 2007/2008 Human Development Report shows.[12]

Thus, in a sense, Jante's Law points to the soft core of what is ultimately a very tough whole. And how the Danes relate to the rest of the world—whether outside their geographical boundaries or inside—is probably quite different than how they relate to each other (Jensen 2008). The Danes are deeply nationalistic, which, seen in the most positive light, translates into an implicit preference for themselves and their culture over others. The recent rise of the *Dansk Folkeparti* (Danish People's Party), with its critical stance toward immigration, suggests that many Danes are far from comfortable with strangers in their midst. It was founded in 1995, precisely when immigration began to be noticeable in the country. In every national elections (and even European-level ones), the party has increased its share of seats. In the latest, in 2009, the *Dansk Folkeparti* won in a landslide a second seat in the European Parliament. The ascendancy of the party has coincided with a toughening of immigration laws in the 1990s (Green-Pedersen and Odmalm 2008: 375), which gave the country one of the most exclusive and restrictive immigration regimes in Europe (Østergaard-Nielsen 2003). Whether "others" can really join the Danish tribe remains to be seen (Kuttner 2008). But these are considerations about the origins and limitations of the Danish approach to competition. They do not undermine the basic fact that, for Danes at least, the tribe comes first and most issues related to winning and losing must prove harmless, if not beneficial, to the Danish community and its well-being.

Back to the United States

Things could hardly be more different in the United States, of course. We could summarize much of what we have discussed in this book by saying that we stand practically *opposite* to the Danes. Consider Jante's Law first. We compete so that we can be in a position to do exactly what Jante's Law asks Danes not to do. We want to win so that we may:

1. Think that we are special
2. Think that we are not of the same standing as everyone else
3. Think that we are smarter than everyone else
4. Fancy ourselves better than the rest
5. Think we know more than the rest
6. Think we are more important than everyone else
7. Think that we are good at something
8. Laugh at others
9. Believe that others care about us
10. Think that we have something to teach.

We learned this in chapters 2, 3, and 4: we want to feel special (principle 1), stand higher physically and mentally in relation to others, (principle 2) and thus fancy (indeed, prove!) ourselves to be better and more important than the rest (principles 4 and 6). Victory also shows us and the world that we are right—about the competitive challenges before us but also the world and life in general. This was the lesson from chapter 3. Thus, yes, we know more than the rest (principle 5), are smarter (principle 3), and therefore have something we could teach to others (principle 10) perhaps at times with a small (or big) dose of arrogance (principle 8).

And we want to prove that we are good at something (principle 7) and, in so doing, win the admiration of others and ultimately ensure that they care about us (principle 9). Indeed, as chapters 7, 8, and 9 showed, we take others very much into consideration when fighting for our very own self. We need others to see us win, to understand the importance and mechanics of what is happening, to appreciate how hard we fought, to support us, and be part of what we are striving to achieve.

Driving us in our intense pursuit of victory are a few core beliefs that once again differ dramatically from those of the Danes. While the Danes put a premium on participation and modesty, we saw that our approach is about *arriving first*. Participation is about the group. Arriving first is about separation. We are clearly not interested in the social aspect of competition. We are interested in establishing something for ourselves. Competition is first and foremost about "me." And we, along with everyone else, understand and accept this. We tell our children to compete and dream "big" for themselves, not their communities. The pursuit of happiness is a private, not collective, affair. In our minds when most of us compete is the desire to distance ourselves from others in just about every way—we want more physical and mental space, more money, more honors, more of this and of that. Adam Smith taught us more than two centuries ago that societies flourish the most when each individual looks after himself (Smith 1993: 291–92). In the United States, this is an accepted and celebrated fact of life.

If, in turn, the Danes try to minimize the hierarchical implications generated by competitive events, we embrace them. A central function of competition—a key raison d'être—is to *make distinctions*, to differentiate among people in a normative (better versus worse, good versus bad, right versus wrong) manner. When competing, our hopes are to emerge from the event in higher standing than when we came in. We aspire to distinction, as we have seen many times in this book (Nelson and Shavitt 2002). The start of a competitive event represents for us a moment of equality, sameness, and parity—and, indeed, as many have noted, the very birth and early years of the United States can be said to have been such a moment (Tocqueville 2003; Greenfeld 1992: 449). Recall here our discussion in chapter 2 about the importance of close rivalries: as individuals and as a society, we find most meaning in those competitions where the competitors are, at the beginning, very close to each other in skills and abilities. Winning against others whom we know beforehand to be far weaker than us is not very interesting. This illustrates clearly the objective of competition: to allow the winners to differentiate themselves from those whom others and themselves thought to be potentially like them. The end of a competitive event is therefore marked by the disappearance of similarities and the arrival of differences. The winner is happy because victory helped her distinguish herself. The audience, too, is pleased to have witnessed someone succeed in what we all aspire to do: to draw new boundaries (quite literally sometimes, as we saw in our discussion of "space" in chapter 4) between them and others. As to the losers, they must go back into the world of anonymity. Their sadness reflects their failure to achieve their goals: the tragedy of their loss lies in their failed attempt to distinguish themselves. We are happy with differences, then, and see little reason that we should devote collective energies—as the Danes do—to eliminate them. Thus, when asked in the General Social Survey whether "those in need have to learn to take care of themselves and not depend on others," more than 50 percent of Americans agree with the statement, and only 23 percent think the opposite.[13]

It follows that competition for us is therefore about *establishing something new* and, thus, challenging the status quo. New and valuable information emerges as we win or lose. Competition is designed to upset the social order and reposition us in that new order. Indeed, we are in the first instance rather clear that that order is never really quite set. Our mythology tells us that the poor, beaten, and fallen of today could be the rich and powerful of to-morrow, and that today's winners will have to continue to prove themselves to remain winners. Americans believe—erroneously, it turns out—that social mobility in their country is far greater than in other advanced industrialized nations (Blanden et al. 2006: 7). According to the World Values Survey, Americans are much more likely than people in other major industrialized countries to think that society needs radical changes.[14] And, as Tocqueville observed correctly in his classic analysis of the United States, "The feeling of instability is perpetuated when order has been established" (Tocqueville 2003: 729).

Thus the bigger the change that competition engenders, the better. The best stories for us are those of the underdogs who reach the top after being at the bottom. A recent story in the *New York Times* featured Wings of America, "an unlikely collection of athletes . . . a group of American Indians [high school students] from reservations around the country [that has] won a boys or a girls national title 20 times since first attending a championship meet in 1988." Why were these achievements worth reporting in the leading national newspaper? Because they stand in sharp contrast to a long history of loss: "The history of Native Americans in the United States," wrote the article's author, is one of loss: "losing land, losing language, losing culture and losing family members." These young American Indians are seeking to undo a situation of doom, they are literally "running from despair" (Spring 2008). Competition is supposed to "rock the boat" and create a new social order: that is its function and mission.

But, again, competition never settles anything in a definitive matter. The very moment that we have a winner and a loser is the start of a new challenge. The end of one competitive event simply provides everyone with a new target for everyone's ambitions. Even the "defending" champion is not expected to merely protect things in their current form. In his fight to stay on, he will try to improve whatever records he himself has set—thus making his own achievements something that have to be surpassed. We may say that the true winner is he who keeps fighting until the end to surpass himself despite constantly coming out on top. Hence the motivational posters in our offices and gyms urge us never to sit and rest. Michael Jordan simply *had* to flash his fingers and think about the possibility of a sixth championship even before the sweat from the final game of his fifth victorious season had dried. Most of us would not want it any other way. We like flux and mobility, as we saw in chapter 9, and we fear stillness and having nothing to work toward. How else to interpret the fact that more than 70 percent of respondents, when asked in the General Social Survey whether they would keep on working if they had enough money to live comfortably for the rest of their lives, answered "yes"?[15]

"Me," "distinctions," and "change": these three concepts are one way of capturing quite well our love for victory and fear of loss, our drive to compete, and what competition is all about in our society. Winning is about the perennial advancement and assertion of the self—or, as we said at the very beginning of this book, about establishing our place in the world, over and over again. Losing is about the perennial worry of falling behind and becoming irrelevant. As the comparison with Denmark made clear, this is a rather particular approach to competition. We have explored this mind-set in detail throughout this book. We should now spell out its advantages, disadvantages, and how we could alter our stance.

Assessing the American Mind-Set

Our embrace of victory and disdain of loss has certain advantages. The most important has to do with some of the results it produces. The mind-set generates intensity and determination. Unconcerned by (because largely unaware of and uninterested in) the complexity of things, many of us do not stop and contemplate things. We are instead constantly and resolutely working toward our next victory. With this kind of mind-set, we are bound to succeed, to achieve, to obtain things for ourselves that we would otherwise not have. It would be a mistake to dismiss those things as superfluous or somehow irrelevant. With an unwavering winning mentality, we are more likely to obtain better-paying jobs, earn the respect of others, accomplish impressive feats (like running a marathon, for instance, or climbing a mountain) that help us learn about ourselves and the world, start new and valuable businesses, achieve prominence in our professions, be more productive, cure ourselves of serious diseases, and much more. As we learned in chapter 5, winning means acquiring ownership, access, and control—all of which can surely help us live better lives. At the more aggregate level, in turn, our individual achievements translate into impressive advancements for society as a whole. Our communities and country benefit from what individuals—driven by great ambition and much more—manage to accomplish.

A competitive mind-set also fills our lives with meaning while relieving us from the painful task of wondering how else we would mobilize ourselves. We could certainly argue over the true quality of that meaning. Some of us, including this very author, may find it shallow or ultimately irrelevant. But psychologists have consistently shown that human beings benefit from having a sense of direction: the specific nature of that direction is of secondary importance (Sommers and Vodanovich 2000; Bargdill 2000). Boredom and aimlessness are surely worse than excited pursuit motivated by dreams of better things. And Americans, according to the World Values Survey, are especially inclined to wonder about the meaning and purpose of their lives.[16] There might be ways of making our lives meaningful other than through winning and losing, of course, as many Danes would argue. But the competitive mind-set seems to be doing a good job for a vast number of people in our country. Their lives have purpose and a direction.

The third advantage has to do with entertainment. As we saw in chapter 2, a good dose of uncertainty infuses most competitive events. We do not know how things will turn out. We experience a certain pleasure in flirting with danger—with the possibility of failure. As long as we actually do not fail, we are interested in being exposed to what we fear. And the possibility of failure gives victory its real flavor: we could have lost, but we have won. We imagine alternative universes and revel in the fact that things turned out well for us. As members of the audience, we are attracted to competitive events for similar reasons. We enjoy witnessing the possibility of failure as well as actual failure (not ours, of course), as well as victory. With a certain amount of sadism, we are entertained by the sight of others giving their very best to succeed. A thrilling event is thus a close event, where potentialities remain open until the end and competitors exhaust themselves to prevail. This sort of entertainment is real: it is part of human history, it draws from powerful drives and instincts. It should therefore be taken seriously.

But our competitive mind-set has serious problems as well. Two stand out as especially serious. We encountered them already at various points in this book. The first is that, by pitting us against so much in the world, it generates enormous tension in our lives and is therefore utterly exhausting. The second is that, despite all that it asks of us, it actually fails to satisfy us in a definitive manner. When we consider these two problems together, we realize that our approach is rather inefficient. Let us examine each problem in some detail.

The Problem of Exhaustion

The language of winning and losing exhausts us. Why? Because it causes enormous tensions in our lives. How? To begin, it is adversarial in nature. As we have seen, when we approach something—a task before us, a challenge, a person—with our competitive mind-set we stand against it, we start out (and also finish) in a state of disharmony with it. We are not interested in establishing bonds or even experiencing whatever connections might naturally be formed in our interactions with it. We are not motivated by a sense of togetherness. Instead, we are defiant. As psychologists have shown, our hormone levels get higher and stay that way for some time after the end of the competition (Mazur et al. 1992). We assume a position of aggressiveness toward the world.

Thus, if I intend to win a marathon, the marathon (along with the other runners and even myself, to some extent) becomes an object of my aggression. If I am competing for a job, the job itself (not to mention the other candidates) becomes the object of my apprehension and emotional investment. As Kohn wrote, "We

197

seem to have reached a point where doing our jobs, educating our children and even relaxing on the weekends have to take in the context of a struggle" (Kohn 1986: 3).

This adversarial quality of our competitive mind-set would not be problematic if we were thoughtful and selective about our use of it. But, as I have shown in this book over and over again, we simply deploy it without much thought in countless areas of our lives. "Competition," Kohn observed, "is a deeply ingrained, profoundly enduring part of our lives" (Kohn 1986: 3). This means that we are seldom at peace with the world. Though our mental stance can prove fruitful, as just discussed, it also generates considerable anxiety and emotional imbalance. Rather than being in harmony with the world, we are drained by it.

Our language about winning and losing exhausts us in another way: it introduces an element of deep uncertainty in our lives. As long as we view our activities in life as tests of our worth, we will be constantly doubtful about ourselves. Anytime we think that something can reveal to us whether we are winners or losers, we admit that we do not know who we really are. More fundamentally, we fear that we are losers—a sensation that is sure to take a toll on us if constantly present in our minds. We push our children to beat those of our neighbors at baseball because we are not sure of their worth and, by reflection, of ours. We found great relief when Bobby Fischer beat Boris Spassky at chess during the height of the Cold War because we were not sure that our capitalist, democratic system was really superior to communism. As a recent report showed, profound insecurities and not self-confidence drive CEOs of many major American corporations. "I am driven by fear of failure," admitted Dennis Manning, CEO of the giant Guardian Life Insurance Company of America, which has annual revenues in excess of $7 billion. "It is a strong motivator for me" (Jones 2007).

Thus, whenever we pursue victory, we entertain the possibility of loss. But, in a sense, even when we win the notion of "loss" lingers on in our minds. When we think of ourselves as winners, somewhere in our minds we have notions of us being a loser as well. Put differently, it is impossible to live only in a world where there is only victory: wherever there is victory, there is loss. And to the extent that we dislike loss, we continue to live in a world where things may one day turn against us.

But uncertainty creeps in even on those rare occasions when victory is pure and absolute—that is, free from any links to loss. The biggest is the "what is next?" problem. The pursuit of victory generates a certain type of stability in our lives, a good amount of inertia. Much like a motorcycle traveling at high speeds, our propulsion forward prevents us from falling by the wayside. We have a purpose and need not stop and think too much. When we actually accomplish something—winning a championship, finally becoming CEO of a company, or becoming a multimillionaire—a void quickly comes into our lives. Suddenly, we are directionless and aimless. We no longer know what to do or where to go. We are profoundly unsure. Similar observations apply to losing in any definitive sense. When we lose and give up any hopes whatsoever of winning, we no longer have a compass. Losers experience great disorientation: what they thought might have been true about themselves needs revisiting. Old assumptions have proven wrong. Somewhere, our strategies and calculations have failed us. We dislike losing because it forces us to face new questions and begin the painful search for new answers.

Our competitive mind-set, then, generates a good deal of uncertainty and, therefore, tension. To the extent that we approach much of our life with our competitive mind-set, we enter into very tentative relationships with people, things, and ourselves. We are fearful of the process and the outcomes. Rather than welcoming our experiences, we stand at a distance, held back by skepticism and an instinct to protect ourselves from unwanted turns of events. We are aggressive rather than peaceful. Without question, our stance is therefore a recipe for exhaustion.

The Problem of Dissatisfaction

In the World Values Survey, only 15 percent of Americans state they are fully satisfied with their lives. The number for Denmark is almost 30 percent.[17] Our competitive mind-set surely contributes to this general failing of dissatisfaction. The language of winning and losing provides us, after all, with a set of "prefabricated" assumptions and conclusions about us: namely, that we are naturally inclined to compete and are therefore very eager to prove ourselves winners and not losers. We do not create those assumptions; instead, they are thrust on us. The problem is that these assumptions and conclusions do not correspond to reality. In many cases, as we have seen many times throughout this book, we are not really interested in winning or worried about losing. We are after something that is quite different.

We have talked at length about our desire to find our place in the world. That is our paramount objective, to be sure. But a set of other things also matter. For instance, often times we are actually interested in knowing that we can do something very well. In other instances, we are looking for ways to stretch and push ourselves. We are interested in doing our very best, discovering our limits and character. On other occasions, we may be really after feeling like we are part of a team. In yet other cases, we are interested in achieving something in the most effortless, noncompetitive way possible. There certainly are several alternatives. And, behind each alternative lie our true inclinations, fears, insecurities, and loves. The point here is that our propensity to view—often automatically and without consciousness—many of our engagements with the world as competitive affairs prevents us from reflecting about, and coming to know, ourselves. The result is that what comes out of competition does not satisfy us in any definitive way. Rather, it makes us quite uneasy.

As an illustration of this, consider the example of a friend of mine (let us call him Paul) passionate about photography who submitted a beautiful photo he had taken to a competition. Most of us would say that he did so out of a desire to win the prize. That seems like a reasonable assumption; it is wrong, however. If we looked closely at the matter, we would learn that Paul was primarily after something else: an external recognition of his skills, some validation (to present to his partner) for his time-consuming and expensive hobby, and proving to himself and to his close friends his credentials as a nature lover (the photo was of a rare and very beautiful bird). To view Paul's submission of his picture as a manifestation of Paul's interest in winning would simply be inaccurate. If we—those witnessing it—were to do so, our error would be one of interpretation. If Paul himself were to do it, it would be an error of self-understanding—a failure to know his inner drives, impulses, and needs.

So it is highly unlikely that we will ever feel fully satisfied by any given activity when we have failed to consider what really moves us to engage in it *and,* instead, believe we are led by desires we do not have. Our energies are misdirected. Something inside of us does not feel fully right. We sense that there is something else at work but do not dare to investigate it further: we cannot get too distracted, after all, and forget what seems to matter most—winning. We thus neglect important parts of ourselves and push ourselves to like that which actually is not to our taste. We do all of this without really being aware of it. It is in most cases a matter of habit. But our true constitutions cannot be changed by habit, as Jean Baptiste Lamarck once erroneously assumed when trying to explain the evolution of humans and other animals.

Many of us would therefore feel a great sense of relief if we were told that we could leave behind the language of winning and losing—that we could go about our lives, at least for a little while, without having to worry about competing. We would feel *free* from having to twist and push ourselves so as to "step up" to the call of competition. That is, we would welcome the opportunity to just be ourselves and pursue what really matters to us. All of which tells us that competitive events often push us to be what we are not, what we prefer not to be. And that their results, even when positive, often do not satisfy us in a definitive manner. Now we know why most competitors feel the necessity to keep on winning even after streaks of impressive victories. They may announce their decisions to keep on going in positive terms—with excitement and enthusiasm. But it is clear that further victories are not what they need.

Our competitive mind-set is problematic, then. We can call it inefficient: it generates some good results but at a very high cost. Could we do better? Could we obtain good results without feeling exhausted and perennially dissatisfied? In the next section, I discuss the elements of an alternative approach.

A New Mind-Set

Despite being practically opposite, the Danish and American approaches to competition actually share one important characteristic: they make it very difficult for individuals to express themselves in a genuine manner. The Danish approach does so by keeping the individual as close to the pack as possible. Any aspiration to distancing oneself from the group is met with great disapproval. The collective comes first, the individual second. The American approach appears in the first instance to be different. It surely does push individuals to propel themselves forward and stand in front of the world with great pride. But, to the extent that it thrusts on individuals a single, monothematic formula for how they should think about their lives and conduct themselves, it deprives them of the opportunity to find out what, exactly, they want for themselves. The enormous pressure it exerts on them strips them of their deliberative faculties—of the process by which they explore who they are, what they like and dislike, how they wish to relate to the people around them, and the activities they engage in. This is ultimately why it is both exhausting and dissatisfying.

My fundamental proposition, then, is that *the process of self-discovery, followed by the pursuit of activities that match our true inclinations and desires, is fundamental for the flourishing of the individual.* The power and prevalence in American society of the language of winning and losing means that we do not engage in such a process of self-discovery and that we settle, in turn, with an approach to life that is tiring and fails to fulfill us fully.

What, then, should we do? Nietzsche warned us against the dangers of cultural moulds—against the stifling air of established values and ideas. He urged us to be creators of our own conceptual

worlds, distance ourselves from established patterns, and find soli-
tude so as to chart new courses where words no longer possess us
but, instead, we pursue truths that are closer to our genuine hearts
and minds (Nietzsche 1990). In some respects, and rather counter-
intuitively perhaps, the message of a number of Eastern thinkers—
from Lao Tsu to Buddha—was the same. "Therefore," wrote Lao
Tsu, "to see beyond boundaries to the subtle heart of things, dis-
pense with names, with concepts" (Lao Tzu 1995: chapter 1). For
Nietzsche, passive acceptance of established values led to a mean-
ingless life. The Eastern philosophers believed it led to unnecessary
pain. I subscribe to both viewpoints and put forth three recommendations that are in line with those insights. The recommendations, which draw from existing research in psychology and other
disciplines, have to do with "conceptual hygiene," discovery, and
alignment.

I should say right away that these recommendations do not involve changing, in top-down fashion, how our workplaces, political system, athletic events, education system, and other institutions
operate. Such large-scale initiatives would have an impact, to be
sure—and good ideas on what those might be already exist.[18]
What I have described mostly in this book is a particular sort of
mind-set. I therefore prefer to discuss what each of us could do at
the individual level. This is, of course, an initial foray into—rather
than a treatise on—a different approach.

Conceptual Hygiene

For decades now, psychologists have described the negative effects
of cognitive dissonance—of entertaining in our minds as valid contradictory concepts about things, including the world and ourselves—
on our well-being (Aronson 1997). We are more productive, satisfied, and at peace when there is consistency in our perspectives
(Ulrich et al. 2007). I have argued many times in this book that our
concepts of winning and losing do not really "match" our internal
ambitions and drives. We hold on to words that do not fit how we
really see things. There is confusion, in other words, in our perspectives and outlooks.

My first recommendation, therefore, has to do with *conceptual hygiene*. We should aim to use our language of winning and losing only when we truly want to pursue victory at something. In all other cases, we should avoid using it. We should "clean the air" of our ideas of winning and losing—much like the Futurists, taking their cues from Nietzsche, asked us to do for old culture in general at the turn of the last century. When we are tempted to use those words in our lives, we should stop and wonder what we really mean. Assume, for example, that I receive the "best employee of the year" award at my job this year. For that, I could call myself a "winner." But adopting such a label turns the others around me into losers, raises the question of what I would be if I had not received the award (a loser?), and (unless my goal was to truly *win* the award) introduces new meanings and interpretations (in my mind and the minds of others) for my actions and motivations. All this creates a good deal of conceptual pollution, of unnecessary confusion. A better approach would be to say that the company chose to recognize my hard work and impressive accomplishments, and that I gladly accept that recognition. That combination of words might be closer to reality and would make it easier for me to relate to the award in a more genuine fashion.

When we hear others use it—in everyday language, movies, sports events, work, politics, and so on—we should, in turn, resist the temptation to acquiesce with their worldviews and interpretations. There has been much talk about "winning" in Iraq in recent months. The situation in Iraq is obviously a very serious matter. Our language should be as precise as possible. "Winning the peace," to name one popular slogan, is the exact opposite of precise. What does it mean to win the peace? Do we wish to own it for ourselves? That is hopefully not the case. If we lost it, could someone else win it? That is not what we intend to say. Is peace like a battle, which can be won or lost? But then peace would have fighting parties in it trying to dominate each other. Peace is the opposite of that. So, when we think of peace in those terms we run the risk of misunderstanding what needs to happen for things to turn the way we really want them to, for what we should do to achieve our real goals, for how we should treat others. Again, how do Iraqis feel about us saying that we need to win the peace in their country? We need to do away with such sloppy language. In the case of peace, it would be much more constructive for everyone to say that we want to *help bring about* peace in the country. We recognize that there is conflict (with us as part of it) and wish for an end to the conflict. We are interested in doing what we can to ensure that. Now, such language introduces ideas of humility, responsibility, and cooperation. It also identifies much more clearly what we want as an outcome. The approach is bound to be more successful and in line with our real intentions.

For a second example, consider Jillian Michaels's best-selling book on fat, *Win by Losing* (Michaels 2005). The title presumably suggests that we can become winners by losing fat. While the meaning of "losing fat" is fairly clear (we let go of something we previously had), the "win" part of the title is utterly puzzling. It obviously suggests that we are losers if we fail to lose the fat we do not want on our bodies. But why are we losers? What have we lost? Against whom? Similar questions then emerge in the case of victory. Are we winners now that we are skinnier? Are skinny people winners? Again, some conceptual cleaning up is in order. A better approach would be to say that some of us are overweight and very much wish to shed some of the fat on our bodies. If we succeed in this effort, we will feel better about ourselves. If not, we will feel unhappy about our bodies. We are not at war with them, nor will we be losers if the fat stays on. We will have just not achieved our goals. We will therefore reconsider our strategies and proceed. During all of this, there is no obvious reason to perceive ourselves as losers (or winners).

The more we resist the language of winning and losing, the more we will feel a sense of relief. We will finally come to see with clarity the mismatch between reality and our competitive language. The competitive mind-set will begin to look odd, "forced," one-sided. What was once subject to a single interpretation will now stand on its own two feet waiting for more varied and insightful engagement. Finally, parents will be able to view their children applying

to colleges as neither winners nor losers but as young people looking for a way to receive a good college education. We will think of
our struggle against terrorism not as matter of victory or loss, but
as a messy and complex entanglement involving highly frustrated
individuals and groups of people. We will no longer automatically
think of very rich people as "winners" but will instead ask who
they really are, where they come from, and where they are headed.
We will no longer think of defeated political candidates as losers
who should exit the scene as fast as possible but, instead, as people
who tried extremely hard to pursue something that clearly mattered to them. We will hopefully look at our own successes and
failures—at work, with our friends, with money—in a different way.

We will certainly enjoy this new freedom. But it will also take us
some time before we can fill the void that will almost certainly follow our conceptual cleanup. Deprived of our habitual vocabulary,
we will be at a momentary loss for words. Because our words
often embody feelings and beliefs (Sacerdote and Zidar 2008), we
will also be confused about who, exactly, we wish to be. This will
be an important moment for us: we will face ourselves naked, as it
were, much like a room feels empty after we remove all the bric-a-
brac that has cluttered it for years. It is easy to "hide" behind
clutter, behind the language of winning and losing and not face
ourselves. This is so especially when we win. As Fellman noted
recently, when we can call ourselves "winners" we need not wonder about what lies beneath our pedestal—about our desires, emotions, and vulnerabilities (Fellman 1998: 50). Indeed, is not this
the reason why so many of us instinctively like to win? But without that language being available to us, we will need to ask ourselves a somewhat uncomfortable question: what are we really after
when we pursue something—a work contract, a lover, an award at
our workplace, a top-notch performance by our kids in school or
in athletics, peace in Iraq?

We will have to embark on a new process of discovery. How are
we to interpret things now? More important, how are we to engage in life? What impulses and desires will drive us now? What
do we really want? Taking the time to answer these questions is

bound to be highly productive. But it is also a form of kindness and respect toward ourselves.

Discovery

Under the right conditions, introspection and self-understanding are key ingredients for healthy minds (Schieman and Van Gundy 2001; Welker 2005). The process of internal inquiry generates self-respect. It often yields valuable insights as well. My second recommendation, therefore, has to do with discovery. We should spend time and energy discovering what lies behind our love of winning, fear of losing, and general embrace of competition.

We must inquire about our needs and drives. All of us are likely to generate a very personal list of things. But, if we were to compare our answers with each other, we would discover that a few basic patterns would emerge. Why do we want that job promotion? Why are we proud when our children win the science club award for best scientist in their school? Why do we feel happy when our favorite baseball team wins a game? What prompts us to train for that marathon?

Early in this book, we discussed our need for physical and mental space, for proofs that we are right about the world in general, for differentiation. In chapter 8, we talked about worth. We then reasoned that all these amount to a need for finding our place in the world, for confirmation that we are competent and legitimate people. We should certainly keep these needs at the very front of our minds. We should get to know them well, ascertain which ones matter most to us, and why. We should then acknowledge that we compete for other reasons as well—less fundamental ones, perhaps, but surely worthy of our attention. These are often related to the more fundamental needs, but deserve to be handled individually.

One such driver is our desire for the *admiration and approval* of others. It is tempting to characterize that desire as something that we should work on eliminating—to suggest that, once we are cognizant of its existence, we ought to learn to feel good about ourselves regardless of what others think. But matters are more complex, of course. It is natural to long for the positive opinion of others, in the early stages of life but also as adults. Excessive dependence is problematic and should, therefore, be addressed. But even if addressed, it is unlikely to disappear in short order. Thus in most cases we can only benefit from understanding this drive as a legitimate need—one that we may want to control and probably try to diminish in intensity, but something that should be taken seriously nonetheless (Crocker et al. 2003). We ought to understand it further and find constructive and healthy ways of satisfying it. Our habitual pursuit of victory—done while blind to our needs—will not do the trick. We must instead be aware of what we are after and find activities and situations that will genuinely address our need. Normally, those tend to be ones where our other needs (creativity, for example) are also met.

So, for instance, we should commend the person who, aware of her strong need for the attention of others as well as her deep passion and talent for music, decides to become a jazz singer. She is putting her strengths and weaknesses to good use. And for this she is likely to feel good about her life. We should feel equally positive about the person who, realizing that he wishes to impress those around him and has a genuine interest in finance, decides to take on a job in investment banking. Once again, that person stays true to his needs and, at the same time, makes constructive use of his talents and weaknesses.

A second and very important driver concerns our need to have *accomplished* something. The psychologist Erik Erikson proposed an eight-stage view of life. The theory remains central to much psychoanalytical research and writing (Berzoff 2008). The seventh is one of the longest (it begins when one is in his twenties and ends in his late fifties) and centers around our need to produce—to make things, to contribute to society, to create. Erikson stressed the importance of producing for one's mental health. I would like to alter slightly Erikson's theory by suggesting that what is important for all of us is to have a sense that we have *done* something: that, moved by a fundamental desire to interact with reality, we have successfully spent time and energy toward the making of something—much like a sculptor uses his hands to make a statue.

It matters little what that "something" is or even whether others are aware of us doing this. What is crucial is that, looking back, we know we interacted with the world—that we put ourselves into it and sought to shape it. In that vein, failing to accomplish something can be highly problematic—as George W. Bush reminded us in May 2003 when, dressed in pilot gear after a dramatic sunset landing on the aircraft carrier USS *Lincoln,* he stood under a huge banner bearing a slogan meant to sum up the situation in Iraq: "Mission Accomplished" (Kornblut 2003).

We should understand as well that the key source of the pleasure has to do with the infinite quality of it all. We delight in the definitive dimension of our feats. "I have done something" means "I will no longer be here, but that which I have done will forever be that." Now, it is precisely this that hides sometimes behind our love of victory and fear of loss. Winning feels good because it is something we have done and, as the expression we so often hear goes, "no one can take that away from me." Losing feels bad because it represents our failure to achieve that sense of eternity. My point here is that we would be far better off recognizing what we are really after—making, infinity, completion—and what is but a manifestation of it—winning. We will be clearer about our pleasures and pains, our choices, and ultimately our selves.

A third and very important driver is a desire *to know ourselves* better. This may seem like a cliché, but it is true that we often compete to discover what we are capable of doing, our limits, our strengths and our weaknesses. We are interested in exploring ourselves. This is in part a reflection of the fact that we do not really know ourselves very well at any point in time *and* that we continuously change over time (thus any knowledge we may gather at particular points in time can quickly become outdated). It also reflects our evolving curiosity. As a young person, we may not be curious to explore our ability to discern white wine vintages, for example. But we may develop that curiosity later in life. Then, after taking classes in wine tasting, we pay to participate in blind tasting events. Regardless of how we arrive to it, competition creates an environment of learning: we see how we behave in new situations, we are pressured to push ourselves in new ways, we discover that we can go further (or less far) than we thought.

Several other things drive us to compete. Some of us are moved by aggression or the feeling we sense when we "get" something for ourselves. Others feel a desire to belong to something bigger—a team, a tournament, an organization, etc. Yet some others of us enjoy (or are even addicted to) the thrill associated with risk and uncertainty. My main message here is that we should take the time to discover what really moves us. The answers to these questions will enable us to be far more accurate in our selection of activities and far more satisfied with ourselves and our lives. Indeed, clarity about our objectives will provide us, by itself, with significant amounts of satisfaction *regardless* of outcomes—of whether we actually achieve those objectives. In the case of success, we will rejoice from having gotten what we wanted. But if we do not attain our objectives, our failure will be quite acceptable to us (provided that we tried earnestly to succeed): our efforts were genuine attempts to take good care of our true selves.

Alignment

My final recommendation concerns *alignment*. After some conceptual clean up and some introspection about what really lurks behind our competitive spirit, we should seek to *match* our real drives with the activities that best suit them. Theorists of organizational dynamics have spent enormous resources and time investigating how to best match the behavior of individual actors in any given organization with the true interests and objectives of that organization (Colvin and Boswell 2007). They have recognized that there is a problem of misalignment in those settings: people do things that do not advance the interests of their organization. Very much the same can be said about us at the individual level, as those researchers working in the area of "positive psychology" tell us (Seligman 2002; Becker and Marececk 2008). By adopting and then following "prepackaged" value-systems and instructions we often embark on paths that do not address our real drives and needs.

We should all ensure that in our public and private lives we engage in activities that satisfy our true and genuine drives and needs. If we are looking for evidence that we belong, that we have a legitimate claim to be in this world, then we should probably immerse ourselves in jobs, relationships, and even hobbies where out competencies are best put to use, where our skills are appreciated but also further honed, where others communicate to us their appreciation for what we have done. This may have very little to do with competition. If, in turn, we really want to be surrounded by others and feel their admiration, then we should choose professions that serve others (like medicine or education) and join service-oriented organizations. If we want to know more about our own limits and qualities, then we should look for physical and mental challenges that provide us with the answers we need. If accomplishing something gives us enormous pleasure, then we might do well in engaging in project-based jobs and activities. If we are really interested in getting things for ourselves, then we should engage in activities that will help us get things. We could go on.

We will then be in positive territory. Instead of exhausted, we will now feel energized (Seligman 2002). Alignment means establishing a proper relationship with the outer world—one that is honest and direct, as well as purposeful. We will finally see in our activities a reflection of ourselves. Thus we will be more respectful of others and the things around us as well. Rather than assuming an antagonistic stance toward the world, we will be peaceful. Rather than being against something, we will be with something. Our actions will originate from a place of affirmation and not fear.

We will also experience a good deal of satisfaction. The competitive mind-set produces dissatisfaction in us because it produces outcomes that we are not really interested in. When we are properly aligned, the outcomes will please us. They are what we are looking for. But even if we fail, we will be in a better position than if we think of ourselves as having lost. We will know that our pursuit was a legitimate one. Rather than serving a foreign master, we were kind and respectful to ourselves. Having carefully listened to ourselves, we sought to engage in the world in a meaningful fashion. Results aside, such a state of mind is sure to bring us and those around us a good deal of benefit.

In Sum

Behind our intense desire to win and avoid loss lie profound doubts about our proper place in the world. But neither victory nor loss can provide us with the answers we are looking for. Faulty logic and erroneous assumptions, coupled with confusion about what we are really after and what winning and losing are all about, ensure that we receive no definitive answers about ourselves from competition. This state of affairs, I have argued, is consistent with a general restlessness that has characterized American society since its early days.

Not everything is wrong with this approach, of course. But we could do better. In this chapter, I proposed three steps—conceptual hygiene, exploration, and alignment—for the development of an alternative mind-set. The language of winning and losing has "hijacked" most of us. Rich with meaning and with its advantages and limitations, it permeates much of our lives. I called for a re-evaluation of our stance. Rather than passively accepting this language, I ask that we become cognizant of it. The primary objective of this book was to clarify that language. My second objective was to urge readers to do away with that language whenever possible, to develop some understanding of their true desires and needs, and to engage in the world in ways that truly fulfill them. So much about life is not about winning and losing: it is about feeling like a human being, expressing ourselves in genuine and productive ways, and interacting with our surroundings in good and healthy ways. We should all keep this in mind as we make our way in the world.

Notes

Chapter One. The Problem

1. The World Values Survey is an ongoing project funded by the U.S. government and directed by a team of social scientists investigating the cultural, moral, religious, and political values of people from more than 90 countries around the world. Most of the data are available on the project's Internet website (http://www.worldvaluessurvey.org/). All claims and comparisons I make in this book come from my own analysis of the data, unless otherwise stated.

2. When it comes to satisfaction (question A170 in the survey), Denmark comes in second (after Puerto Rico), the United States thirteenth. When it comes to happiness (question A008), Denmark comes in seventh, the United States thirteenth again.

3. Around 90 percent of Americans think often or sometimes about the direction of their lives. In Denmark, Finland, Germany, Italy, Japan, Mexico, and Great Britain—to name a few countries—the figure is considerably lower. Only eight countries in the world reported figures higher than 90 percent. All but one (South Korea) are developing countries (for instance, Nigeria, Zimbabwe, and Vietnam). Question F001.

4. I rely on macro-level data typical of many social scientific studies to reveal basic facts about our approach to winning and losing: statistical surveys from governmental and nongovernmental organizations (the General Social Survey and the World Values Survey above all), analyses of existing legal systems and regulatory frameworks (in business, politics, and beyond), results from psychological experiments, and more. At the same time, in order to reveal some of the subtler but perhaps more important aspects of winning and losing, I engage in extensive interpretations of a wide variety of written texts (such as the Bible, the U.S. Declaration of Independence, motivational books on how to always win, college and business websites, newspaper articles, advertisements, etc.), personal interviews (with public officials, business people, coaches, parents, teachers, and more), historical and current events (in politics, economics, sports, and more), statements of leading figures, and more.

Chapter Two. Differentiation

1. All references to the General Social Survey in this book refer to cumulative data from 1972 (the first year of the survey) to 2006 (most recent year available). For all references, I report the relevant survey question by its variable code. In this case, it was variable "usclass7."

2. Interestingly, recent research suggests that significant variation exists between women and men in the extent to which they doubt themselves before competitive events: men approach those events with more self-confidence than women. This may in part explain why women are on the whole less interested than men in participating in those events (Niederle and Vesterlund 2007).

3. We are reminded, with all of this, of Thomas Hobbes, the seventeenth-century British political philosopher who famously observed that our neighbor's misery is our delight. "Men," he wrote, "take pleasure to behold from the shore the danger of them that are at sea in a tempest, or in fight, or from a safe castle to behold two armies charge one another in the field . . . [they] usually are content . . . to be spectators of the misery of their friends" (Hobbes 1999 [1650]: 58). We can revise those words to say that *our potential* misery, once foregone, is the source of our delight. Of course, if our victory happens at the expense of others, we need not work too hard to imagine the misery we have avoided. As Hobbes suggested, they will remind us of that.

4. Variables "opoutcme," "equalize," "usclass8," and "richpoor."

5. Variable "attsprts."

6. See, for instance, Gan et al. (1997) regarding levels of spectator excitement in close and not-so-close athletic events.

7. The research on this topic is extensive, with important nuances and variations. In one of the most interesting studies, Kahneman and Tversky (1979) proposed convincingly that risk aversion does occur when people are facing questions of gains. When, however, they have to choose with regard to losses, they take on more risk.

8. Variable "life."

9. When we view political races as being of real importance to us, for instance, we are more than happy to know ahead of time that our preferred candidate will win by a landslide.

10. See Hareli and Weiner (2002) and Daly and Wilson (2007) for a discussion of recent research. See Raney and Depalma (2006) for an interesting study of violence in athletic competition: audiences report more pleasure from viewing sports events that have violent components in them than sports events without violence.

11. There is little doubt that close competition motivates the competitors and, as such, ensures a high level of performance, as we shall discuss in chapter 10. When this happens in business, education, government, and scientific research, it can prove beneficial to people who are not even aware of the competition, since it generates outputs (new products or discoveries, for instance) that are useful to many others.

12. These rankings also make it possible for schools themselves to compete against peer institutions.

CHAPTER THREE. I WIN, THEREFORE I AM RIGHT

1. Most current research on this topic no longer focuses on demonstrating that losers feel badly about themselves but on identifying factors that account for vari-

ance in the intensity of such feelings. These include gender, initial levels of self-esteem, types of feedback gathered during competitive events, and more. See, for instance, Mills and D'Alfonso (2007) and Zhang and Baumeister (2006).

2. Of course, the United States is not unique in this rather liberal—in the sense of generous and loose—interpretation of events in the battlefield. Other countries very much engage in it. The tortuous history of the Middle East offers many precious—and quite tragic—examples. The words of Itzhak Rabin in 1967, as he accepted on behalf of the Israeli armed forces an honorary degree from Hebrew University in Jerusalem soon after their incredible victory over their Arab neighbors, captured much of the spirit of that conflict:

> Our soldiers prevailed not by the strength of their weapons but by their sense of mission, by their consciousness of the justice of their cause, by a deep love of their country, and by their understanding of the heavy task laid upon them: to insure the existence of our people in their homeland, and to affirm, even at the cost of their lives, the right of the Jewish people to live its life in its own state, free, independent and in peace. (Rabin 1967)

Israel's soldiers won because they were right about their mission, about what was being asked of them, about the meaning of the war, and about justice and Israel's place in the world. The Arabs must have lost, instead, partly because they held on to a wrong interpretation of things.

3. For several of these polls, see: http://www.pollingreport.com/clinton-.htm.

4. A final, rather powerful example is Martin Luther King's struggle for civil rights. It borrowed heavily from Mahatma Gandhi's vision for India's independence movement from Great Britain during the 1930s and 1940s, following nearly two centuries of subjugation. Gandhi called his movement Satyagraha. The term itself derives from the Sanskrit words *satya* (truth) and *grah* (to grasp or hold on to). Gandhi's struggle was political, but he clearly believed that at stake was the truth itself and that, crucially, those with the correct view would ultimately prevail. King's vision was unambiguously similar: the movement for the liberation of blacks would prevail because it was based on a right, accurate philosophy about race and, more generally, the world and life.

5. Quote from the BBC's website (accessed on January 18, 2008): http://news.bbc.co.uk/2/hi/europe/2182926.stm.

Chapter Four. The Quest for Space

1. Variable "privacy."

2. Those studies often measure our interest in "space" in terms of our strong passion for "privacy." The two concepts are obviously not identical but closely connected. For interesting studies, see Larson and Medora (1992), Solove (2008), and Weigel-Garrey et al. (1998).

3. Most sociologists of sports, for instance, focus on questions of gender, race, class, power, and politics. The literature is extensive. See Foley (1990) for an example.

4. Of course, winning market share in new, unexplored countries is also highly prized. Thus, commenting recently on Proctor & Gamble—the United States' largest household product maker—and its amazing financial performance across the world but especially China, analyst Bill Schmitz of Deutsche Bank North America observed the following: "If anyone knows developing markets, it's P&G. . . . They know the consumer better than anyone else and they have the broadest product range. They are on top of the world right now" (Cornwell 2005).

5. Variables "execrank" and "unsklrnk."

6. The text of the speech is available on Barack Obama's official website (accessed on December 1, 2008): http://www.barackobama.com/2008/11/04/remarks_of_presidentelect_bara.php.

7. The text of the speech is available on the White House's Internet site (accessed on October 5, 2007): http://www.whitehouse.gov/news/releases/2004/11/20041103–3.html.

8. Ecologist Jim Motavalli has written extensively about our attitudes toward public transportation. See Motavalli (2001).

9. Interestingly, a recent study suggests that males seem more prone than females to view competitive events as occasions for the generation of mental hierarchies. Boys improved their performance at a given task (solving a computer maze) much more than girls when they were rewarded not on the basis of their individual achievements but in relation to how others did. Clearly, the arrival of *comparison* motivated those boys (Gneezy and Rustichini 2004).

Chapter Five. Powers and Limitations

1. See Anderson and McChesney (2003) for a valuable introduction to the evolution of private property and property rights in Western societies.

2. For example, winners of the Stanley Cup in hockey are expected to treat that trophy with respect for as long as it remains in their possession.

3. See Honoré (1961) for a classic treatment of the freedoms and powers that come with ownership.

4. The literature on the ownership of abstract objects is voluminous. See, for instance, Christman (1994: 16).

5. See, for instance, Zuroff et al. (2007).

6. Studies show, for instance, that gender, one's own level of self-esteem prior to entering the competitive events, and even levels of testosterone prior to competition all shape how losers react to loss. See, for instance, Mehta et al. (2008) and Navaro and Schwartzberg (2007).

Chapter Six. Types of Winners and Losers

1. From the homepage of the Christopher and Dana Reeve Foundation (accessed on August 31, 2007): http://www.christopherreeve.org/site/c.geIMLPO pGjF/b.1097025/k.6FF5/Christopher_and_Dana_Reeve.htm.

2. In this regard we could add that there may exist a fifth path to eternal victory: failing once when trying to do something utterly impressive and even courageous. The losers may then be remembered as winners. Recall, for instance, how people turned into winners the crew of the shuttle Challenger after they tragically died in January 1986 a minute after takeoff—even though hardly anyone knew who they were beforehand.

3. According to a Fox News poll, only 35 percent of Americans approved of Rumsfeld's performance in April 2006. See (accessed on October 9, 2008): http://www.foxnews.com/story/0,2933,192468,00.html.

4. Variable "whypoor2."

Chapter Seven. Process versus Outcomes

1. From the official Internet site of the U.S. Soccer Federation (accessed on October 29, 2007): http://www.ussoccer.com/articles/viewArticle.jsp_2555913.html.

2. From Dartmouth College's Internet site (accessed on November 8, 2007): http://www.dartmouth.edu/home/about/mission.html.

3. Variable "owndoing."

4. Question A173. I calculated the percentage of people who answered with either a 9 or 10 (out of 10, with 10 being "a great deal") to the question of how much freedom and choice they have over their lives. Mexico, Venezuela, and Puerto Rico scored more positively than the United States.

5. As Freud puts it, "Civilization is built upon the renunciation of instinct" (Freud 1989: 51–52).

6. Variable "successz."

7. Hence, the owner of Bond's record-breaking home-run ball (fashion designer Marc Ecko) has marked it with an asterisk after asking baseball fans to vote on its fate. The asterisk is intended to symbolize doubt.

8. The poster in fact says more than reward makes success all the sweeter. It also says that nothing that is worthwhile can be gained without effort. This is a very odd view of things: surely some worthy things come our way without us fighting for them.

9. See, for instance, Seligman (2006) and Touhey (2007).

10. Variables "optimist," "anomia6," and "anomia2."

Chapter Eight. Injecting Value

1. Variable "lfegod."

2. Who can recall, after all, a loser stating that they take their loss as a sign of God's disapproval or condemnation of them?

3. Here we are reminded of Weber's classic study of capitalism's birth and the stance of Protestants in Europe and North America toward success in business: profit and the accumulation of money were seen not merely as signs of good business skills but of having been selected by God for heaven (Weber 2002).

4. Variable "godsport." While 60 percent approve, only 25 percent disapprove.

5. And, we should add, it is the easiest to manipulate in interesting ways. After all, if there is no clear logical connection between the actual outcome of a competitive event and these higher-order prizes, one can be very creative on how that connection is made. Sometimes the connection is made *before* an event; when the outcome proves unfavorable, the connection is simply dismissed. At other times, losses in the first steps of the ladder can be somehow interpreted as positive for prizes higher in the ladder. This can happen, for instance, when a competitor redefines, adds to, or subtracts from the higher prizes that are at stake. This occurred in the wake of the Republican Party's major defeat in the congressional midterm elections of 2006, for instance, when some Republicans stated that the defeat was actually a victory for truly conservative ideals: the party lost the vote count, in other words, because the voters felt that the party had betrayed its core values. This was the perspective of Senator John McCain, for example, and many other party leaders (Nagourney 2006).

6. Variable "amsports."

7. Variable "life."

8. Question F001.

9. Variable "satjob."

10. Thus, after infusing events with much meaning, members of the audience are quick to "move on" and forget outcomes, especially if these did turn out to be negative (while they may indulge in positive outcomes a little longer).

Chapter Nine. Awareness and Competition

1. See, for example, Heaton and Sigall (2006). To keep matters simple, I am taking here the perspective of us as competitors and not members of the audience. Let us just note that audience members too, of course, are aware of competition and play a role in its making.

2. See, for instance, Saint-Phard et al. (1999) on perceptions of self among NCAA women athletes.

3. Thus the presence of an audience causes stress for competitors. See, for instance, James and Collins (1997).

4. Question C018.

5. Accessed on November 1, 2007: http://www.swarthmore.edu/x18.xml.

6. Accessed on February 1, 2008: http://www.spellingbee.com/finishers.asp.

7. Thus the NLF fined Coach Bill Belichick the maximum penalty of $500,000 in September 2007 and the New England Patriots were ordered to pay $250,000 for spying on an opponent team's defensive signals. What made the infraction especially bad? NFL Commissioner Roger Goodell stated that "this episode represents a calculated and deliberate attempt to avoid long-standing rules designed to encourage fair play and promote honest competition on the playing field" (Pedulla 2007). The problem, then, was the "calculated" and "deliberate" nature of the breach: it was the conscious disregard of the rules.

In a similar way, Senator Hillary Clinton lost significant capital (this time political) when her campaign camp for the 2008 presidential election tried to undermine Senator Barack Obama's credibility by informing the public that Obama misled the public when he said he had not been planning to run for president: he had written an essay in kindergarten, Clinton's campaign staff noted, titled "I want to become President." It was a violation of etiquette, of an informal rule about what we can question and publicly investigate about a candidate. And the public would not forgive her for that.

8. From the Internet site of *Sports Illustrated* (accessed on January 22, 2008): http://sportsillustrated.cnn.com/2004/golf/specials/masters/2004/04/12/mickel son.win/index.html.

9. From the Internet site of CBS News (accessed on September 14, 2009): http://www.cbsnews.com/elements/2003/09/22/in_depth_showbiz/photoessay 574575_0_15_photo.shtml.

CHAPTER TEN. OUR RESTLESSNESS

1. Question E039. The countries with lower scores than Denmark were Finland, Japan, the Netherlands, Northern Ireland, and the United Kingdom.

2. Until then, teachers work out an "individual pupil plan" (*individuelle elevplaner*) for each student. These are development plans based on the student's abilities and potential. Parents, teachers, and students also hold two conferences a year.

3. Accessed on August 26, 2009: http://www.eng.uvm.dk/Aktuelt/News/Eng/ 090731%20Welfare%20courses%20are%20Danish%20students%20favoured %20choice.aspx.

4. As Queen Margaret II once said, "We are very proud of our modesty. It is our inverted megalomania. It is highly sophisticated" (Askgaard 1992: 8, as quoted in Nelson and Shavitt 2002: 454).

5. Accessed on February 13, 2008: www.carlsberg.com.

6. Though it must also be said that, should a person fail miserably to capitalize in some way on all that the system has offered to him, he will be judged in the harshest of terms. It is therefore considered unacceptable in Danish society to receive unemployment benefits for extended periods of time (though those are available for up to four years), or to stay idle in one way or another for long. Indeed, according to the World Values Survey, the Danes are among the most critical people in the world of those who claim government benefits (question F114). That person will be castigated and deemed to be a loser in the most definitive way—more so, in fact, than in the United States. This explains why around 20 percent of Danes work when, should they claim unemployment, they would receive more income.

7. Such satisfaction leads Danes, curiously, to feel a fairly strong sense of superiority vis-à-vis the rest of the world. Hence, as a collective one could say that the Danish approach to competition is quite different from what happens inside that society.

8. Question A008.

9. See (accessed on October 17, 2008): http://www.reuters.com/article/health News/idUSN3045469520080701 and http://edition.cnn.com/2008/HEALTH/07/02/nations.happiness/index.html.

10. The ministry's website discusses these and other wars. Accessed on February 8, 2008: http://www.denmark.dk/en/menu/AboutDenmark/History/The+Period1720 1900/TheSchleswigIssue/TheWarOf1864.

11. See the recent volume by Campbell et al. (2006) for a fascinating and comprehensive study of Danish history, culture, and politics.

12. Accessed on February 7, 2008: http://hdr.undp.org/en/media/hdr_2007 2008_en_complete.pdf.

13. Variable "careself."

14. Question E034.

15. Variable "richwork."

16. Question F001.

17. Question A170.

18. See, for instance, Alfie Kohn's suggestion for the removal of incentives at the workplace and elsewhere (Kohn 1993), or the work of Joshua Margolis and James Walsh on how we can encourage corporations to be competitive in the marketplace but also more aware of what humanity needs (Margolis and Walsh 2003).

References

Anderson, Dave. 2004. "Sports of The Times: A Sweet Victory, One That Went According to Plan." *New York Times*, April 12.

Anderson, Jared R., and William J. Doherty. 2005. "Democratic Community Initiatives: The Case of Overscheduled Children." *Family Relations* 54 (5): 654–65.

Anderson, Jenny. 2006. "Wall St. Bonuses: So Much Money, Too Few Ferraris." *New York Times*, December 25.

Anderson, Terry L., and Fred S. McChesney, eds. 2003. *Private Property: Cooperation, Conflict, and Law*. Princeton: Princeton University Press.

Aristotle. 1976. *Ethics*. New York: Penguin Books.

Aronson, Elliot. 1997. "Review: Back to the Future: Retrospective Review of Leon Festinger." *American Journal of Psychology* 110 (1) 127–37.

Askgaard, Helle. 1992. "As Denmark Sees Herself and Is Seen by Others." In *Discover Denmark—On Denmark and the Danes: Past, Present and Future*, ed. Per Himmelstrup et al., 7–26. Herning, Denmark: Copenhagen and Systime.

Atkinson, Michael. 2002. "Fifty Million Viewers Can't Be Wrong: Professional Wrestling, Sports-Entertainment, and Mimesis." *Sociology of Sport Journal* 19 (1): 47–66.

Baker-Ward, Lynne E., et al. 2005. "Young Soccer Players' Reports of a Tournament Win or Loss: Different Emotions, Different Narratives." *Journal of Cognition and Development* 6 (4): 507–27.

Bargdill, Richard W. 2008. "The Study of Life Boredom." *Journal of Phenomenological Psychology* 31 (2): 188–219.

Beck, Peter. 2005. "Britain and the Cold War's 'Cultural Olympics': Responding to the Political Drive of Soviet Sport, 1945–1958." *Contemporary British History* 19 (2): 169–85.

Becker, Dana, and Jeanne Marecek. 2008. "Positive Psychology: History in the Remaking?" *Theory and Psychology* 18 (5): 591–604.

Belluck, Pam, and Katie Zezima. 2004. "With Nothing Left to Win, Fans of Red Sox Suddenly Feel a Loss." *New York Times*, October 29.

Berger, Peter. L., and Thomas Luckmann. 1967. *The Social Construction of Reality: A Treatise in the Sociology of Knowledge*. Garden City, NY: Anchor Books.

Berkow, Ian. 1994. "A Humbled Jordan Learns New Truths." *New York Times*, April 11.

Berlin, Isaiah. 1969. *Four Essays on Liberty*. New York: Oxford University Press.

Bernstein, Aaron. 2003. "Waking Up from the American Dream." *Business Week*, December 1.

Berzoff, Joan. 2008. "Psychosocial Ego Development: The Theory of Erik Erikson." In *Inside Out and Outside In: Psychodynamic Clinical Theory and Psy-

chopathology in Contemporary Multicultural Contexts, ed. Joan Berzoff et al., 99–120. Lanham, MD: Jason Aronson.

Blanden, Jo, et al. 2005. "Intergenerational Mobility in Europe and North America." Sutton Trust (accessed on October 13, 2008 at http://www.suttontrust .com/reports/IntergenerationalMobility.pdf).

Boehm, Christopher. 2000. "Conflict and the Evolution of Social Control." *Journal of Consciousness Studies* 7 (1–2): 79–101.

———. 2001. *Hierarchy in the Forest: The Evolution of Egalitarian Behavior.* Cambridge, MA: Harvard University Press.

Bourdieu, Pierre. 1984. *Distinctions: A Social Critique of the Judgment of Taste.* Cambridge, MA: Harvard University Press.

Brooks, Larry. 2000. "Devils' Big Three Been There Before." *New York Post*, May 14.

Broström, Stig. 1998. "Kindergarten in Denmark and the USA." *Scandinavian Journal of Educational Research* 42 (2): 109–22.

Bush, George W. 2007. *Weekly Compilation of Presidential Documents* 43 (17), April 30.

Byrnes, Nanette, et al. 2006. "The Great CEO Exodus." *Business Week*, October 30.

Caillois, Roger. 2001. *Man, Play, and Games.* Urbana: University of Illinois Press.

Campbell, John L. 2004. *Institutional Change and Globalization.* Princeton: Princeton University Press.

Campbell, John L., et al., eds. 2006. *National Identity and the Varieties of Capitalism: The Danish Experience.* Montreal: McGill University Press.

Campbell, John L., and Ove K. Pedersen. 2007. "The Varieties of Capitalism and Hybrid Success: Denmark in the Global Economy." *Comparative Political Studies* 40 (2): 307–32.

Carnegie, Dale. 1981 [1937]. *How to Win Friends and Influence People.* New York: Pocket Books.

CDC News. 2006. "CDC Influenza Expert Selected as Federal Employee of the Year." Retrieved on March 8, 2007 from: http://www.cdc.gov/about/news/2006_ 09/cox.htm.

Christiansen, Peter Munk. 1998. "A Prescription Rejected: Market Solutions to Problems of Public Sector Governance." *Governance* 11 (3): 273–94.

Christman, John. 1994. *The Myth of Property: Toward an Egalitarian Theory of Ownership.* New York: Oxford University Press.

Cohn, Jonathan. 2007. "Great Danes." *New Republic* 236 (1–3): 13–17.

Colvin, Alexander J. S., and Wendy R. Boswell. 2007. "The Problem of Action and Interest Alignment: Beyond Job Requirements and Incentive Compensation." *Human Resource Management Review* 17 (1): 38–51.

Corn, David. 2001. "Al, Don't Run." *The Nation*, September 17/24.

Cornwell, Lisa. 2005. "Health, Bany, and Family Care Sales Drive P&G's Higher Third-Quarter Profit." Associated Press, April 28.

Crocker, Jennifer, et al. 2003. "Contingencies of Self-Worth in College Students: Theory and Measurement." *Journal of Personality and Social Psychology* 85 (5): 894–908.

Crouse, Karen. 2006. "For 2 Star Running Backs, Leaving Isn't Easy." *New York Times*, November 2.

Daly, Mary, and Daniel Wilson. 2007. "Relative Comparisons and Economics: Empirical Evidence." *FRBSF Economic Letter* 30: 1–3.

Davey, Ian, and Rob MacAskill. 1997. *September 1972* (film, Polygram Video).

David, Paulo. 1999. "Children's Rights and Sports—Young Athletes and Competitive Sports: Exploit and Exploitation." *International Journal of Children's Rights* 7 (1): 53–81.

Diamond, Jared. 1999. *Guns, Germs, and Steel: The Fates of Human Societies.* New York: W. W. Norton.

Dorman, Larry. 1997. "The 61st Masters; Woods Tears up Augusta and Tears down Barriers." *New York Times*, April 14.

Drape, Joe. 2006. "Bailey Rides Off Into the Sunset at the Top of His Sport." *New York Times*, January 19.

Dribben, Melissa. 2007. "Her Frantic Call for Help Aided a Victim—A Heartless Attack, Then a Swift, Brave Act." *Philadelphia Inquirer*, October 7.

Dumas, Jean E., et al. 2005. "Home Chaos: Sociodemographic, Parenting, Interaction, and Child Correlates." *Journal of Clinical Child and Adolescent Psychology* 34 (1): 93–104.

Dunning, Eric. 1999. *Sport Matters: Sociological Studies of Sport, Violence, and Civilisation.* London: Routledge.

Durkheim, Emil. 1982 [1895]. *The Rules of Sociological Method.* New York: Free Press.

———. 1965 [1912]. *The Elementary Forms of the Religious Life.* New York: Free Press.

Economist. 2006. "The Alan and Ben Show." *Economist*, February 18.

———. 2007. "Lexington: The Spirit of Christmas." *Economist*, December 22.

———. 2009. "Lands of Opportunity." *Economist*, March 14.

Edelman, Robert. 1993. "Stalin and His Soccer Soldiers." *History Today* (February): 46–51.

Egelund, Niels. 2005. "Educational Assessment in Danish Schools." *Assessment in Education: Principles, Policy, and Practice* 12 (2): 203–12.

Erikson, Erik. 1968. *Insight and Freedom: The Ninth T. B. Davie Memorial Lecture Delivered at the University of Cape Town on 6 August 1968.* Cape Town: University of Cape Town.

———. 1969. *Gandhi's Truth: On the Origins of Nonviolence.* New York: W. W. Norton.

Eskenazi, Gerald. 2004. "The Miracle on Ice: A Hockey Moment Frozen in Time." *New York Times*, February 3.

Estavillo, Maricel E. 2006. "Google's Uncompromising Premiums to Stay on Top." *BusinessWorld*, February 21.

Fellman, Gordon. 1998. *Rambo and the Dalai Lama: The Compulsion to Win and Its Threat to Human Survival.* Albany: State University of New York Press.

Fligstein, Neil. 1996. "Markets as Politics: A Political-Cultural Approach to Market Institutions." *American Sociological Review* 61: 656–73.

Foley, Douglas E. 1990. "The Great American Football Ritual: Reproducing Race, Class, and Gender Inequality." *Sociology of Sport Journal* 7 (2): 111–35.

Frank, Robert H., and Philipp J. Cook. 1995. *Winner-Take-All Society: Why the Few at the Top Get So Much More than the Rest of Us*. New York: Penguin Books.

Frazier, Jimmy A., and Eldon E. Snyder. 1991. "The Underdog Concept in Sport." *Sociology of Sport Journal* (8): 380–88.

Freud, Sigmund. 1989 [1930]. *Civilization and Its Discontents*. New York: W. W. Norton.

Gan, Su-lin, et al. 1997. "The Thrill of the Game: Who Enjoys It and Who Doesn't?" *Journal of Sport and Social Issues* 21 (1): 53–64.

Gavin, Robert. 2005. "MIT Professor Named Top Economist under 40." *Boston Globe*, June 15.

Geertz, Clifford. 1973. *The Interpretation of Cultures*. New York: Basic Books.

Gherardi, Francesca, and William H. Daniels. 2003. "Dominance Hierarchies and Status Recognition in the Crayfish Procambarus Acutus Acutus." *Canadian Journal of Zoology* 81 (7): 1269–81.

Gilbert, Alfred Todd. 2006. *Stumbling on Happiness*. New York: Alfred A. Knopf.

Gilbert, Brad, and Steve Jamison. 1993. *Winning Ugly: Mental Warfare in Tennis— Tales from the Tour and Lessons from a Master*. Secaucus, NJ: Carol.

Gingrich, Newt. 2005. *Winning the Future: A 21st Century Contract with America*. Washington, DC: Regnery.

Gneezy, Uri, and Aldo Rustichini. 2004. "Gender and Competition at a Young Age." *American Economic Review* 94 (2): 377–81.

Goldman, Adam. 2006. "You're Not Fired! Trump Lets Miss USA Hang on to Her Tiara." Associated Press, December 20.

Gould, Daniel, et al. 1993. "Life at the Top: The Experiences of U.S. National Champion Figure Skaters." *Sport Psychologist* 7 (4): 354–74.

Greenfeld, Liah. 1992. *Nationalism: Five Roads to Modernity*. Cambridge, MA: Harvard University Press.

———. 2005a. "When the Sky Is the Limit: Busyness in Contemporary American Society." *Social Research* 72 (2): 315–38.

———. 2005b. "Nationalism and the Mind." *Nations and Nationalism* 11 (3): 325–41.

Green-Pedersen, Christoffer, and Pontus Odmalm. 2008. "Going Different Ways? Right-Wing Parties and the Immigrant Issue in Denmark and Sweden." *Journal of European Public Policy* 15 (3): 367–81.

Habermas, Jürgen. 2003. *The Future of Human Nature*. Cambridge: Polity Press.

Hall, John A., and Charles Lindhom. 1999. *Is America Breaking Apart?* Princeton: Princeton University Press.

Hareli, Shlomo, and Bernard Wiener. 2002. "Dislike and Envy as Antecedents of Pleasure at Another's Misfortune." *Motivation and Emotion* 26 (4): 257–77.

Heaton, Alan W., and Harold Sigall. 2006. "Self-Consciousness, Self-Presentation, and Performance under Pressure: Who Chokes, and When?" *Journal of Applied Social Psychology* 21 (3): 175–88.

Heeren, John W., and Marylee Requa. 2001. "Winning Ways: Constructing Values on a Girls High School Field Hockey Team." *Journal of Sport and Social Issues* 25 (4): 417–29.

Helman, Scott. 2008. "Obama, Clinton Sound a Conciliatory Tone on Controversies." *Boston Globe*, January 15.

Heyman, James, et al. 2004. "I Was Pleased a Moment Ago: How Pleasure Varies with Background and Foreground Reference Points." *Motivation and Emotion* 28 (1): 65–83.

Hirt, Edward R., et al. 1992. "Costs and Benefits of Allegiance: Changes in Fans' Self-Ascribed Competencies after Team Victory and Defeat." *Journal of Personality and Social Psychology* 63 (5): 724–38.

Hobbes, Thomas. 1999 [1650]. *Human Nature and De Corpore Politico*. Oxford: Oxford University Press.

———. 1985 [1651]. *Leviathan*. London: Penguin Books.

Hofferth, Sandra L., and John F. Sandberg. 2001. "Changes in American Children's Time, 1981–1997." In *Children at the Millennium: Where Have We Come From, Where Are We Going?* ed. Sandra L. Hofferth and Timothy J. Owens, 193–29. Kindlington, Oxford: Elsevier Science.

Homer. 1974. *The Iliad*. New York: Anchor Books.

Honoré, A.M.A. 1961. "Ownership." In *Oxford Essays in Jurisprudence*, ed. Anthony Gordon, 107–47. Oxford: Clarendon Press.

Huizinga, Johan. 1955. *Homo Ludens: A Study of the Play-Element in Culture*. Boston: Beacon Press.

Ikenberry, G. John. 2001. *After Victory: Institutions, Strategic Restraint, and the Rebuilding of Order after Major Wars*. Princeton: Princeton University Press.

Irish Times. 2008. "Bush Pledges Continued Backing for Afghanistan." December 16.

Jackson, Phil. 1995. *Sacred Hoops: Spiritual Lessons of a Hardwood Warrior*. New York: Hyperion.

James, Benjamin, and David Collins. 1997. "Self-Presentational Sources of Competitive Stress during Performance." *Journal of Sport and Exercise Psychology* 19 (1): 17–35.

Jefferson, Thomas. 1999. *Jefferson: Political Writings*, ed. Joyce Oldham Appleby and Terence Ball. Cambridge: Cambridge University Press.

———. 2003. *Quotations of Thomas Jefferson*, ed. U Inspire. Bedford, MA: Applewood Book.

Jensen, Tina Gudrun. 2008. "To Be 'Danish,' Becoming 'Muslim': Contestations of National Identity?" *Journal of Ethnic and Migration Studies* 34 (3): 389–409.

Jones, Del. 2007. "Could Insecurity Be the Secret to CEOs' Success?" *USA Today*, January 2.

Jørgensen, Martin. 2005. "Boosting Growth through Greater Competition in Denmark." Economics Department Working Paper No. 431. Paris: OECD.

Kahneman, Daniel, and Amos Tversky. 1979. "Prospect Theory: An Analysis of Decision under Risk." *Econometrica* 47: 263–91.

Kant, Immanuel. 1998 [1781, 1787]. *Critique of Pure Reason*. Ed. Paul Guyer and Allen W. Wood. Cambridge: Cambridge University Press.

Kanter, Rosabeth Moss. 2004. *Confidence: How Winning Streaks and Losing Streaks Begin and End*. New York: Crown Business.

Kennedy, Helen. 2001. "N.J. Hero's Call: I Love You, We're Going to Stop Them—3 Passengers Likely Saved 4th Target." *Daily News* (New York), September 13.

Kohn, Alfie. 1986. *No Contest: The Case against Competition*. New York: Houghton Mifflin.

———. 1993. *Punished by Rewards: The Trouble with Gold Stars, Incentive Plans, A's, Praise, and Other Bribes*. New York: Houghton Mifflin.

Kornblut, Anne E. 2003. "The President's Address: Bush Proclaims a Victory in Iraq Turns Tide in War on Terrorism." *Boston Globe*, May 2.

Kurzer, Paulette. 2001. *Markets and Moral Regulation: Cultural Change in the European Union*. Cambridge: Cambridge University Press.

Kuttner, Robert. 2008. "The Copenhagen Consensus." *Foreign Affairs* 87 (2): 78–94.

Lao Tzu. 1995. *Tao Te Ching*. New York: St. Martin's Press.

Larson, Jeffrey H., and Nilufer Medora. 1992. "Privacy Preferences: A Cross-Cultural Comparison of Americans and Asian Indians." *International Journal of Sociology of the Family* 22 (1): 55–66.

Layard, Richard. 2003. "The Secret of Happiness." *New Statesman*, March 3.

Leibovich, Mark. 2006. "Plea of the Democratic Pariah: Forgive My Defeat." *New York Times*, May 21.

Levine, Donald, N., ed. 1971. *Georg Simmel: On Individuality and Social Forms*. Chicago: University of Chicago Press.

Low, Setha. 2003. *Behind the Gates: Life, Security, and the Pursuit of Happiness in Fortress America*. London: Routledge.

Lozano, Juan A. 2007. "Biggio Will Retire after Season." *Austin American Statesman*, July 25.

Madison, James. 2006. *Selected Writings of James Madison*, ed. Ralph Ketchnam. Indianapolis: Hackett.

Mager, Robert. F. 1983. *Goal Analysis: How to Clarify Your Goals So You Can Actually Achieve Them*. Atlanta, GA: Center for Effective Performance.

Mahoney, James. 2000. "Path Dependence in Historical Sociology." *Theory and Society* 24 (4): 507–48.

Mandel, Robert. 2007. "Reassessing Victory in Warfare." *Armed Forces and Society* 33 (4): 461–95.

Margolis, Joshua D., and James P. Walsh. 2003. "Misery Loves Companies: Rethinking Social Initiatives by Business." *Administrative Science Quarterly* 48 (June): 268–305.

Marx, Karl. 1978. "Economic and Philosophical Manuscripts of 1844." In *The Marx-Engels Reader*, ed. Robert C. Tucker, 66–125. New York: W. W. Norton.

Mazur, Allan, et al. 1992. "Testosterone and Chess Competition." *Psychological Quarterly* 55 (1): 70–77.

McAlpine, Robert Alistair, and Kate Dixey. 2003. *Triumph from Failure: Lessons from Life for Business Success*. New York: Texere.

McIntyre, Mary G. 2005. *Secrets to Winning at Office Politics: How to Achieve Your Goals and Increase Your Influence at Work*. New York: St. Martin's Press.

McLean, Bethany, and Peter Elkind. 2003. *The Smartest Guys in the Room: The Amazing Rise and Scandalous Fall of Enron*. New York: Penguin.

McPherson, James M. 2004. "Antebellum Southern Exceptionalism: A New Look at an Old Question." *Civil War History* 50 (4): 418–33.

Mehta, Pranjal H., et al. 2008. "The Social Endocrinology of Dominance: Basal Testosterone Predicts Cortisol Changes and Behavior Following Victory and Defeat." *Journal of Personality and Social Psychology* 94 (6): 1078–93.

Mento, Anthony J., et al. 1992. "Relationship of Goal Level to Valence and Instrumentality." *Journal of Applied Psychology* 77: 395–405.

Meyer, Joyce. 1995. *Battlefield of the Mind: Winning the Battle in Your Mind*. Fenton, MO: Warner Faith.

Michaels, Jillian. 2005. *Winning by Losing: Drop the Weight, Change Your Life*. New York: HarperCollins.

Michelli, Joseph. 2007. *The Starbucks Experience: Five Principles for Turning Ordinary into Extraordinary*. New York: McGraw-Hill.

Miller, Michael. 1997. "American Football: The Rationalization of the Irrational." *International Journal of Politics, Culture and Society* 11 (1): 101–27.

Mills, Jennifer S., and Sante R. D'Alfonso. 2007. "Competition and Male Body Image: Increased Drive for Muscularity Following Failure to a Female." *Journal of Social and Clinical Psychology* 26 (4): 505–18.

Miniter, Richard. 2002. *The Myth of Market Share: Why Market Share Is the Fool's Gold of Business*. New York: Crown Business.

Moore, John. 2006. *Tribal Knowledge: Business Wisdom Brewed from the Grounds of Starbucks Corporate Culture*. Chicago: Kaplan.

Mortimore, Peter. 2009. "Danish and English Education Systems: What Lessons Can We Learn?" *Education Review* 21 (2): 47–59.

Motavalli, Jim. 2001. *Breaking Gridlock: Moving Toward Transportation that Works*. San Francisco: Sierra Club Books.

Nagourney, Adam. 2006. "McCain Tells Conservatives GOP's Defeat Was Payback for Losing 'Our Principles.'" *New York Times*, November 17.

Navaro, Leyla, and Sharan L. Schwartzberg, eds. 2007. *Envy, Competition, and Gender: Theory, Clinical Applications, and Group Work*. New York: Routledge.

Nelson, Michelle R., and Sharon Shavitt. 2002. "Horizontal and Vertical Individualism and Achievement Values: A Multimethod Examination of Denmark and the United States." *Journal of Cross-Cultural Psychology* 33 (5): 439–58.

New York Times. 1996. "Excerpts from President Clinton's Victory Address at Arkansas Statehouse." November 6.

Nickolas, Davis W., and Barbara B. Meyer. 2008. "When Sibling Becomes Competitor: A Qualitative Investigation of Same-Sex Sibling Competition in Elite Sport." *Journal of Applied Sport Psychology* 20 (2): 220–35.

Niederle, Muriel, and Lise Vesterlund. 2007. "Do Women Shy Away from Competition? Do Men Compete Too Much?" *Quarterly Journal of Economics* 122 (3): 1067–101.

Nietzsche, Friedrich. 1997 [1881]. *Daybreak: Thoughts on the Prejudices of Morality*, ed. Maudemarie Clark and Brian Leiter. Cambridge: Cambridge University Press.

———. 1990 [1886]. *Beyond Good and Evil: Prelude to a Philosophy of the Future*. New York: Penguin Books.

O'Connor, Ian. 2005. "'Miracle on Ice' Is Still a Marvel to Goalie Craig." *USA Today*, February 15.

OECD. 2000. *Message from PISA*. Paris: OECD.

Østergaard-Nielsen, Eva. 2003. "Counting the Costs: Denmark's Changing Migration Policies." *International Journal of Urban and Regional Research* 27 (2): 448–54.

Park, Robert Ezra. 1964 [1950]. *Race and Culture*. New York: Free Press.

Pedulla, Tom. 2007. "Belichick Tries to Silence Talk of Spying Scandal." *USA Today*, September 14.

Plato. 1989a. "Socrates' Defense." In *The Collected Dialogues*, ed. Edith Hamilton and Huntington Cairns, 3–26. Princeton: Princeton University Press.

———. 1989b. "Laws." In *The Collected Dialogues*, ed. Hamilton and Cairns, 1225–513. Princeton: Princeton University Press.

Pollock, Susan. 1999. *Ancient Mesopotamia*. Cambridge: Cambridge University Press.

Pritchett, Price. 2006. *Hard Optimism: How to Succeed in a World Where Positive Wins*. New York: McGraw-Hill.

Rabin, Itzhak. 1967. Address by Rav Aluf Itzhak Rabin upon Receiving Hebrew University Honorary Doctorate at Mount Scopus, Jerusalem.

Rafael, Dan. 2004. "Lewis Retires, Saying He Has Nothing Left to Prove." *USA Today*, February 9.

Raney, Arthur A., and Anthony J. Depalma. 2006. "The Effect of Viewing Varying Levels and Contexts of Violent Sports Programming on Enjoyment, Mood, and Perceived Violence." *Mass Communication and Society* 9 (3): 321–38.

Reilly, Jim. 2002. "'Jordan' Soars with Michael." *Post-Standard* (Syracuse, NY), March 8.

Rhoden, William C. 2005. "Young Blood Makes Yankees Rush into First." *New York Times*, September 30.

Riess, Marc, and Jim Taylor. 1984. "Ego-involvement and Attributions for Success and Failure in a Field Setting." *Personality and Social Psychology Bulletin* 10 (4): 536–43.

Robbins, Liz. 2005. "Year after Winning Trophy, Kuznetsova Can Feel Its Weight." *New York Times*, August 29.

Roberts, John Owen. 2002. *Repentance: The First Word of the Gospel*. Wheaton, IL: Crossway Books.

Rose, Pete. 2004. *My Prison without Bars*. New York: St. Martin's Press.

Ross, Dennis. 2007. *Statecraft: And How to Restore America's Standing in the World*. New York: Farrar, Straus, and Giraux.

Rousseau, Jean Jacques. 1968 [1762]. *The Social Contract*. London: Penguin Books.

Runciman, W. G., ed. 1978. *Weber: Selections in Translation*. Cambridge: Cambridge University Press.

Sacerdote, Bruce, and Owen Zidar. 2008. "Campaigning in Poetry: Is There Information Conveyed in the Candidates' Choice of Words." Unpublished paper.

Saint-Phard, Deborah, et al. 1999. "Self-perception in Elite Collegiate Female Gymnasts, Cross-Country Runners, and Track-and-Field Athletes." *Mayo Clinic Proceedings* 74: 770–74.

Sandomir, Richard. 2001. "How 'Miracle on Ice' Helped Restore Faith." *New York Times*, February 2.

Saul, Michael, and Helen Kennedy. 2008. "Hey, Let's Get Civil." *New York Daily News*, January 15.

Schieman, Scott, and Karen Van Gundy. 2001. "Introspectiveness, Psychosocial Resources and Depression." *Social Behavior and Personality* 29 (2): 105–12.

Schmidt, Martin B. 2006. "When It Comes to the World Series, Luck Conquers All." *New* York Times, November 5.

Seligman, Martin E. P. 2002. *Authentic Happiness: Using the New Positive Psychology to Realize Your Potential for Lasting Fulfillment*. New York: Free Press.

———. 2006. *Learned Optimism: How to Change Your Mind and Your Life*. New York: Vintage Press.

Simmel, Georg. 1971. *Georg Simmel on Individuality and Social Forms*, ed. Donald N. Levine. Chicago: University of Chicago Press.

Smith, Adam. 1993 [1776]. *An Inquiry into the Nature and Causes of the Wealth of Nations*. Oxford: Oxford University Press.

Solove, Daniel, J. 2008. *Understanding Privacy*. Cambridge, MA: Harvard University Press.

Sommers, Jennifer, and Stephen J. Vodanovich. 2000. "Boredom Proneness: Its Relationship to Psychological- and Physical-Health Symptoms." *Journal of Clinical Psychology* 56 (1): 149–55.

Sparks, Debra. 1996. "The Cowboy's New Clothes." *Financial World* 165 (14): 36.

Spring, Joe. 2008. "Running from Despair." *New York Times*, February 16.

Stanley, Alessandra. 2004. "Bush Shows a Different Side, but Not His Best One." *New York Times*, October 9.

Staples, Walter. 1993. *Think Like a Winner!* Chatsworth, CA: Wilshire.

Statistics Denmark. 2009. *Denmark in Figures: 2009*. Copenhagen: Statistics Denmark.

Still, Bob. 2002. *Officials under Assault: Update 2002*. Racine, WI: National Association of Sports Officials.

Stoiber, Julie, and Christine Schiavo. 2006. "Truly 'Good Man' is Laid to Rest." *Philadelphia Inquirer*, May 13.

Stroman, James, et al. 2007. *Administrative Assistant's and Secretary's Handbook*. New York: AMACOM.

Suedfeld, Peter, and Dennis A. Rank. 1976. "Revolutionary Leaders: Long-term Success as a Function of Changes in Conceptual Complexity." *Journal of Personality and Social Psychology* 34 (2): 169–78.

Thomsen, Lotte, et al. 2007. "Interpersonal Leveling, Independence, and Self-Enhancement: a Comparison between Denmark and the US, and a Relational Practice Framework for Cultural Psychology." *European Journal of Social Psychology* 37 (3): 445–69.

Tocqueville, Alexis de. 2003 [1835, 1840]. *Democracy in America*. London: Penguin Books.

Touhey, Kevin. 2007. *The Miracle of Optimism: Change Your Perspective, Transform Your Life*. Chicago: Miracle Press.

Tresniowski, Alex, and Kathy Ehrich Dowd. 2007. "The Truth at Last." *People*, October 22.

Ulrich, Stangier, et al. 2007. "Intrapersonal Conflict in Goals and Values of Patients with Unipolar Depression." *Psychotherapy and Psychosomatics* 76 (3): 162–70.

Union Leader. 2000. "At a Glance." *Union Leader* (Manchester, NH), January 26.

U.S. Department of Defense. 2003a. "Prepared Statement for the Senate Armed Services Committee: Helping Win the War on Terror." September 9. Retrieved on October 31, 2006 from http://www.defenselink.mil/Speeches/Speech.aspx?SpeechID=524.

———. 2003b. "Secretary Donald Rumsfeld Town Hall Meeting in Baghdad." April 30. Retrieved on October 31, 2006 from http://www.defenselink.mil/transcripts/index.aspx?mo=4&yr=2003.

U.S. Government Accountability Office. 2007. "Premium Class Travel: Internal Control Weaknesses Governmentwide Led to Improper and Abusive Use of Premium Class Travel." Retrieved on June 2, 2008 from http://www.gao.gov/new.items/d071268.pdf.

Van de Vliert, Evert, and Onne Janssen. 2002. "Competitive Societies Are Happy if the Women Are Less Competitive than the Men." *Cross-Cultural Research: The Journal of Comparative Social Science* 36 (4): 321–37.

Wann, Daniel L. 2006. "Examining the Potential Causal Relationship between Sport Team Identification and Psychological Well-being." *Journal of Sports Psychology* (29) 1: 79–95.

Weber, Bruce. 2005. "For Players, Fast Pulses: For Parents, Raw Nerves." *New York Times*, January 22.

Weber, Max. 2002 [1920]. *The Protestant Ethic and the Spirit of Capitalism*. Los Angeles: Roxbury.

———. 1978a. "Protestant Asceticism and the Spirit of Capitalism." In *Max Weber: Selections in Translation*, ed. W. G. Runciman, 138–73. Cambridge: Cambridge University Press.

———. 1978b. "The Types of Legitimate Domination." In *Economy and Society: An Outline of Interpretative Sociology*, ed. Guenter Roth and Claus Wittich, 212–301. Berkeley: University of California Press.

Weigel-Garrey, Cindy J., et al. 1998. "Children and Privacy." *Journal of Family Issues* 19 (1): 43–64.

Welch, Jack. 2006. *Winning.* New York: HarperCollins.

Welker, Robert L. 2005. "The Fundamental Importance of Simple Operational Definitions of Introspection and Empathy." *Psychoanalytic Quarterly* 74 (3): 767–99.

Wiese, Bettina S., and Alexandra M. Freund. 2005. "Goal Progress Makes One Happy, or Does It? Longitudinal Findings from the Work Domain." *Journal of Occupational and Organizational Psychology* 78: 287–304.

Wood, Sylvia. 1999. "Genetics Researcher Joins the Elite." *Times Union* (Albany, NY), June 4.

Zeleny, Jeff, and Kate Zernike. 2006. "For Democrats, Time to Savor Victory at Last." *New York Times*, November 8.

Zhang, Liqing, and Roy F. Baumeister. 2006. "Your Money or Your Self-Esteem: Threatened Egotism Promotes Costly Entrapment in Losing Endeavors." *Personality and Social Psychology Bulletin* 32 (7): 881–93.

Zientek, C. Cates, and G. M. Breakwell. 1991. "Attributional Schema of Players before and after Knowledge of Game Outcome." *Journal of Sport Behavior* 14 (3): 211–22.

Zoysa, Richard. 2005. "America's Foreign Policy: Manifest Destiny or Great Satan?" *Contemporary Politics* 11 (2/3): 133–56.

Zuckerman, Mortimer B. 2006. "A Sad Litany of Failures." *U.S. News and World Report* 141 (15): 68–68.

Zuroff, David C., et al. 2007. "Depression, Perceived Inferiority, and Interpersonal Behavior: Evidence for the Involuntary Defeat Strategy." *Journal of Social and Clinical Psychology* 26 (7): 751–78.

INDEX

Page numbers in italics refer to tables or figures in the text.